TIME CAPSULE/1968

TIME CAPSULE/1968

STORY OF THE YEAR CONDENSED FROM THE PAGES OF TIME

TIME-LIFE BOOKS, NEW YORK

TIME / **1968**

EDITOR-IN-CHIEF *Hedley Donovan*
SENIOR STAFF EDITOR *Ralph Graves*
MANAGING EDITOR *Henry Anatole Grunwald*
EXECUTIVE EDITOR *James Keogh*
SENIOR EDITORS *A. T. Baker, Jesse L. Birnbaum, Champ Clark,*
George G. Daniels, Michael Demarest, John T. Elson, Edward L. Jamieson,
Cranston Jones, Marshall Loeb, Peter Bird Martin, Jason McManus,
Richard Seamon, Robert Shnayerson
ASSOCIATE EDITORS *Douglas Auchincloss, Harriet Bachman,*
Laurence I. Barrett, Gurney Breckenfeld, Gilbert Cant, Spencer Davidson,
Timothy Foote, Barker T. Hartshorn, Bruce Henderson, Charles P. Jackson,
Leon Jaroff, Robert F. Jones, T. E. Kalem, Ray Kennedy, John Koffend,
Ronald P. Kriss, Ed Magnuson, Robert McLaughlin, Martin O'Neill,
Charles Parmiter, John M. Scott, David B. Tinnin, Edwin G. Warner

EDITOR *Maitland A. Edey*
EXECUTIVE EDITOR *Jerry Korn*
TEXT DIRECTOR *Martin Mann*
ART DIRECTOR *Sheldon Cotler*
CHIEF OF RESEARCH *Beatrice T. Dobie*

SERIES EDITOR *John Dille*
ASSISTANT *Rosemarie Conefrey*
DESIGNER *Arnold Holeywell*
ASSISTANT DESIGNER *John Woods*

PUBLISHER *Rhett Austell*

EVENTS OF THE YEAR

Editors' Note

As the list of major events on page 5 attests, 1968 was one of the most turbulent years in recent history. Rarely has the world been jolted so often by news of tragedy and upheaval. There was violence in Viet Nam, in Nigeria, in the Middle East and on campuses in half a dozen countries. The U.S. experienced student revolts, racial riots and two shocking assassinations—as well as an unexpectedly dramatic election campaign.

Because of the way in which this volume is organized, accounts of some of these events and the names of the leading figures crop up over and over again. References to the murder of Senator Robert F. Kennedy, for example, appear in several places, notably in a section dealing with Assassinations that starts on page 24, and in another section devoted to Politics that begins on page 53. The same holds true of the war in Viet Nam. Detailed battle accounts appear in a chapter beginning on page 121. First reports on the progress toward peace talks are carried in The Presidency section. Three major events—the Israeli attack on Beirut [page 148], the return of the crew of the U.S.S. *Pueblo* [page 166], and the fabulous voyage of Apollo 8 to the moon [page 203]—took place so close to the end of 1968 that they were reported in the Jan. 3, 1969 issue of TIME and are included in this 1968 Capsule.

■

TIME CAPSULE/1968 is one of a series of volumes, each adapted and condensed from a year's contents of TIME, the Weekly Newsmagazine. The words, except for a few connecting passages, are those of the magazine itself. The book is divided, like the magazine, into departments, and is organized so that each department forms a chronological chapter for the entire year. The dates in the margin are the issue dates of the magazine.

THE NATION

The Presidency

For President Lyndon Baines Johnson the year 1968 was probably the most painful of his life. Having swamped his Republican opponent Barry Goldwater in the presidential election four years earlier, and having been swept into office on a wave of national popularity, he embarked on an ambitious program of social legislation designed to implement what he and his aides referred to as "the Great Society." However, during the years that followed his popularity sank steadily. The Great Society seemed only to produce growing unrest throughout the country, particularly among Negroes and young people. Worse, the President presided over a steady escalation of the U.S. military effort in Viet Nam, and by the start of 1968 the national dismay over that far-off war had driven his prestige to an all-time low.

JAN. 5 **BELEAGUERED:** Even if the television tube and a ubiquitous Texan had yet to be conceived, the President of the U.S. in the latter third of the 20th century would almost certainly be the world's most exhaustively scrutinized, analyzed and criticized figure. Whatever his role, in the age of instant communication he inevitably seems so close that the viewer can almost reach out, pluck his sleeve and complain: "Say, Mr. President, what about prices? Napalm? The draft?"

For Lyndon Johnson's 200 million countrymen, the year 1967 produced an unprecedented crop of complaints, based largely on the two great crises that came into confluence. Abroad, there was the war in Viet Nam, possibly the most unpopular conflict in the nation's history and the largest ever waged without specific congressional consent. At home, the Negro, more aware than ever of the distance he has yet to travel toward full citizenship, vented his impatience in riots that rent 70 cities in a summer of bloodshed and pillage. The U.S. was vexed as well by violence in the streets, rising costs, youthful rebelliousness, pollution of air and water and the myriad other maladies of a post-industrial society that is growing ever more bewilderingly urbanized, ungovernable and impersonal. With so many problems flowing together, the nation was battered by a flood tide of frustration and anxiety. And more than ever before in an era of material well-being, the nation's discontent was focused upon its President.

It was sometimes hard to tell whether the rancor aroused by Johnson stemmed from his policies or his personality. An immensely complex, contradictory and occasionally downright unpleasant man, he has never managed to attract the insulating layer of loyalty that a Roosevelt or a Truman, however beleaguered, could fall back on. Whenever he left his desk and sallied forth among the people who only three years ago gave him the greatest outpouring of votes in history, he attracted angry pickets. Hardly a day passed without a contumelious attack. Wherever he went, from a speaking engagement in Los Angeles to a cardinal's funeral in Manhattan, he was dogged by shouts of "Murderer!" or chants of "Hey, hey, L.B.J., how many kids did you kill today?" Black Power Apostle Stokely Carmichael called him a "hunky," a "buffoon," and a "liar." Stokely's successor as head of the ill-named Student Nonviolent Coordinating Committee, H. Rap Brown, suggested that the President—and Lady Bird—ought to be shot.

With so many harpoons filling the air, Johnson prudently stuck to his bunker for much of 1967. He spent two months at the L.B.J. ranch and even in Washington made himself scarce for long periods. But he went on working hard at his job. Unlike Ike, who set up military lines of command and delegated considerable responsibility, Johnson wants to be in on everything. His "night reading," often a five-inch-thick stack of memos and cables, covers everything from the latest CIA intelligence roundup to a gossipy report on a feud between two Senators. "Not a sparrow falls," says a former aide, "that he doesn't know about." He speaks of "my Government" and "my army" and "my taxes." The Presidential Seal has been emblazoned on his twill ranch jackets, his cowboy boots, his cuff links, even on plastic drinking cups.

Johnson is acutely aware of how much is expected of him as President—and of the fact that, in the eyes of many, he has fallen short. "In all candor," he conceded, "I cannot recall a period that is in any way comparable to the one we are living through today. It is a period that finds exhilaration and frustration going hand in hand—when great accomplishments are often overshadowed by rapidly rising expectations."

A difficult problem that the President had to deal with was a deficit in the balance of payments, which weakened the dollar abroad and led to a dangerous drain in U.S. gold reserves. [See Business, page 218.]

AN. 12 **STANCHING THE FLOOD:** The dollar-bolstering campaign that President Johnson sprang on an unsuspecting world during the first day of 1968 was conceived in secrecy worthy of a major military maneuver. When the finishing touches were finally completed, newsmen were summoned to the airplane hangar at the L.B.J. ranch for what they were told would be an important New Year's Day announcement.

Johnson greeted them with somber words. Continued deficits in the balance of payments, he warned, could "endanger the strength of the entire free-world economy and thereby threaten our unprecedented prosperity at home." With that, the President moved to stanch the dollar drain with the most Draconian measures yet. He outlined a five-point program aimed at cutting the deficit by $3 billion in the year ahead. Principal features: a reduction in U.S. investment abroad to save $1 billion; a cutback in U.S. loans to foreigners to save $500 million; scaled-down Government expenditures overseas—by the Pentagon, by heavily staffed U.S. embassies and by G.I.s and their dependents—to save $500 million; deferment for two years of all but what the President called "the most important, urgent and necessary" travel outside the Western Hemisphere to save $500 million of the $4 billion now being spent abroad each year by U.S. tourists.

AN. 19 **TUNING IN ALL CHANNELS:** If waging a war in Asia has been a frustrating exercise for Americans, trying to end it has proved almost as stultifying. Through dozens of channels last week, President Johnson was exploring Hanoi's recent statement that a halt in U.S. bombing of North Viet Nam "will" result in peace talks. But nobody could determine for certain whether the Communists were interested in launching negotiations that could end the war or in scoring a propaganda coup. "We could be on the threshold of something big," said one U.S. official, "but as of now it looks more like a cheap political ploy to get the bombing turned off for nothing."

Skeptical though it was toward Hanoi's latest stance on talks, the Administration repeatedly emphasized that it was determined to explore the matter thoroughly—but with as little fanfare as possible. "If I discuss private contacts," said Secretary of State Rusk in a speech at San Francisco's Fairmont Hotel, whose walls were splattered with red paint by some 400 antiwar demonstrators, "then they are no longer either private or contacts."

LYNDONTHINK: While the thoughts of Red China's leader are JAN. available to American readers in the little red booklet *Quotations from Chairman Mao Tse-tung,* they have no such access to the accumulated wisdom of Lyndon Johnson. To fill this obvious gap—and turn a profit in the process—Journalists Jack Shepherd, 30, and Christopher Wren, 31, set out to anthologize *Quotations from Chairman L.B.J.*

Carefully following the original Red format, the two editors —Democrats both—grouped Johnson's sayings under 30 categories such as "The Long March Toward the Great Society" and "Humble Origins of the People's Servant." Under the chapter head "Humility and Self-Criticism," there is a meaningful blank space. All told, Shepherd and Wren gathered about 300 quotations from Johnson—his folksiest and most fulsome.

❡ LET A HUNDRED FLOWERS FLOURISH. "Even in our own country we do not see everything alike. If we did, we would all want the same wife—and that would be a problem, wouldn't it?"—Washington, Feb. 11, 1964.

❡ BENIGN DESPOTISM. "I have the ablest staff that ever served any President in my memory. There's not a playboy among them. They aren't sitting around drinking whisky at 11 o'clock at night. They aren't walking around with their zippers unbuttoned."—Washington, July 14, 1965.

❡ ULTIMATE REFLECTION. "I'm the only President you've got." —Washington, April 27, 1964.

FEB. 9   **BAD WEEK:** At the height of the Communists' savage Viet Nam offensive against the U.S. Marine outpost at Khe Sanh [see page 121], Lyndon Johnson's low-key performance was a cool effort to mask one of the most trying weeks of a crisis-ridden presidency. Amid all the tumult around him, Johnson still found time to present the Heart of the Year Award to Actress Patricia Neal, who suffered three near-fatal strokes three years ago. And he went to the annual presidential prayer breakfast, where he said: "America never stands taller than when her people get to their knees. I can tell you that in these long nights your President prays."

After news of the enemy attacks reached Washington, Johnson kept constant alert, pouncing on reports that were rushed to him through the evening and night. At 5 a.m., he was up for a briefing in the basement Situation Room of the White House. Before breakfast, he was on the phone twice to Defense Secretary Robert McNamara. Said Presidential Press Secretary George Christian: "He's working like a dog, keeping tabs on everything."

For all the troubles swirling about him, Johnson was still quick to bristle at charges that his Great Society is being sacrificed to foreign crisis. "It's just a bunch of blarney," he declared. "It's just like saying I can't take care of Luci because I have Lynda Bird."

MARCH 8   **FLY NOW, TELL LATER:** Thanks to some of the most elaborate security measures in memory, there were no crowds on hand to greet Lyndon Johnson last week as a six-car procession bore him down Stemmons Freeway on his first visit to Dallas since Nov. 22, 1963. As his aquamarine limousine passed within 200 yards of the building from which Lee Harvey Oswald fired the bullets that killed John F. Kennedy, the President seemed determined to curtain his memories of that terrible day and spot. With Daughter Luci in the back seat, he chatted lightly about his mongrel Yuki, perched on the ledge behind his head.

Inside Dallas Memorial Auditorium, delivering his first campaign stump speech of 1968, the President assumed the stance that he now apparently plans to maintain until Election Day. The Great Society, said Johnson—invoking a term that has been notably missing from recent presidential pronouncements —is "taking root. It is thrusting up; it is reaching out to

President Lyndon Johnson, on nationwide TV, delivers the political surprise of the year: "I shall not seek, and I will not accept, the nomination."

banish need and to bring new hope into millions upon millions of lives."

Another emerging, and perturbing, pattern for the 1968 campaign is the prospect that violently hostile demonstrations will rule out the handshaking style of campaigning amid big crowds that Johnson likes. His secret journey to Dallas even took local lawmen by surprise. Police Chief Charles Batchelor received only one hour's warning from the Secret Service. Johnson intends to announce none of his trips in advance, will honor speechmaking invitations only at the last moment.

BOWING OUT: "I shall not seek, and I will not accept, the nomination of my party. . . ." Thus on nationwide television this week, almost as a throwaway line, in one of the most painful speeches that he has ever delivered to the American people, did the 36th President of the U.S. declare his intention to bow out of the 1968 presidential race. APRIL

THE RENUNCIATION: Lyndon Johnson's renunciation of a second term as President dumfounded all but a score of relatives and top aides, who suspected that it might be coming. It was not included in the advance text of his bombing-pause speech. And by the time Johnson reached the crucial passage 35 minutes after his address began, many Americans had already APRIL

Barry Goldwater. He heard L.B.J.'s news—and "had another drink."

Senator Dirksen. The Democrats, he says, forced L.B.J. to quit.

switched off their television sets. Others had grown heavy-lidded. Then, with the particular relish he derives from surprises, the President jolted his countrymen out of their Sunday somnolence with the biggest surprise of all. Said he, in a sentence that may have earned its place among historic American quotations: "I shall not seek, and I will not accept, the nomination of my party for another term as your President."

Johnson had long toyed with the idea of renouncing a second term. According to White House Press Secretary George Christian, Lady Bird "thought it best that her husband step out after one elected term—but she didn't pressure him. She's not that kind of woman." But plainly, the President was stung by the savagery of the criticism aimed at him. Early in his presidency, he had declared: "I want to do only one thing in this job. I want to unite this country." But deepening troubles at home and abroad finally persuaded the President to take the step he did.

When the announcement came, politicians, uncharacteristically, were at a loss for words. "I don't know quite what to say," stammered Bobby Kennedy. Said McCarthy: "I think I'm surprised." Barry Goldwater had a more down-to-earth reaction: "I went and had another drink." Senate Minority Leader Everett M. Dirksen bitterly noted that the "personal and sometimes ugly" criticism of the President by his fellow

Democrats helped drive him to his decision. Said Dirksen: "The harpies of the shore shall pluck the eagle of the sea." Outside the White House, a group of youths unfurled a banner reading "THANKS, L.B.J." In Kansas City, a photographer wrote: "Congratulations. It was the best thing you could possibly have given up for Lent."

The next morning the President felt, as he told friends, like a man who had shed a sack of cement. He flew out to Chicago to address the National Association of Broadcasters, and in a notably restrained speech, he made an uncharacteristically modest confession: "I understand, far better than some of my severe and perhaps intolerant critics would admit, my own shortcomings as a communicator." That night he went to bed early, for the first time in memory did not bother to wade through his thick stack of official reports, even overslept the next morning. Relaxed, almost jaunty, he told a group at the Department of Agriculture: "I am a Hereford breeder. I sell registered calves. I am going to have a lot of time to work on it pretty soon."

HOPEFUL HALF STEPS: After three years of ever more furious combat, after dozens of feints and one-sided gestures toward conciliation, the U.S. and North Viet Nam finally moved in the same direction at the same time. The first half step came last week when President Johnson dramatically restricted the U.S. bombing of North Viet Nam without demanding any reciprocal restraint by the Communists. North Viet Nam, in turn, agreed to the first significant face-to-face diplomatic contact with the U.S. since embassy-level talks in Moscow 14 months ago, although its insistence upon an end to all attacks on its territory had not been met. The entire exchange took just 68 hours.

Even the first half step proved difficult for each side. Bombing of the North has been a constant impediment to any peace talks—not to say one of the most emotional issues of the war. Between May 1965 and February 1967, the U.S. suspended the bombing—"Operation Rolling Thunder"—five times, the halts ranging in duration from two to 37 days. None of them cracked diplomatic ice. On Feb. 1, President Johnson depicted a grim situation if the U.S. stopped bombing: "The enemy force in the South would be larger. It would be better equipped.

The war would be harder. The losses would be greater."

The chief reason for limiting the bombing this time was a strong hunch that Hanoi might finally cooperate. The Communists' *Tet* offensive [see page 122], despite its savagery and shock effects, cost the North Vietnamese and the Viet Cong heavily. Recently, a 9th Infantry Division brigade captured a revealing critique of the *Tet* fighting. Issued by Hanoi's Central Office for South Viet Nam, it said: "We failed to seize a number of primary objectives and to destroy mobile and defense units of the enemy. We also failed to motivate the people to stage uprisings."

Then Radio Hanoi issued a 1,000-word statement bristling with the clichés of intransigence. But nestled in the bombast was a bombshell: "However, for its part, the government of the Democratic Republic of Viet Nam declares its readiness to appoint its representatives to contact the U.S. representatives with a view to determining with the American side the unconditional cessation of the U.S. bombing raids and all other acts of war against the Democratic Republic of Viet Nam so that talks may start."

The North Vietnamese statement electrified Washington. After conferences with key aides, Johnson went on television to announce: "We will establish contact with the representatives of North Viet Nam. Consultations with the government of South Viet Nam and our other allies are now taking place."

RIL 19 **A PLACE TO TALK:** Like two boxers at the opening bell, the U.S. and North Viet Nam warily circled the ring, each testing the other's reach. Striking a prizefighter's pose, Lyndon Johnson said: "I'm holding my left hand open and out in front of me, saying, 'Come on, let's talk.' And I'm keeping my right up high to protect myself and to hit." The pose had a certain drama about it. But the noisy dispute over a site where American and North Vietnamese negotiators could meet for preliminary talks on ways to end the war recalled what the late John Foster Dulles said about negotiating with Asian Communists: "Progress is always slow and seldom spectacular."

Initially, Johnson suggested Geneva. Without rejecting the Swiss city outright, Hanoi came back with Pnompenh. Johnson, in turn, pointed out that Cambodia's capital has serious communications shortcomings and that neither the U.S. nor

South Viet Nam has an embassy there. Instead, he proposed four other Asian sites (Vientiane, Rangoon, Djakarta and New Delhi). North Viet Nam's next reply: Washington's reluctance to accept Pnompenh "cannot but cause wonder, because the U.S. has repeatedly expressed willingness to send its representatives to any point on the globe."

This was a reference to Johnson's repeated statements that he would send U.S. representatives "anywhere, any time," to "any spot on this earth." Accusing the U.S. of a "stubborn and perfidious attitude," Hanoi at week's end rejected as "not convenient" all the sites suggested by Washington. During this diplomatic *pas de deux*, Johnson sought to emphasize that the U.S. had its right hand "up high." After conferring with Johnson, Defense Secretary Clark Clifford announced that 24,500 Army, Air Force and Navy reservists and National Guardsmen were being called up. At the same time, Clifford announced that the U.S. force level in South Viet Nam would increase within the next five months, from the presently authorized total of 525,000 men to 549,500.

But there were signs that Johnson was wigwagging his open left hand as well as prominently displaying his clenched right fist. U.S. planes, having ranged as far as the 20th parallel after the President declared a partial bombing pause, last week went no farther north than the 19th parallel—a difference of nearly 70 miles. For its part, however, Hanoi offered no sign that it was prepared to make a reciprocal gesture.

THE VERY FIRST STEP: It was just after 1 a.m. when the phone MAY shrilled at Lyndon Johnson's White House bedside. Drowsily the President lifted the receiver. An instant later, he was wide awake. At the other end of the line was National Security Adviser Walt W. Rostow with the news that Hanoi was at last prepared to send representatives to Paris to get the long-delayed negotiations under way. Nine hours later, the President announced: "I have sent a message informing Hanoi that the date of May 10 and the site of Paris are acceptable to the U.S." He added somberly: "I must, however, sound a cautionary note. This is only the very first step. There are many, many hazards and difficult days ahead."

For the U.S., the chief negotiator in what is likely to prove a harrowing test of endurance, patience and skill will be Roving Ambassador Averell Harriman, who at 76 boasts not only a long record of successful negotiations with Communist diplomats but astonishing stamina as well. Backing up Harriman will be Cyrus R. Vance, 51, until last year the Deputy Secretary of Defense. As its chief representative, Hanoi designated Xuan Thuy, 55, a veteran diplomat and journalist who retired as Foreign Minister three years ago.

BITING THE BULLET: For most of his press conference last week, the President seemed unwontedly subdued, as if he had prepared himself with one Miltown too many. Then a newsman asked him about that vexed, vexatious tax-boost bill which the President has been trying to get [see Congress, page 84], and Lyndon Johnson all at once was his old self again. For eight gesticulatory minutes he urged Congressmen to "stand up like men" and vote, to "bite the bullet" no matter how much it hurt. Oddly enough, until he spoke, they had seemed ready to do just that. The principal roadblock, apart from popular feeling against tax boosts and congressional reluctance to raise the rates in an election year, has been the fiscal conservatives' demand for a substantial cutback in federal expenditures. With military spending still going up and the needs of the cities paramount in the minds of most liberals, there seemed little room for maneuver. Massive cuts, liberals believed, would gut too many socially oriented programs that have already been pared to the bone.

There matters stood until last week, when the President first met with House leaders and, with great reluctance, worked out an agreement for a slash of $4 billion in cash from the 1969 budget and a hefty cut of $18 billion in promised allotments for future budgets. Both cutbacks were then ratified by the key House Appropriations Committee. Wilbur Mills, chairman of the House Ways and Means Committee, wanted even larger retrenchments: $6 billion in cash and $20 billion in promised money. Economizing on this scale, countered the President, "would really bring chaos to the Government. I am the coach," he protested at one point—referring to Mills, who has replaced Senator William Fulbright as his chief nemesis—"and I send in signals for a pass to my quarterback and he runs a play off tackle."

In fact, a compromise had seemed imminent until the President's news-conference tirade. Angry as they are, most Congressmen now realize, like it or not, that higher taxes are mandatory if the economy and the dollar are to be saved. But like it or not, Lyndon Johnson also will have to bite the bullet and accept cutbacks that will maim some of his proudest programs.

DR. JOHNSON, HIS OWN BOSWELL: When Lyndon Johnson re- MAY treats to his Texas ranch and his reflections next January, he will carry with him the most exhaustive record of a presidency ever compiled. As grist for a planned treatise on his life in politics of from three to four volumes, he has a lode of documents that already overflows 8,000 filing-cabinet drawers. Perhaps because he has always been mistrustful of how others may interpret his stewardship, Johnson has been a kind of auto-Boswell, chronicling virtually his every waking minute in the White House. Squirreled away in the Executive Office Building are Johnson's letters, memos, speeches, citations, directives and doodles. There are transcripts of thousands of his telephone calls, notes taken by aides at secret parleys, notations of every visitor logged in and out of his office, even timetables of presidential repasts, catnaps and dips in the White House pool.

Almost every night in her sitting room, Lady Bird dutifully augments her husband's historical hoard by dictating her own Johnsoniana to what she calls a talking machine. There are miles of films of L.B.J. in action given by television networks and more than 500,000 pictures of the President snapped by ubiquitous White House photographers. This plethora of memorabilia and trivia, together with hundreds of official gifts from visiting dignitaries, will be housed in a special Johnson library at the University of Texas in Austin. L.B.J. also aims to help set up an institute of public affairs at the school, aided by foundation grants, emphasizing a redefinition of the nature of the U.S. presidency. Dr. Johnson—he has 35 honorary doctorates—has yet to delineate his future role at the university. "If Lyndon Johnson came here to teach government," sniffed a coed studying political science, "I'd change my major to journalism."

CALLS FOR COOPERATION: Lyndon Johnson last week ad- JUNE 2 dressed two appeals to the Kremlin for progress on arms controls, a subject he clearly holds vital to the peace effort of his last months as president. Flying into rain-soaked Manhattan, the President made a calculated surprise visit to address the U.N. General Assembly, whose members had just voted, 95 to 4, to endorse the nuclear nonproliferation pact. When it is signed by the U.S., Russia, Britain and 40 non-nuclear countries, the treaty will prohibit traffic in nuclear arms and war matériel between the atomic haves and have-nots, and at the same time encourage the spread of peaceful know-how and materials. Although two atomically armed nations—France and Red China—will not sign the treaty, Johnson nonetheless hailed it as "the most important international agreement in the field of disarmament since the nuclear age began."

Later, at a ceremony in the White House Secretary of State Dean Rusk and Soviet Ambassador Anatoly Dobrynin exchanged papers ratifying a U.S.-Russian consular agreement. The new accord calls for separate negotiations on the opening of consular offices outside Moscow and Washington and constitutes the first bilateral agreement between the two nations since the U.S. granted diplomatic recognition to Russia in 1933.

OV. 8   **THE BOMBING HALT:** The Viet Nam war has divided and demoralized the American people as have few other issues in this century. It led, on March 31, to Lyndon Johnson's renunciation of the presidency in the realization that he might well have been defeated for re-election. Thus it came as the supreme irony of the Johnson Administration that, as Americans prepared to go to the polls this week to vote for another President, the agony of Viet Nam appeared about to be alleviated.

In a televised address to the nation that may rate as the high point of his career, the President announced: "I have now ordered that all air, naval and artillery bombardment of North Viet Nam cease," effective twelve hours after he spoke. "What we now expect—what we have a right to expect—are prompt, productive, serious and intensive negotiations." Presumably there was some *quid pro quo,* but in order to spare Hanoi embarrassment among its allies, most notably Peking, the U.S. may keep the specific terms secret as long as possible. Still, the President made it clear that if North Viet Nam takes advantage of the pause—such as massive violation of the Demilitarized Zone or the shelling of cities—the U.S. will not hesitate to resume the bombing. "We could be misled—and we are prepared for such a contingency," he said.

Johnson's announcement climaxed days of roiling activity. In Saigon, officials would not even say whether U.S. Ambassador Ellsworth Bunker had been conferring with South Viet Nam's President Nguyen Van Thieu—when everybody in town knew that he had. To attend one White House conference, Defense Secretary Clark Clifford drove to the State Department in his chauffeured limousine, met Secretary of State Dean Rusk in the basement, then with Rusk hopped into a nondescript Chevrolet for the half-mile drive to 1600 Pennsylvania Avenue. The ruse failed; newsmen sighted them anyway.

As the week began, Washington received word from Hanoi that the North Vietnamese were amenable to Johnson's latest proposals. Before making a final decision, however, the President decided to review the picture once more. General Creighton W. Abrams [who had replaced General William Westmoreland as commander of U.S. forces in Viet Nam in June], responded to an urgent summons from Johnson. "Get him over here as soon as you can," the President had ordered. The general hastily boarded a four-jet C-141 StarLifter for an unannounced flight to Washington. During an all-night session at the White House with Johnson and several top aides that began at 2:38 a.m. Abrams noted that the situation in the field has improved vastly in recent months, and that a bombing halt might now be militarily tolerable.

RETURN OF THE NATIVE: When Lyndon Baines Johnson enters the voting booth this week at the Pedernales Electric Co-op in Johnson City, his name, for a change, will not be on the ballot. After 31 years in Washington and ten consecutive election victories, L.B.J. will be coming home. His fellow-Texans in Johnson City will be pleased to have him back. They should be. During Lyndon Johnson's three decades in Washington, the community has been transformed from a decaying, unpaved cow town into a humming tourist mecca. As Congressman, Senator, Vice President and President, Johnson City's native son has showered largesse on his home hill country. In New Deal days came the Lower Colorado River Authority, whose dams harnessed and tamed waters that had ravaged the countryside. Then he won for Johnson City the Pedernales Co-op, which today provides power from the authority's steam plants to some 18,500 customers in seven counties. Lately there has been more: a handsome 50-unit $650,000 housing development for the aged and the poor, and an $840,000 federal grant for a badly needed 30-bed hospital, and a small, as yet unannounced federal building that will house the post office and local federal agencies. There is also a Lake Lyndon B. Johnson in nearby Kingsland, a Lyndon B. Johnson High School, a Lyndon Baines Johnson State Park, and several roads bearing the presidential name. In the Texas state capital of Austin— an hour's drive from Johnson City—there will be the Lyndon Baines Johnson Library at the University of Texas.

V. 15 **THIEU BALKS:** When Lyndon Johnson announced the bombing halt to the American people, he prudently cautioned that the U.S. could be seriously disappointed in its efforts to find peace in Viet Nam. At first, his admonition seemed unwarranted. From most of the world's capitals, including Moscow, came only praise for the President's action.

But then, to Washington's dismay, the U.S. peace initiative foundered on the obduracy of its principal allies, the South Vietnamese, and last week's scheduled session in Paris was canceled. The man who dashed the diplomatic hopes was South Viet Nam's President Nguyen Van Thieu. Until two days before the announcement of the bombing pause, Thieu seemed to go along with the U.S. plan. Then he hardened his stand, bluntly barring South Viet Nam's participation in the Paris talks.

The sticking point is the participation of the National Liberation Front, which is the political arm of the Viet Cong. As Saigon sees it, the participation of the N.L.F. as an equal member in any peace talks is tantamount to recognizing that the Communists represent a portion of the population of South Viet Nam. Such an admission would be a serious loss of face for Thieu's regime and might force the Saigon government into the position of having no alternative to the acceptance of Communists in a coalition government. [President Thieu later agreed to send a delegation to Paris, and the expanded talks began. For a report on the new phase of negotiations, see page 127.]

Assassinations

The year was overshadowed by two tragic and violent deaths, the assassinations of Negro leader Dr. Martin Luther King and Senator Robert F. Kennedy. Their passing would have a momentous effect on political events in the months to come and on the nation's search for racial peace.

SYMBOL & SYMPTOM: The murder last week of Martin Luther King was both a symbol and a symptom of the nation's racial malaise. The proximate cause of his death was, ironically, a minor labor dispute in a Southern backwater: the two-month-old strike of 1,300 predominantly Negro garbage collectors in the decaying Mississippi river town of Memphis. The plight of the sanitation workers, caused by the refusal of Memphis' intransigent white Mayor Henry Loeb to meet their modest wage and compensation demands, first attracted and finally eradicated Dr. King, the conqueror of Montgomery, Birmingham and Selma.

The Eastern Airlines jet that carried King to Memphis was delayed 15 minutes before takeoff while crewmen checked its baggage for bombs that anonymous callers had warned were aboard. That was nothing particularly unusual for a man whose life had been threatened so often, but when King arrived in Memphis he met a different challenge. Some newspapers had emphasized during the previous week that the prophet of the poor had been staying at a luxurious Holiday Inn hostelry on the Mississippi's east bank, which charges $29 a night for a suite. To repair his image, King checked into the Negro-owned Lorraine, a nondescript, two-story cinderblock structure where King and his entourage paid $13 a night for their green-walled, rust-spotted rooms.

Across Mulberry Street from the Lorraine, on a slight rise, stands a nameless rooming house adorned only with a metal awning whose red, green and yellow stripes shade an equally nameless clientele. Into that dwelling—actually two buildings, one for whites, the other for Negroes, and connected by a dank, umbilical hallway—walked a young, dark-haired white man in a neat business suit. "He had a silly little smile that I'll never forget," says Mrs. Bessie Brewer, who manages the rooming house. The man, who called himself John Willard, carefully chose Room 5, with a view of the Lorraine, and paid his $8.50 for the week with a crisp $20 bill—another rarity that stuck in Mrs. Brewer's mind.

Back at the Lorraine, King and his aides were finishing a long, hot day of tactical planning for the next week's march—one that would be carried out in defiance of a federal district court injunction. In the course of the conference, King had assured his colleagues that, despite death threats, he was not afraid. "Maybe I've got the advantage over most people," he mused. "I've conquered the fear of death." After the strategy session, King washed and dressed for dinner. Then he walked out of Room 306 onto the second-floor balcony of the Lorraine to take the evening air. Leaning casually on the green iron railing he chatted with co-workers readying his Cadillac sedan in the dusk below. To Soul Singer Ben Branch, who was to perform at a rally later that evening, King made a special request: "I want you to sing that song *Precious Lord* for me—sing it real pretty." When Chauffeur Solomon Jones naggingly advised King to don his topcoat against the evening's chill, the muscular Atlantan grinned and allowed: "O.K., I will."

Then, from a window of the rooming house across the way, came a single shot. "It was like a stick of dynamite," recalled

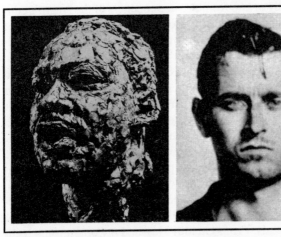

Martin Luther King. A report "like dynamite"—and a great leader is dead.

James Earl Ray. Q.: "Did you kill Dr. King?" A.: "No, sir." Page 40.

one aide. All of the aides hit the deck. The heavy-caliber bullet smashed through King's neck, exploded against his lower right jaw, severing his spinal cord and slamming him away from the rail, up against the wall, with hands drawn tautly toward his head. Some 30 hard-hatted Memphis police swiftly converged on the motel in response to the shot. In doing so, they missed the assassin, whose weapon (a scope-sighted 30.06-cal. Remington pump rifle), binoculars and suitcase were found near the rooming house. A spent cartridge casing was left in the grimy lavatory. An ambulance came quickly, and raced King to St. Joseph's Hospital 1½ miles away. Moribund as he entered the emergency ward, Martin Luther King Jr., 39, was pronounced dead within an hour of the shooting.

TRANSCENDENT SYMBOL: For Martin Luther King Jr., death came as a tragic finale to an American drama fraught with classic hints of inevitability. Propelled to fame in the throes of the Negro's mid-century revolution, he gave it momentum and steered it toward nonviolence. Yet the movement he served with such eloquence and zeal was beginning to pass him by, and nonviolence to many black militants had come to seem naive, outmoded, even suicidal. Yet if ever there were a transcendent Negro symbol, it was Martin Luther King. Bridging the void between black despair and white unconcern, he spoke so powerfully of and from the wretchedness of the Negro's condition that he became the moral guidon of civil rights not only to Americans but also to the world beyond. Born in a middle-class Georgia family active for two generations in the civil rights cause, he was the second child and first-born son, named after his father, Michael Luther King. The elder King, pastor of Atlanta's Ebenezer Baptist Church, changed both their names when Martin was five to honor the Reformation rebel who nailed his independent declaration to the Castle Church.

At Crozer Theological Seminary in Chester, Pa., where young King was elected class president and outstanding student, he was exposed to the writings of Mohandas Gandhi, whose mystic faith in nonviolent protest became King's lodestar. "From my background," he said, "I gained my regulating Christian ideals. From Gandhi I learned my operational technique." Indeed, Gandhi's word for his doctrine, *satyagraha,* becomes in translation King's slogan, "soul force." Moving on to Boston University, King gained a doctorate and a bride, Antioch College Graduate Coretta Scott, and in 1954 took his first pastorate in Montgomery, Ala. There in 1955, a seamstress' tired feet precipitated the first great civil rights test of power and launched King's galvanic career. The seamstress' arrest for refusing to give her seat on a town bus to a white man led to a Negro boycott of the Montgomery busline. Three hundred and eighty-two days later the busline capitulated. King, a leader in the boycott too new to Montgomery to have enemies in the usually fragmented Negro community, soon became its chief. His march to martyrdom had begun.

VISIONS OF THE PROMISED LAND: Few American orators, black or white, could match the sonorous, soul-stirring resonances of Martin Luther King Jr. From his early sermons to his letter from a Birmingham jail, from the epic address at the Lincoln Memorial during the 1963 March on Washington to his acceptance speech at the 1964 Nobel Prize ceremonies, King's rhetoric rang richly with both the ageless cadences of Negro spirituals and the moral immediacy of the civil rights struggle. His voice was for his time and beyond. Highlights:

❡ ON THE NEGRO IN AMERICA (from Birmingham jail, 1963): "Before the Pilgrims landed at Plymouth, we were here. Before the pen of Jefferson etched across the pages of history the majestic words of the Declaration of Independence, we were here. If the inexpressible cruelties of slavery could not stop us, the opposition we now face will surely fail. We will win our freedom because the sacred heritage of our nation and the eternal will of God are embodied in our echoing demands."

❡ ON MARCHING FOR CIVIL RIGHTS (Selma to Montgomery, 1965): "Like an idea whose time has come, not even the marching of mighty armies can halt us. We are moving to the land of freedom. Let us march on segregated housing. Let us march on segregated schools. Let us march on poverty. Let us march on ballot boxes, until the Wallaces of our nation tremble away in silence. My people, my people, listen! The battle is in our hands."

❡ ON THE DREAM OF FREEDOM (Washington, D.C., 1963): "I have a dream that one day this nation will rise up and live out the true meaning of its creed . . . that all men are created equal. I have a dream that my four little children will one day live in a nation where they will not be judged by the color of their skin but by the content of their character. I have a dream today. And if America is to be a great nation, this must become true. So let freedom ring. From the prodigious hilltops of New Hampshire, let freedom ring. From the heightening Alleghenies of Pennsylvania, let freedom ring. But not only that; let freedom ring from Stone Mountain of Georgia. Let freedom ring from every hill and molehill of Mississippi. And when this happens, when we let it ring, we will speed that day when all of God's children, black men and white men, Jews and Gentiles, Protestants and Catholics, will be able to join hands and sing in the words of the old Negro spiritual:

> *Free at last, free at last,*
> *Thank God Almighty, we're free at last."*

¶ ON HIS OWN FUTURE (Memphis, April 3, 1968): "We've got some difficult days ahead. But it really doesn't matter with me now. Because I've been to the mountaintop. Like anybody, I would like to live a long life. Longevity has its place. But I'm not concerned about that now. I just want to do God's will. And he's allowed me to go up to the mountain. And I've looked over, and I've seen the Promised Land. I may not get there with you, but I want you to know tonight that we as a people will get to the Promised Land. So I'm happy tonight. I'm not fearing any man. Mine eyes have seen the glory of the coming of the Lord."

RAMPAGE & RESTRAINT: In its sweep and immediacy, the shock APR wave of looting, arson and outrage that swept the nation's black ghettos after Martin Luther King's murder exceeded anything in the American experience. By week's end, 168 towns and cities had echoed to the crash of brick through window glass, the crackle of the incendiary's witch's torch, the scream of sirens and the anvil chorus of looters. Yet one sound was remarkable in its very diminuendo. The fierce fusillades of gunfire that exacerbated the disorders of years past were heard only rarely last week. And considering the specter of anarchy looming over every U.S. city, the nation weathered its April agony with remarkable aplomb.

The low "kill rate," to borrow an unhappy term from another war, was due in large measure to lessons learned from three years of urban upheaval. Heeding the advice of the Kerner riot-commission report, which warned that "the use of excessive force—even the inappropriate display of weapons—may be inflammatory and lead to worse disorder," lawmen in most cities refrained from gunplay, and magistrates quickly processed those arrested for rioting, setting low bail as the commission suggested. "It seems to me a high-policy decision was made to trade goods and appliances for human lives," remarked Negro Psychologist Kenneth Clark.

The nation's capital, afflicted for the first time since 1962 by racial turmoil, endured three days of pillaging and burning that brought a force of 15,246 regular troops to its defense—more than twice the size of the U.S. garrison that held Khe Sanh. Total damage to the capital's buildings and property: $13.3 million, highest in the U.S. Arsonists and looters were highly selective, hitting elegant clothing stores or else stripping liquor or grocery shelves and then burning credit records. Ten deaths were counted in the capital. The 711 fires that plumed the city afforded a pyrotechnical spectacle unmatched since British troops burned the capital in 1814.

For the most part, Negroes rejected the call of Black Powermonger Stokely Carmichael to "get your gun." Despite Stokely's call to arms, a number of major cities remained relatively quiet: New York, Detroit, Cleveland, Los Angeles and Milwaukee, among others. In all of them, black militants were the most influential peacemakers. Watts's Ron Karenga, abrasive boss of a black nationalist outfit, supported the "Committee for Operational Unity," which had cooled the ghetto the week before. Harlem's Charles Kenyatta, a chieftain of the American Mau Mau, preached in favor of racial peace.

KING'S LAST MARCH: Not since the funeral of John F. Kennedy had the nation so deeply involved itself in mourning. As is their wont in time of national tragedy, the American people turned to their television sets. An estimated 120 million watched a funeral march that lasted more than three hours, twice as long as that for President Kennedy. Instead of the rolling rifle volleys and gutteral drums that accompanied the President's obsequies, Martin Luther King's funeral was counterpointed by resonant spirituals and the toll of mourning bells.

The only jarring note at the church service came when Mrs. Coretta King unexpectedly requested that a tape of her husband's last sermon delivered in the church be played in memoriam. The mournful mood of the moment was shattered by King's unquenchable rhetoric. "If any of you are around when I have to meet my day, I don't want a long funeral," bellowed the voice on the tape. "Tell them not to mention that I have a Nobel Peace Prize. That isn't important. I'd like somebody to mention that Martin Luther King Junior tried to *love* somebody. That I *did* try to feed the hungry, that I *did* try in my life to clothe those who were naked, that I tried to love and serve humanity."

Then followed a four-mile march to the campus of Morehouse College. On a sharecropper's cart drawn by a brace of mules called Ada and Agnes, King's coffin passed the helmeted, machine-gun-armed cops of Governor Lester Maddox at the Georgia Statehouse. Maddox had refused to close schools on the funeral day and later protested the lowering of the flag to half-staff. The procession terminated at the Negro college where King graduated at the age of 19. There on a quadrangle crowded with 100,000 mourners, Morehouse President Emeritus Benjamin E. Mays, 72, eulogized the man whose eloquence he had expected to ease his own passage. The two ministers had agreed that the one who survived would deliver the last verdict on the other. "Too bad, you say, Martin Luther King Jr. died so young," preached Mays. "Jesus died at 33, Joan of Arc at 19, Byron and Burns at 36. And Martin Luther King Jr. at 39. It isn't how long but how well."

WHO KILLED KING: The world had hardly learned of Martin Luther King's murder before speculation began that the civil rights leader had been the victim of a well-planned conspiracy. The rumor mills were lubricated in part by the assiduously cultivated doubts that some still entertain about the killing of John F. Kennedy. In this case, however, the conspiracy theorists could point to the fact that, though the gunman was clearly identified, he remained—for all the far-flung resources of the FBI—mysteriously at large.

The first putative name broken out of the FBI was that of Eric Starvo Galt. This, it soon became clear, was a pseudonym built up to throw pursuers off the trail. Fingerprints found on the rifle left in the street when the killer fled belong to James Earl Ray, an escaped Missouri convict who has spent prison time for four major crimes, including armed robbery, burglary, forgery of U.S money orders and car theft. The prints were painstakingly checked against the FBI's bank of 53,000 sets of records on wanted men; it took 13 days to find them.

James Earl Ray had fled the Missouri State Penitentiary in April 1967, hiding in a big wooden breadbox to get from the prison bakery to the outside world. He had twice before tried to escape, once placing a dummy in his bed and hiding in a ventilator shaft; once he broke a makeshift ladder trying to scale the wall. Ray's youth in Alton, Ill., had been full of tangles with the law. He dropped out of school in the 10th grade, spent two years in the Army, where he served a term for drunkenness and "breaking arrest," was discharged in 1948, and turned to civilian crime. He was convicted of burglary in Los Angeles in 1949, of robbery in Chicago in 1952, of forgery in Missouri in 1955, and in 1960 had drawn the 20-year term for armed robbery and car theft that he was serving when he made his escape.

After Ray escaped from prison, he eventually showed up— as Galt—in Los Angeles, where he presented two distinctly different personalities. If Galt was remembered as shy and pleasant by some of his acquaintances, others recall him as an obsessive racial bigot, an abrasive patron who belted screwdrivers, dozed on the bar stool and bickered with anyone around. Everyone at the Rabbit's Foot Club remembers Galt's big dispute. A young woman had the temerity to tell him that Negroes were "good people." This so enraged Galt that he grabbed her arm and hauled her to the door, shouting: "I'll drop you off in Watts and we'll see how you like it there!" When another customer followed, Galt fled.

The nation had scarcely recovered from the shock of the King assassination when it was assailed by another.

ONCE AGAIN: Once again the crackle of gunfire. Once again the long journey home, the hushed procession, the lowered flags and harrowed faces of a nation in grief. Once again the simple question: Why? The second Kennedy assassination—almost two months to the day after the murder of Martin Luther King Jr.—immediately prompted, at home and abroad, deep doubts about the stability of America. For the young people, in particular, who had been persuaded by the new politics of Robert Kennedy and Eugene McCarthy to recommit themselves to the American electoral system, the assassination seemed to confirm all their lingering suspicions that society could not be reformed by democratic means.

The killing of Robert Kennedy was horrifying in itself and forever haunting to all who had suffered through the earlier agony. Kennedy was not shot by a white racist angry with his defense of the Negro, or a Negro militant incensed with his white liberalism, or a high-school dropout like Lee Harvey Oswald who felt himself rejected by a capitalist society. The man charged with his murder is a virulent Arab nationalist, whose hatreds stem from the land where he spent the early part of his life, and where political assassination is commonplace and violence as accepted as the desert wind.

That, for most Americans, did not make the loss any easier to bear. Lyndon Johnson, who has more than once brooded late into the night with friends on the subject of violence, seemed shaken and visibly disturbed by the shooting in Los Angeles. He did what he thought had to be done. He promised the stricken family any help that the Government could provide, appointed a commission to study the causes of violence, and called, in the most vigorous language at his command, for an end to the "insane traffic" in guns—a trade, as he observed, that makes instruments of death as readily purchasable as baskets of fruit or cartons of cigarettes [see Law & Order, page 44]. Almost as he spoke, Congress sent him a crime bill with a gun-control section, but the measure was so flabby as to be almost as scandalous as the lack of any legislation in all the previous years. Congress, on Johnson's request, also passed emergency legislation authorizing immediate Secret Service protection for the other major presidential candidates (cost: $400,000 this month alone).

"IF ANYONE WANTS TO KILL ME": The circumstances were cruel enough: son of a house already in tragedy's grip, father of ten with the eleventh expected, symbol of the youth and toughness, the wealth and idealism of the nation he sought to lead—this protean figure cut down by a small gun in a small cause. The anthems and eulogies, the fears and the rumors, the calls for conciliation, for wisdom, all were unexceptional. The United Nations lowered its flag to half-staff—an unprecedented tribute to one of Kennedy's modest official rank. For many, the only solace was tears openly shed.

More than anyone else, Robert Kennedy had long felt the possibility that some day people would no longer be able to mention "the Kennedy assassination" without specifying which one. In 1966, he responded to a question about his long-range political plans by saying: "Six years is so far away. I don't even know if I'll be alive in six years." More recently: "If anyone wants to kill me it won't be difficult." Whether gulping fresh air as a tyro mountain climber or rapids shooter or staring down frenzied crowds at home, he had only a shrug for death. He made a point of declining police protection when it was offered—as it was last week in Los Angeles.

He had just won the California primary. Plans were being made for the campaign's next stages, but first there were some formalities and fun to attend to; the midnight appearance before loyal campaign workers. The winner greeted his supporters with a characteristic mixture of serious talk and cracks. Among Kennedy's last words from the rostrum: "I think we

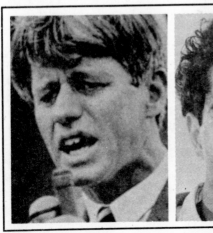

Robert Kennedy: "If anyone wants to kill me it won't be difficult."

Accused assassin Sirhan Sirhan: "I can explain! Let me explain!"

can end the divisions within the United States, the violence."

The next stop was to be the press room. For once, Kennedy did not plunge through the crush to reach the Embassy Room's main door. Bill Barry, his bodyguard, wanted to go that way despite the crowd; he did not like the idea of using a back passageway. Said R.F.K.: "It's all right." So they went through a swinging door and into the hot, malodorous, corridorlike chamber that was to be his place of execution. Kennedy paused to shake hands with a dishwasher, turning slightly to his left as he did so. The gunman managed to prop his right elbow on the serving counter and fire at his victim just four feet away. Kennedy fell. Rafer Johnson, an Olympic champion, knocked the pistol out of the man's hand. "Why did you do it?" he screamed. "I can explain! Let me explain!" cried the swarthy man, now spread-eagled on the counter. Several R.F.K. supporters tried to kill the man on the spot with their hands. Johnson and Roosevelt Grier, a 300-lb. Los Angeles Rams lineman, fended them off. Someone had the presence of mind to shout: "Let's not have another Oswald!" Johnson pocketed the gun. Ethel, shoved back to safety by a hotel employee at the first sound of gunfire, appeared moments later. Finally she got to Bobby. She knelt over him, whispering. His lips moved. She rose and tried to wave back the crush. Someone clamped an ice pack to Kennedy's bleeding head, and someone else made a pillow of a suit jacket. His blue and white striped tie was off, his shirt open, a rosary clutched to his hairy chest. An aide took off his shoes.

With Ethel by his side, Kennedy was taken first to nearby Central Receiving Hospital, where doctors could only keep him alive by cardiac massage and an injection of Adrenalin, and alert the better-equipped Good Samaritan Hospital to prepare for delicate brain surgery. At Good Samaritan, meanwhile, a team of neurosurgeons was being assembled. At this stage, there was still some frail hope that Kennedy would live. It was known that he had been hit twice. One of the .22-caliber "long rifle" slugs had entered the right armpit and worked its way up to the neck; it was relatively harmless. The other had penetrated his skull and passed into the brain, scattering fragments of lead and bone. It was these that the surgeons had to probe for in their operation.

In the intensive-care unit after the operation, Ethel rested on a cot beside him, held his unfeeling hand, whispered into his now-deaf ear. His sisters, Jean Smith and Pat Lawford, hovered nearby. Ted Kennedy, his shirttail flapping, strode back and forth, inspecting medical charts and asking what they meant. More kith and kin gathered. The three eldest children—Kathleen, 16, Joseph, 15, and Robert, 14—were allowed to see their father. The even rise and fall of the patient's chest offered some reassurance; the blackened eyes and the pallor of the cheeks that had been healthy and tanned a few hours before were frightening.

SIRHAN SIRHAN: As the doctors fought for one life, Police Chief Thomas Reddin worried about another. Dallas, 1963, might not have taught the nation how to preserve its leaders, but it had incontestably demonstrated the need to protect those accused of political murder. The man seized at the Ambassador was taken first to a local police station, then to North Los Angeles Street police headquarters. Reddin described him as "very cool, very calm, very stable and quite lucid." John Doe, as he was billed at first when he refused to offer his name, demanded the details of a sexy Los Angeles murder case. "I want to ask the questions now," he remarked. "Why don't you answer my questions?" He talked about the stock market, his belief that criminal justice discriminates against the underdog. After a few hours, the police fed him a pre-dawn breakfast of sausage and eggs and gave up the interrogation.

By then the snub-nosed Iver-Johnson eight-shot revolver, model 55 SA was yielding information. The serial number had been registered with the State Criminal Identification and Investigation Bureau. Within minutes, the bureau's computer system came up with the pistol's original purchaser who had bought the gun for protection in August 1965, after the Watts riot. He informed police that he had given it to his daughter, who gave it to a Pasadena neighbor, who subsequently sold it to someone named Joe—"a bushy-haired guy who worked in a department store." With that lead, the police quickly found Munir ("Joe") Sirhan, 20, in Nash's Department Store. Joe and Adel Sirhan, 29, identified the prisoner as their brother, Sirhan Bishara Sirhan, 24, who goes by the nickname Sol. The identification was confirmed by a check of fingerprints taken when Sirhan applied for a state racetrack job in 1965.

Finally came the news that the family had feared. At 1:44 a.m., Pacific Daylight Time, Bobby Kennedy died under the eyes of his wife, his brother, his sisters Pat and Jean and his sister-in-law Jackie. Sirhan was indicted for murder by a grand jury. Meanwhile, once again, the nation watched the grim logistics of carrying the coffin of a Kennedy home in a presidential Boeing 707.

There remained the final searing day, the day of formal farewell amid all the ancient panoply of Roman Catholic ceremony and all the contemporary irony of American politics. But in all the vastness of St. Patrick's Cathedral, it was from first to last a peculiarly personal Kennedy occasion. The women wore black, their daughters white; the Mass, even for the dead, carries promise of life. Ethel and Rose displayed yet again the steely grace that seems to sustain all women born to or married to Kennedys. Four sons served as acolytes. Eight of their brothers, sisters and cousins bore the bread, the wine and the sacred vessels to the high altar.

It was Ted who acted as paterfamilias. His determinedly brisk voice betrayed him a few times, but the occasional hesitation only added to the power of his eulogy. "He loved life completely and lived it intensely," Ted said, in a reading that was unusual for a Roman Catholic funeral. Frequently using Bobby's own words, Ted concluded with the lines adapted from George Bernard Shaw that Bobby used to end many of his own speeches: "Some men see things as they are and say 'Why?' I dream things that never were and say 'Why not?' "

During the afternoon as the special 21-car train bore the Senator and his family and his friends south to Washington, there were crowds and choirs at many communities along the right-of-way, more tears and dirges—and there was still more death. Two waiting mourners at Elizabeth, N.J., were killed by a train roaring in the other direction. The funeral train inched on and on through the waning day. From the rear platform, Ted Kennedy, with short, sad gestures, thanked the people for coming out. Long after nightfall, the train arrived in Washington. Along the lamplit streets, past a luminescence of sad and silent faces, the cavalcade wound through the federal city and across the Potomac, where in a green grove up the hill in Arlington, John Kennedy's grave looks out over the city and the river. The moon, the slender candles, the eternal flame at

John's memorial laved Robert Kennedy's resting place beneath a magnolia tree. It was 11 o'clock, the first nighttime burial at Arlington in memory. There was no playing of taps, no rifle volley. After a brief and simple service, the coffin flag was folded into a triangle for presentation to Ethel, and the band played *America the Beautiful.*

ARRESTED AT LAST: Among the 96 passengers debarking at Heathrow Airport from BEA's Lisbon-London Flight 75 was Ramon George Sneyd, who went to the Commonwealth immigration desk and presented his Canadian passport. The immigration official took one look at the document, then asked the bespectacled Sneyd to join him in a back room for some "routine" questions. The interrogation was far from routine. Sneyd was found to be packing a loaded pistol in his back pocket, plus another Canadian passport. And when Scotland Yard's crack detective Tommy Butler took over, the alert immigration official's original suspicions were confirmed: fingerprints proved that Sneyd was, in fact, Illinois-born James Earl Ray, 40, alias Eric Starvo Galt, the escaped convict accused of assassinating Dr. Martin Luther King Jr. on April 4 in Memphis.

Since the time that Ray had left his fingerprints on the .30-'06 Remington rifle that killed Dr. King, he had made an elaborate odyssey from justice. He fled to Toronto on April 8, where he checked in and out of two $9-a-week flophouses. He adopted the name Ramon George Sneyd, that of a Toronto policeman, which he possibly picked at random from a city directory. Using his new identity, Ray submitted a passport application. Because of Canada's ludicrously simple passport procedures—which demand, in effect, that the applicant merely swear that he is Canadian—he was granted one. On May 6 he flew by BOAC to London, and the next day on to Portugal.

The FBI, meanwhile, had launched the biggest manhunt in its history, warning officials in Mexico and Canada, favorite hideaways in Ray's tawdry past, to be on the alert. Scotland Yard and Interpol joined the manhunt, and FBI liaison men traveled to Europe and Australia in search of their man. For all the manpower and expense, Ray's trail seemed to grow progressively colder. Then, on June 1, came the first big break. At the U.S.'s request, the Royal Canadian Mounted Police had been checking passport mug shots for the slippery suspect.

After assiduously studying about 300,000, they spotted the face they were looking for.

While all this was going on, Ray was in Lisbon calculating his next move. He apparently attempted to alter his fraudulent passport, but only got as far as changing the *d* in Sneyd to *a*. At the Canadian embassy in Lisbon he told the consul: "My name has been misspelled," and was issued a new passport on May 16. Thus, with the two cards and pistol in pocket, he flew off to London and incarceration at Cannon Row police station, a stone's throw from Big Ben. Facing Ray after his extradition to the U.S. are a Shelby County, Tenn., murder indictment and a federal conspiracy charge. The big, unanswered question is where he got the money for a two-month foray to Europe.

IN THE FAMILY TRADITION: This Monday would have been their 18th wedding anniversary, an occasion for a party in the old frenetic Kennedy style at Hickory Hill, with children and pets much in evidence and perhaps friends in evening clothes ending up spluttering in the swimming pool. Instead, a memorial Mass for Robert Kennedy would be held two days later at a small nearby church. Throughout the week, in public at least, Ethel Kennedy remained gallantly cheerful.

A game of "Kennedy touch" football (forward passing legal anywhere on the field) continued on the broad, sloping lawn. But Ethel Kennedy's best therapy was the exuberance of Christopher, 4, Matthew, 3, and Douglas, 15 months, who, too young to understand what had happened, continued in their usual bouncy style, restoring some feeling of normalcy to the stricken household. Ethel requested that all the tens of thousands of letters of condolence be answered. She also found the time and courage to help close down her husband's Washington campaign headquarters, shaking hands with each volunteer and thanking him for his effort.

At week's end, Ted and Rose Kennedy taped a five-minute television message of thanks to the nation for its condolences. As Patriarch Joseph Kennedy sat speechless beside them in a wheelchair on the lawn of the Hyannisport compound, his youngest and last surviving son said: "It has been the people themselves, with outstretched hands of sympathy and strength, that have most touched the hearts of the members of our family. It is the ones who could give the least who have given the most."

BUILDING A BIOGRAPHY: The accused assassin of Robert Kennedy sat passively in his 12-ft. by 12-ft. maximum security cell at Los Angeles County's Central Jail for Men, reading works on theosophy. Meanwhile, bits and pieces of Sirhan Bishara Sirhan's personality and past began falling into place. Most of the insights came with last week's release of testimony taken by the grand jury, which had convened the day after Kennedy died. Vincent T. Di Pierro, part-time waiter at the Ambassador Hotel, recalled seeing Sirhan at the moment of the murder. "The minute the first two shots were fired," testified Di Pierro, "he still had a very sick-looking smile on his face. That's one thing—I can never forget that."

Three others in the serving kitchen where Kennedy was shot also testified to seeing Sirhan, who crouched on a tray rack and asked repeatedly if the Senator would come that way.

Another witness claimed that he had seen Sirhan at a gun club twelve hours before the assassination. Contrary to range policy, which calls for a pause between shots, Sirhan snapped off 300 rounds in rapid-fire succession with an Iver-Johnson .22-cal. revolver, the same type as that used in the killing.

JUNE 28 **TWO FOR THE ACCUSED:** Before the law, Sirhan Bishara Sirhan and James Earl Ray are simply the accused—no more. Last week, in London and Los Angeles, both men moved to protect their rights under the law by retaining topflight attorneys. For a few days it looked as if Sirhan's trial on charges of assassinating Senator Robert F. Kennedy might become a hippodrome. Four Jordanian lawyers announced that they would fly to the U.S. to assist in the defense of their countryman Sirhan. But before week's end, the Jordanians, under pressure from their own government, had canceled their plans, and Sirhan had a U.S. attorney of impeccable credentials. He was Russell E. Parsons, 73, a Los Angeles criminal lawyer who once defended Gangster Mickey Cohen but is even more famous for his careful appeals work. He is also, according to one admiring colleague, "a totally fair and decent man," and he gave strong proof of that assessment by waiving his usual $10,000 fee to handle Sirhan's case without charge.

In the meantime, former Birmingham Mayor Arthur J. Hanes, 51, and his law partner son Arthur Jr., arrived in London and announced that Ramon George Sneyd, who is presumed in the U.S. to be James Earl Ray, accused assassin of Dr. Martin Luther King Jr., had asked Hanes Sr. to serve as his American counsel. In 1965, Hanes successfully defended Collie Leroy Wilkins and two other Klansmen against Alabama State charges of killing Civil Rights Worker Viola Liuzzo. Despite Hanes' efforts, the three were later convicted of conspiracy in a federal court.

DID YOU KILL DR. KING?:

Q. Did you know Martin Luther King personally?

A. No, sir.

Q. Did you kill Dr. King?

A. No, sir.

Thus, in an unsworn statement, the man whom the U.S. Government claims is James Earl Ray battled last week in London against extradition to face a murder charge in Tennessee. Then a London barrister read into the record depositions and affidavits pointing to Sneyd as the rifleman who pulled the trigger in a second-floor bathroom of a shabby Memphis rooming house to kill King.

An FBI fingerprint expert testified that there were at least eleven points of similarity between the prints belonging to Ray and those of the man held in London as Sneyd. Ray's prints, said an FBI agent, were on a rifle and telescopic sight abandoned in a store doorway near the shooting and also on binoculars wrapped with the weapon. Affidavits from merchants in Montgomery, Ala., and Birmingham pointed to Ray as the man who had purchased the binoculars, rifle and sight.

A VERY IMPORTANT PRISONER: With the wrapped-in-cotton care normally accorded to precious art works, James Earl Ray was flown to Memphis last week to stand trial for the murder of Martin Luther King. A bulletproof vest hung over his plaid shirt and his legs were encased in armored trousering when he was led, handcuffed, from a 6½-ton armored van into Shelby County jail at dawn. A score of deputies with riot guns formed a defensive perimeter. Ray was hustled to an air-conditioned cell on the jail's third floor. Heavy steel plates block cell windows. Closed-circuit television cameras monitor all movements. Prison trusties who ran elevators have been replaced by sheriff's officers.

Such massive protection is more than justified. There is widespread speculation that King's death was plotted by conspirators who are still free. "He won't finish that trial," a Memphis underworldling warned last week. "He's not going to get on that witness chair—and that's the straight word."

Law & Order

A major source of concern to Americans—and a critical issue of the 1968 political campaign—was the rising incidence of crime and violence in the U.S., along with the related problems of gun control and the role of the nation's police forces.

JAN. 5 **CRIME & COUNTERFORCE:** The day after Christmas, Tuesday, Dec. 26, was what police wearily call a "typical" day in U.S. cities—perhaps a cut too typical. In Nashville, Tenn., armed robbers held up two banks. In Chicago, one of the city's 50 aldermen was shot twice in the leg by thugs as he walked the South Side streets, and, just three miles away, another alderman barely escaped from robbers by locking himself inside his garage and screaming for help. New York City registered four murders in the 24-hour period. And in Miami, Police Chief Walter Headley declared: "This is war. We are going to use shotguns and dogs from now on."

Throughout urban America the scene was the same: a rising rate of increasingly violent and audacious crimes—met by a strong public outcry that something must be done. The call was to fight force with force—more police, more guns. New York's Mayor John Lindsay promised to shake up police assignments so that, within a year, 40% more men would be walking beats (instead of riding desks). "We'll whack away at crime with every damn thing we've got," said Lindsay. Meanwhile, a county grand jury in Nashville urged that the death penalty and heavy prison sentences be imposed to halt "the avalanche of crime and arson that has come upon us. Because it appears that we have reached a point in this community where a person is not safe in or out of his home, we recommend that consideration be given to the possibility that every person have a firearm, or firearms, in his home."

"A CERTAIN RESTLESSNESS": Lyndon Johnson was interrupted JAN by polite applause 53 times during his State of the Union address, but only once did he draw from his audience of Congressmen and Cabinet members, judges and generals a prolonged, spontaneous ovation. That was when he declared: "The American people have had enough of rising crime and lawlessness in this country." Increasingly, "crime in the streets"— an omnibus label encompassing all the wellsprings of urban unrest from ghetto riots to muggings in middle-class neighborhoods—looms as one of the nation's prime preoccupations in Election Year 1968. Now, after four summers of holocausts in the nation's largest cities, concern over the Negro's welfare has been largely replaced by consternation at the prospect of anarchy. Nothing more dramatically underscored this shift than the total silence that greeted Johnson's State of the Union plea for several "vital" civil rights laws covering fair jury trials, enforcement of equal-employment opportunity and open housing. By contrast, he was applauded a dozen times when he spoke of curbing crime.

Noting that "Americans are prosperous as men have never been in recorded history," the President added mildly that, nonetheless, "there is in the land a certain restlessness, a questioning." He asked rhetorically: "Why, why, then, this restlessness?" He answered himself with an even greater rhetorical flourish: "Because when a great ship cuts through the sea, the waters are always stirred and troubled. And our ship is moving —and it's moving through troubled and new waters, and it's moving toward new and better shores."

Coming from the bridge, that seemed a peculiarly euphoric position report. But turning to crime, Johnson listed a number of measures aimed at calming the roiled waters. He told Congress that it confronted "no more urgent business" than passage of his Safe Streets Act with a $100 million authorization, double the amount he requested last year. He called for a gun-control law to halt "the trade in mail-order murder." To end "the sale of slavery to the young," he called for a narcotics-control act that would impose harsher penalties for the sale of LSD "and other dangerous drugs," and urged adding to the number of agents in the Narcotics Bureau. In addition, he asked Congress to authorize more FBI agents, for a nationwide strength of 6,718.

CH 15   **PATCH OF BLUE:** The crime rate in downtown Miami reached critical proportions last December. Robberies had almost doubled since the previous December. Police Chief Walter Headley was "fed up." The day after Christmas, he simply "called in all my commanding officers and told them to change some things. I said we should use dogs to accompany men on the beat. And I said I wanted the force in high-crime areas to carry shotguns. And I said I wanted to concentrate men in these high-crime areas, and that I wanted them to use the stop-and-frisk law more." Did the new approach work? The answer was yes. In January, the city's robbery rate dropped 45%, from 299 to 163. In the high-crime areas, the rate went down 62%.

There were problems, of course. High-crime areas in Miami mean Negro slums, and there were rumbles of discontent from militant Negroes who felt that the crackdown was discriminatory. But Negro merchants were generally pleased, and civil rights leaders worked to cool the hotter tempers. Despite the early statistics, however, Miami's solution seems to be little more than an emergency patch of blue. Last week Chief Headley gave out the figures for February. The number of robberies had bobbed back up from 163 to 207. But the rate did not go up in the crackdown areas; all the increase was in previously low-crime areas. Headley thinks that means that the crackdown has driven some criminals into new territory.

RIL 26   **SHOULD LOOTERS BE SHOT?:** Chicago's Mayor Richard J. Daley was hopping mad. Mulling over the massive damage caused by black rioters on the city's West Side after Martin Luther King Jr.'s assassination, Daley came to the conclusion that he had been badly let down by his police. The toll: 162 buildings gutted by arsonists; 268 businesses and homes looted; $9,000,000 in property losses; eleven lives lost. Yet, of the 2,900 Negroes arrested, only 19 were charged with arson. Last week Daley's ire erupted with nationwide reverberations.

"I have conferred with the superintendent of police and given him the following instructions," he said at a press conference. "I said to him very emphatically and very definitely that an order be issued by him immediately to shoot to kill any arsonist or anyone with a Molotov cocktail in his hand, because they're potential murderers, and to shoot to maim or cripple anyone looting." As for young looters, Daley favored the use of Chemical Mace, a canned disabling gas.

Reaction came swiftly. More than 4,500 letters and telegrams running 15 to 1 in favor of the mayor's stand reached his office. Some even suggested that Daley run for President.

MACE QUESTIONS: Police across the country have gratefully MAY adopted Mace, a chemical stun gas in a pressurized can, as a means of coping with rioters and unruly suspects. Used as recommended (from at least 3 ft. away, in 1-sec. bursts), it causes temporary loss of vision and inability to move—effects far less drastic than those of a club or a .38-cal. bullet. Lately, however, questions have arisen about possible long-range effects of Chemical Mace. A San Francisco ophthalmologist, Lawrence Rose, has squirted it at close range into one eye of each of three rabbits, whose eye structure is biologically similar to that of humans; he has caused permanent corneal scarring in one. In Ann Arbor, Mich., the face of a Negro who was sprayed last March is still partially depigmented. A spokesman for Mace's manufacturer explained that although the device has already been used 20,000 to 30,000 times, there has been no evidence of any damage worse than "a burn equivalent to sunburn."

Nonetheless, the police forces of Cleveland, Kansas City, Mo., Madison, Wis., Los Angeles and San Francisco last week stopped using the spray. Pittsburgh Director of Public Safety David Craig took the opposite view. In most cities, newspaper reports of Mace's irritant ability omitted the point that prompt treatment would forestall permanent damage. To Craig, that fact meant that Mace, properly used, was now clearly the safest weapon in his arsenal and "the first feasible nonlethal hand weapon since the caveman invented the wooden club."

THE GUN UNDER FIRE: Forget the democratic processes, the ju- JUNE dicial system and the talent for organization that have long been the distinctive marks of the U.S. Forget, too, the affluence (vast, if still not general enough) and the fundamental respect for law by most Americans. Remember, instead, the Gun. That is how much of the world beyond its borders feels about the U.S. today. All too widely, the country is regarded as a blood-drenched, continent-wide shooting range where housewives pack pearl-handled revolvers, and political assassins stalk their victims at will.

Emulating their forebears, who did pack a lot of guns on the wild frontiers, Americans have turned their country into an arsenal. Today they own somewhere between 50 million and 200 million pistols and revolvers, shotguns and rifles, as well as uncounted machine guns, hand grenades, bazookas, mortars, even antitank guns. At least 3,000,000 more are bought each year, some two-thirds through the mails. Said Maryland's Democratic Senator Joseph Tydings last week in an appeal for more effective legislation to curb this traffic: "It is just tragic that in all of Western civilization the U.S. is the one country with an insane gun policy."

Spurred largely by fears of racial violence, Americans are engaged in a manic internal arms race. Close to 500 Dearborn, Mich. women are taking regular pistol practice; similar distaff firearm courses are under way from Redondo Beach, Calif., to Dallas, where 1,000 women have completed a pistol program in recent months. Increasing numbers of guns are falling

Women of Dearborn, Mich. at target practice. Americans own up to 200 million small arms, plus uncounted machine guns, hand grenades, bazookas, mortars.

into the hands of juveniles; in Chicago last year, 1,293 youths, one only eight years old, were arrested with guns in their possession. Last week in Oklahoma, two brothers, 12 and 10, were charged with shooting a 49-year-old grocer to death. Startling accidents happen, especially around inexperienced gun handlers. A Detroit man heard footsteps in his home, saw the knob of his bedroom door open slowly, leveled his bedside pistol—and fatally drilled his three-year-old daughter through the head.

Attempts to tighten the absurdly loose laws which permit such violence have repeatedly been defeated, largely due to the efforts of the 1,000,000-member National Rifle Association. Two years before he became President, John F. Kennedy unsuccessfully sought a ban on imports of foreign weapons—which would have kept out of the U.S. the $12.78 Mannlicher-Carcano Italian rifle that killed him in 1963. Senator Robert F. Kennedy testified in favor of a bill to tighten controls on handguns—such as the .22-cal. Iver-Johnson eight-shot revolver that felled him on June 4.

DANGER AT HOME: Laws to register and license firearms seemed JULY within reach during the days of shock that followed Robert Kennedy's assassination. That prospect is now dimming with each passing day. Spurred by lobbyists of the National Rifle Association, foes of gun controls reversed the earlier avalanche of congressional mail in favor of stricter gun laws. In the Senate Judiciary Committee, a coalition of conservative Midwesterners and Southerners, ramrodded by South Carolina's Republican Strom Thurmond, riddled Joseph Tydings' gun-control bill with escape-clause amendments, leaving little hope for enactment of a meaningful law.

Crime

THE GIRL IN THE BOX: Feeling ill, Barbara Jane Mackle, 20, a DEC. tall, slender, attractive brunette, abruptly excused herself from an exam at Atlanta's Emory University last week. She checked in at Roseway Inn, a motel near the campus, there joined her mother Jane, who had arrived earlier from Coral Gables, Fla., to take Barbara home for Christmas. During the evening, Barbara's boy friend and fellow student, Stewart Woodward, drove over in his white Ford for a visit. After Woodward left, mother and daughter sat up in their beds talking. They were still awake at 4 a.m. when a man who identified himself as a detective knocked on the door and said he had information about an auto accident involving a man in a white Ford. Thinking that Woodward had been hurt, Mrs. Mackle opened the door and found herself confronted by a masked man carrying a shotgun, and a smaller person wearing a ski mask, who, Mrs. Mackle thought, might be a twelve-year-old boy. After binding Mrs. Mackle hand and foot, the kidnapers seized Barbara and hustled her into a car. Mrs. Mackle freed herself in minutes and phoned the police. Almost at once, the FBI mobilized agents in Georgia and Florida.

The kidnaped girl belongs to one of Florida's wealthiest families. Her father Robert and his brothers own and run the $65 million Deltona Corp., one of the biggest home-building companies in the U.S. The three brothers are friends of President-elect Nixon, and they own the Key Biscayne Hotel where Nixon has often stayed. Robert Mackle made it clear that he wanted to deal with the kidnapers as fast as possible to ensure his daughter's safe return. Contact was made and Mackle stuffed a large suitcase with old $20 bills to the amount of $500,000. Following orders, he dropped it into Biscayne Bay on Thursday morning, just offshore from a stretch of overgrown lots south of downtown Miami. A local resident, wakened at 5 a.m. by the sound of an approaching outboard, saw a white Boston Whaler being beached on a neighbor's lawn and, because of a recent rash of burglaries, phoned the police. Because the FBI had not bothered to notify the police of the ransom dropoff, two officers responded to the call. They spotted what appeared to be two men, one carrying a duffle bag, the other a suitcase and a carbine. At the appearance of the police, the two dropped everything and escaped. The duffle bag contained scuba diving gear. In the suitcase was Mackle's $500,000.

Despite the bungling of the ransom delivery, the police and FBI now had an important clue. A blue Volvo parked nearby—and containing scuba gear—was found to be registered to one George D. Deacon, 28, a research technician at the Institute of Marine Science across the bay. It was from the Institute that the Boston Whaler had been stolen earlier that night. Indefatigable Robert Mackle tried once again to pass the money to the kidnapers and, on Thursday night, finally succeeded. For twelve hours after the ransom was delivered, the family and the FBI waited in vain for the release of Barbara Jane. Then the FBI issued warrants for the arrest of Gary Steven Krist, 23, an escaped convict from California who had been using the alias of George D. Deacon, and Ruth Eisemann Schier, 26. A petite 5 ft. 3 in., Miss Schier may have been mistaken for a boy by Mrs. Mackle.

Barbara Jane was found at week's end when the kidnapers telephoned the FBI and said that she could be located in a wooded area some 20 miles northeast of Atlanta. The kidnapers had hidden her well. Barbara Jane had been placed in a coffinlike box which had then been buried under 18 inches of earth. Her tomb had been equipped with food, water, two flexible vent tubes which protruded above ground, a fan, a small light which failed some hours before she was found. She had spent an estimated 80 hours underground. Still wearing the red-and-white nightgown that she had on when she was abducted, Barbara Jane was reported in good condition and was immediately flown to her distraught parents in Coral Gables, while the FBI pressed a nationwide hunt for Krist and Schier. [Krist was apprehended a few days later and all but $3,000 of the $500,000 ransom was recovered.]

Poverty

Despite a massive infusion of federal funds and many programs for its alleviation, there was widespread poverty across the country. To dramatize the plight of the nation's poor, the Rev. Martin Luther King Jr. had planned to lead thousands of impoverished citizens in a great march on Washington. Although King was assassinated before the march began, his associates went ahead with the plan.

MISERY AT VORTEX: Bathed in the unforgiving harshness of FEB. 23 massed TV lights, Senator Robert F. Kennedy pounded a table to still the chatter of shabby, tieless white folk crowded into the one-room schoolhouse at Vortex, Ky. The New Yorker, lowest-ranking Democrat on the Senate's Labor and Public Welfare Committee, had come to assess the plight of once-proud Appalachian mountaineers who rank today among the poorest of America's poor. For two days last week, Bobby and a caravan of 36 cars crammed with reporters, committee staffers and electronic gear burned up the dirt-topped back roads of eastern Kentucky's poverty-blighted counties, halting in hidden hollows at weather-bleached shanties sagging with neglect. And in spavined one-horse communities named Neon, Grassy Creek, Mousie, Fisty, Jackhorn and Cody, ragged, slack-eyed men and women and listless children with bellies taut from hunger spoke of their need. Why, Kennedy was asked in the township of Pippa Passes, was a man reared to a multimillionaire's comforts concerned with the plight of Kentucky's poor? "I can't answer that question," Bobby confessed. "Sorry."

Yet neither cynics nor the little girl who thrust a scrawled note into his hand pleading "Bobby, please run for President" could soften the facts of east Kentucky's poverty or blot out the reality of Appalachia's misery statistics. Some 5,000 of Wolfe County's 6,500 people exist beneath the poverty line, able to afford little more than a dime for each meal. "Whenever you get another kid to feed," advised Cliston Johnson, 48, a partially disabled miner struggling to raise 15 children on $60 a month, "just add a little more water to the gravy." The result, says Harlan County Pediatrician Doane Fischer, is that 30% of the children he treats are undersized, half are infested with worms and intestinal parasites, and over 60% have rotting teeth.

Federal aid to Appalachia, totaling $450 million since 1965, has done little to alleviate the mountain folks' plight. "Welfare's not the answer," rasped Bobby. "It's jobs. It is a basic responsibility of our society to give every man an opportunity to work." The poor people of Vortex cheered loudly. Even the cynics were moved.

AY 17 **A NATION WITHIN A NATION:** The accouterments of affluence are everywhere: Americans possess more than 60 million automobiles, 70 million television sets (10 million with color),

$500 billion worth of common stock. At least two-thirds of U.S. families own their homes. Yet in the midst of this unparalleled abundance, another nation dwells in grinding deprivation. It comprises the 29,700,000 Americans who are denied access to the wealth that surrounds them—a group three times the population of Belgium. They are the men, women and children—black, white, red, yellow and brown—who live below the "poverty line." [An arbitrary guideline used by economists, the "poverty line" varies according to the specific area and situation. A city family with 11 children which exists on an annual income of $7,910, for example, can be considered "poor." So can a single male farm worker who receives $1,180 per year.]

Clearly, American poverty is unique, both in its scope and its symptoms. According to a U.C.L.A. study "people who fall below the norm do not necessarily consider themselves to be poor, and people who are above the norm may feel poverty stricken." There are, in other words, two kinds of poverty: physical and psychological. The poor make up 15% of the U.S. population. And contrary to the impression given by riots and all the other conspicuous problems of the slums, Negroes are not the major component of that group, at least not in numbers: two out of every three poor Americans are white. As a result, one adverse effect of the War on Poverty has been to set deprived minorities in competition with one another for federal aid. Militancy becomes a weapon for winning attention; and the minorities grow increasingly jealous and imitative of one another's extremism. "We've tossed a few crumbs in the middle of millions of the nation's people and said, 'Folks, you fight for it and may the best man win,' " says one high-ranking poverty warrior. "That's a disgrace."

CHALLENGING THE PHARAOH: Last week, stepping out from shantytowns and slums throughout the nation, more than 1,200 marchers of the Poor People's Campaign began the trek toward Washington. Some were weathered field hands who had never before left the cotton-blown bottoms; others were rambunctious teen-agers splitting from a desperate scene. "By the time we're through in D.C.," cried March Coordinator Hosea Williams, "white folks gonna say, 'Where's Dr. King? Wake up, Dr. King!' These white folks killed the dreamer, but we're gonna show these white folks what become of the dream. The poor people are marching to challenge the Pharaoh." Led by Williams and the Rev. Ralph David Abernathy, the poverty pilgrims wound through back-country roads in buses, battered cars and behind farm wagons drawn by mules named Stennis and Eastland, George Wallace and Jim Clark (for the former Selma, Ala., sheriff who bloodied many a black head during earlier civil rights marches).

Even a man of the cloth like Abernathy felt no compunction about wearing the marchers' arm band reading "Mississippi God Damn." In Boston, where 1,000 poverty marchers mustered en route to Washington last week, a self-styled "Polish Freedom Fighter" named Joseph Mlot-Mroz, 53, picketed the parade with a sign reading, "I Am Fighting Poverty. I Work! Have You Tried It?" In a sorry scuffle, the bow-tied anti-protester was stabbed and hospitalized in fair condition.

AY 24 **THE SCENE AT ZIP CODE 20013:** In an elm-lined meadow between the Lincoln Memorial and the Washington Monument, the 15-acre "Resurrection City" slowly began to take shape last week. As thousands of poor Negroes, Indians, Mexican-Americans and a few Appalachian whites wound toward the capital in eight separate caravans, the enterprise could not be underrated as an imaginative appeal to the nation's conscience, but it was clearly headed for trouble. An air of bedlam hung over the encampment. There were too few shelters. Sewage lines were uncompleted. Only two shower units were available to the nearly 1,000 people on hand at week's end. But there were power lines, portable latrines and phone booths. Mobile clinics were scheduled to wheel up to dispense medical, dental and psychiatric care. Resurrection City even boasted the ultimate insignia of identity: a ZIP code number (20013).

JNE 7 **TURMOIL IN SHANTYTOWN:** "We will not abandon this place!" cried the Rev. Ralph Abernathy in Resurrection City. Abernathy and his lieutenants were not notably successful at maintaining order. One group of 150 poor people marched into the cafeteria of the Agriculture Department, piled their trays high with food, then refused to pay the $292.66 tab. "We're going to balance it off against what the Agriculture Department owes us for all the lunch programs that we didn't get," said the Rev. Jesse Jackson. Next day Abernathy hurried over to the department to pay the bill. The campaign was also plagued by internal dissent. There was an angry flare-up over the black monopoly on policy-making. "Black militants have taken over, and nobody else gets a chance to talk," protested Reies Lopez Tijerina, leader of a group of 200 Mexican-Americans. He complained that brown, red and white Americans were being bossed around by the Negroes and shouted down at meetings. Abernathy finally promised Tijerina a larger voice for nonblack groups.

SOLIDARITY & DISARRAY: Five hundred buses converged on JUN the muggy capital. A vast crowd—half white, half black— marched from the Washington Monument to the Lincoln Memorial. Placards identified them as "Sisters of Watts" and "Concerned Citizens from Slippery Rock"; costumes identified them as Indians and Mexican-Americans, hippies and middle-class citizens of all shades. For all that, last week's Solidarity Day, the climactic event of the Poor People's Campaign, bore little resemblance to the famous March on Washington in August 1963. Though the turnout was an impressive 55,000, it did not even come close to the 200,000 of the earlier march. More important than size was spirit. The 1963 demonstration was suffused with the hope that the last vestiges of legal segregation would soon disappear. The 1968 rally was motivated by disillusionment and despair.

Mrs. Coretta King, dressed in black in memory of her slain husband, sang *Come by Here, My Lord,* then launched into a 25-minute speech dwelling at length on the war in Viet Nam— "the most cruel and evil war in the history of mankind." The Rev. Ralph Abernathy, who has bumbled in his efforts to lead the campaign begun by Mrs. King's husband, talked for 65 minutes. He did not much care, he cried, whether the Government renewed its permit for Resurrection City, the poor people's waterlogged campsite by the Lincoln Memorial. "I received my permit a long time ago," said Abernathy, "from God Almighty."

Nevertheless, the campaign can point to some limited successes with the Administration. The Agriculture Department agreed to speed up food relief programs in 256 of the country's poorest counties. The Labor Department hurried a plan to create 100,000 new jobs. The Office of Economic Opportunity found $25 million more for the Head Start school program and emergency food and health care. Still, it was pretty thin fare for a crusade that set for itself no less a task than the conquest of poverty. The National Capitol Parks Police estimate that 100 assaults and other violent incidents have occurred since the shacks were set up in mid-May. "There are rapes, robberies and cuttings every day," said Alvin Jackson, who resigned in anger last week as the camp's chief security marshal, "and there is nothing we can do about it." Even so, by toning down his demands to include those things that are within reach and by exaggerating his successes, Abernathy has also left open the door to retreat. Thus the marchers can leave with some claim to victory, though, sad to say, it is mostly illusory.

Politics

As the presidential election year began it seemed certain that the opposing candidates would be Lyndon B. Johnson and Richard M. Nixon (who, after four years of careful fence-mending, held a commanding lead over a small field of Republican contenders). At first there was widespread apathy among the voters, and an unexciting campaign was predicted everywhere. But then Senator Eugene McCarthy, who had declared his candidacy the year before in order to register his opposition to the Viet Nam war, entered the Democratic primary in New Hampshire. McCarthy made an amazingly strong showing, and overnight the race turned into one of the most hectic and unpredictable election campaigns in many years.

N. 19 **WAITING FOR ROCKY:** Few politicians know the twists and bumps in the road to a presidential nomination better than Nelson Rockefeller. In 1960 and 1964 he ventured onto it, found more ambushers than adherents, and dropped out before the Republican Convention began. This year the Governor of New York chose to promote Michigan's George Romney and wait upon events. [But Romney campaigned ineptly and withdrew from the race. Another Republican hopeful, Senator Charles

Percy of Illinois, never became an effective contender, nor did Governor Ronald Reagan of California. That left Rockefeller —and Richard Milhous Nixon.]

NIXON'S RE-ENTRY: If Richard M. Nixon's noisy exit from elective politics in 1962 was a classic example of gracelessness, his re-entry last week was the very model of dignified restraint. There was no formal news conference, no crush of reporters. The announcement came by means of an open letter that was delivered by messenger boys to the Associated Press and United Press International in Manhattan. As a personal touch, 150,-000 copies were mailed to voters in New Hampshire. Addressed "to the citizens of New Hampshire," Nixon's letter recalled his 14 years of Washington service and the forced retirement that followed his narrow defeat for the presidency in 1960 and his rout in California's 1962 gubernatorial race. During those private years, he wrote, he had had "a chance to reflect on the lessons of public office, to measure the nation's tasks and its problems." "I believe," he concluded, "that I have found some answers."

The day after his announcement, Nixon was in New Hampshire beginning his eighth run for public office in 22 years. He opened a press conference with some of the disarming self-mockery that has become a trademark recently. Yes, he conceded, he must erase his loser's brand. But, at the risk of sounding "insufferably conceited," he predicted: "I will be the decisive winner of the primaries. I will go on and win the nomination. And I will beat Lyndon Johnson."

ROCKY CONFUSED: Increasingly, New York Governor Rockefeller looms as the only real challenger to Nixon and the only candidate who can offer G.O.P. moderates a voice at the convention. In the opinion of many party professionals, he is also the only Republican with any chance of defeating Lyndon Johnson next November. But if Rockefeller is the G.O.P.'s most electable candidate, he is also its least nominatable one. His short-lived attempt to derail Nixon in 1960 and his failure to back Barry Goldwater in 1964 still rankle among party workers. Said one Midwestern G.O.P. state chairman: "If Rocky reaches for the nomination, a thousand people will try to cut off his hand."

CH 22   **THE NEW CONTEXT:** In a single week, the entire political context of 1968 changed almost beyond recognition. Out of New Hampshire's frozen farm lands and bucolic hamlets emerged a new equation for the Democratic Party: what had once been a cakewalk was now a slashing dogfight. As a result of the nation's first primary, three men now figured in the new Democratic equation:

❡ EUGENE J. MCCARTHY, Senator from Minnesota, presidential candidate from out of nowhere, who confounded everybody by scoring heavily in the New Hampshire voting and demonstrating that the divisions within the Democratic Party were indeed deep.

❡ ROBERT F. KENNEDY, Senator from New York, all along the likeliest man to challenge the President, but inhibited by a fear that to join the fray would sunder the party and expose him to charges of opportunism.

❡ LYNDON B. JOHNSON, the President, the greatest vote-getter in U.S. history, now in serious trouble because of an arduous war abroad, a racial crisis of alarming proportions at home, and a gyrating economy that seems to be getting out of hand.

And three's a crowd. The ingredients for an intraparty explosion were already there, but it was McCarthy who pulled the trigger with his New Hampshire showing. Before the debris had settled, Kennedy moved to shoulder him aside. Scarcely a month after he had unequivocally denied speculation that he would challenge the President, the Senator from New York announced: "I am reassessing my position." Then, in the chandeliered Senate Caucus Room, where his brother had launched his campaign eight years earlier, he began with the identical words that John F. Kennedy had used: "I am announcing today my candidacy for the presidency of the United States." Ticking off a list of Johnsonian policies that had brought "despair" to the nation and "the growing risk of war" to the world, he declared: "I run because it is now unmistakably clear that we can change these disastrous, divisive policies only by changing the men who make them. For the reality of recent events in Viet Nam has been glossed over with illusions. The report of the riot commission has been largely ignored. The crisis in gold, the crisis in our cities, the crisis on our farms and in our ghettos, all have been met with too little and too late."

UNFORESEEN EUGENE: He was laughed off as a windmill tilter, shrugged off as a lackluster campaigner, written off as a condescending cynic. But last week, when the votes in New Hampshire's presidential primary were counted, Minnesota's Democratic Senator Eugene J. McCarthy came off—to practically everyone's surprise—a hero. He polled a stunning 42.2% of the Democratic vote to Johnson's 49.4%. With an additional 5,511 Republican write-ins (McCarthy, astonishingly, ran third on the G.O.P. ticket), he trailed the President in the overall tally by a scant 230 votes, 29,021 to 28,791. THE UNFORESEEN EUGENE proclaimed a placard toted by one of his fans after the balloting, and that said it all.

CRUSADE OF THE BALLOT CHILDREN: Not since the civil rights march on Mississippi in the summer of 1964 had so many young Americans committed themselves so fervently to a major national cause. In an era when many younger Americans are turning away from involvement in the democratic process, by dropping out either to psychedelia or to the nihilism of the New Left, the cool, crisply executed crusade of Gene McCarthy's "ballot children" provided heartening evidence that the generation gap is bridgeable—politically, at least.

McCarthy demanded hard work and personal self-sacrifice from his young workers. To escape the hippie image, miniskirted girls went midi, and bearded boys either shaved or stayed in the back rooms, licking envelopes or compiling address lists to the accompaniment of muted Beatle music. The students, of course, had slogans of their own. Posters announced: "God Isn't Dead—He's Just Lonely—But He Might Commit Suicide March 12th. It's Up to You."

Most of McCarthy's staffers are outraged by Bobby Kennedy's candidacy. Blue-eyed Ann Hart, 20, a diminutive self-described "dropout and cop-out," who is the daughter of Michigan Senator Philip Hart, argues that McCarthy's idealism is the only answer to the nation's malaise. "We wouldn't do this cruddy work for anybody but Gene McCarthy," says Ann, who lost 18 lbs. during her New Hampshire duty. "We've sworn ourselves to him."

BOBBY'S GROOVE: They screamed. They applauded wildly on MARC and off cue. They tore off his cuff links and nearly toppled him from the podium. They waved signs proclaiming KISS ME BOBBY, BOBBY IS GROOVY. In his first week as a presidential candidate, Kennedy shrewdly chose four university campuses as his major stops. The greetings he received ranged from unbridled ecstasy at the University of Kansas to friendly acceptance in the potentially hostile territory of the University of Alabama. It was a double demonstration: Eugene McCarthy has no monopoly on collegiate affection; Kennedy can still wow 'em.

Governor Rockefeller. He no longer has any stomach for the fight.

Senator McCarthy. His New Hampshire brush fire smokes out L.B.J.

GENE'S BIND: As he fought gamely to spread nationwide the brush fire he started in New Hampshire, it was difficult to tell whether Eugene McCarthy was running harder against Lyndon Johnson or Robert Kennedy. Most of his gut thrusts were reserved for Kennedy. He termed Kennedy's style a belated "crash course to great ideas." Kennedy's popularity? "I don't have the enemies in the party that Bobby has—or in the country, for that matter." Even Kennedy's athletic prowess came in for the McCarthy treatment. "He plays touch football," said McCarthy. "I play football. He skates in Rockefeller Center. I play hockey." Then, at the University of Wisconsin's Racine campus, McCarthy mused aloud that, if eliminated himself he might be neutral next fall. "I have a commitment," McCarthy cracked, "as chairman of the [Senate] subcommittee on Africa that I might honor at the time with a last great safari."

ROCKY'S EXIT: While Democratic presidential candidates thronged to the race, Republican contenders seemed more concerned with getting out. Last week Nelson Rockefeller abruptly and all but finally removed himself from contention. "Quite frankly," declared the New York Governor to a nationwide television audience, "I find it clear at this time that a considerable majority of the party's leaders want the candidacy of former Vice President Richard Nixon."

Rocky still maintained that he was willing to "answer any true and meaningful call," should the party demand his candidacy. But for all practical purposes, Rockefeller is finished as a presidential contender—not because he is a loser, but because he no longer has any stomach for the fight. As he confided to an aide with all too evident relief: "I never really wanted this anyway."

HUMPHREY RENEWED: From the moment Lyndon Johnson APR dropped out of the presidential race, there was little doubt that Hubert Humphrey would claim the right of succession. Last week the Vice President withheld his formal declaration for tactical reasons, but made clear to the nation that he was a candidate for the Democratic nomination. In making it a three-way contest with Senators Robert Kennedy and Eugene McCarthy, Humphrey began to emerge from the shadows of three years of veepship, during which many had dismissed him as an overly obsequious vice regent. "I will do everything I can for the cause of peace in the world," he told a wildly enthusiastic audience of A.F.L.-C.I.O. leaders. "I will do everything I can to keep social progress moving forward in America. And I ask your help." It was the old Humphrey and a revivified politician on the march, offering his traditional recipe of pugnacity and eloquence.

ROCKY'S RETURN: New York's Governor Nelson Rockefeller last week was clearly back in the lists as an active presidential candidate. In the changed game that ensued after President Johnson's rejection of a second term, Rocky was still playing his hand cagily. Nonetheless, he was unmistakably doing—if not saying—the things Americans traditionally expect from a presidential candidate. He flew down to Atlanta for the funeral of Martin Luther King. And he gave his tacit approval to the formation of a blue-chip Rockefeller for President Committee whose members include four Senators, four Governors, five former Republican national chairmen and 14 noted businessmen. Said Kentucky's Senator Thruston Morton, who was instrumental in organizing the committee: "We'll have more delegates lined up in four weeks than a mule can haul."

AY 3 **UPBEAT NOTE:** "The time has come to speak out on behalf of America—not a nation that has lost its way, but a restless people striving to find a better way." On that characteristically upbeat note, Hubert Horatio Humphrey volunteered last week to serve his nation as chief pathfinder. Eight years ago, he was the first to announce for the Democratic presidential nomination and the first to be eliminated, long before the convention. Now he is the third entry in a far more bitter contest. This time, no one doubts that he has the strength to battle it out to the end next August.

He will need it. Apart from Robert Kennedy and Eugene McCarthy, Humphrey has history against him: no Vice President has succeeded to the White House by the elective process since Martin Van Buren turned the trick in 1836. Moreover, he has built-in problems of his own. Humphrey's early reputation as a sectional, dogmatic, abrasively self-righteous radical evaporated some time ago, to be replaced by an equally detrimental image as the uncritical apologist for an unpopular Administration. Many have denounced him for out-Lyndoning Johnson on the war. Others think that he is really too nice a guy to run a successful national campaign, too soft to fire anyone who needs firing. In the TV age, he remains a master of the meeting-hall peroration. In an era when a fresh face and youthful persona are worth 1,000 platitudes and millions of votes, Humphrey, who will be 57 this month, is the old man of the competition, in danger of seeing his many and distinguished accomplishments of 23 years in elective office dissipated by overexposure.

AY 24 **SEVERAL BOBBYS:** They pronounce his boyish name with fear and derision or else with adoration and awe. To many enemies, he is more his father's son than his brother's brother. Indeed, it was old Joe himself who observed, "He hates just like I do." By this reckoning, Robert Kennedy is the spoiled dynast, reclaiming the White House as a legacy from the man he regards as a usurper. There are several Bobbys within that slim, taut, toothy exterior. He can communicate with the disinherited as few others of his race or rank are able to do. He can be morose or merry, expansive or petty, merciless or magnanimous—all to an extreme degree. Says Lawrence O'Brien: "The pendulum just swings wider for him than it does for most people." For every Machiavellian maneuver there is a graceful gesture; for every half-truth or hyperbole there is a disarming pinch of self-deprecation: "You see what sacrifices I am willing to make to be President? I cut my hair."

Last week, following up victories in the Indiana and Washington, D.C., Democratic primaries, Kennedy scored a smashing success in Nebraska and won 51% of the vote, against 31% for Senator Eugene McCarthy. Hubert Humphrey poohpoohed the results, saying that they would have been "a little different" if he had been an active contender. But the "unauthorized" Nebraska write-in campaign on Humphrey's behalf clearly bombed. And every Kennedy victory puts Humphrey's present delegate lead in greater jeopardy. To increase Humphrey's danger, Kennedy has become the most frenetic campaigner on the road today, starting his days before 7 a.m., often skipping lunch, frequently chugging on until 3 the next morning before allowing himself food and rest. "He looks tired," the motherly types in the crowds say. "He looks like he needs a square meal." Another common observation: "He looks like a little kid." And from younger women: "Beautiful!" Late at night, in his chartered Boeing 727, Bobby, 42, looks neither young nor beautiful. Deep lines mark the brow. Stumping in the sun has turned his nose pink; lack of sleep has dulled and reddened his eyes. The grey wires in his tawny hair grow more visible.

But Kennedy's campaign is running smoothly. At the proper moment, kids stream on cue from every door, engulfing the candidate, filling the lenses. During his first days as an announced candidate, particularly before Lyndon Johnson withdrew from the race, he wobbled a bit. His attacks on Johnson sometimes bordered on the demagogic. He realized his error and soon pulled back. He also ceased invoking Jack's memory. His very presence is enough to evoke the old mystique anyway, and the press, which had given Bobby a bad time for the way in which he entered the race, was quick to pick up his obvious use of New Frontierisms. "There is such a thing as evocation of the great dead," wrote Columnist Murray Kempton, "and there is also such a thing as the exploitation of corpses. Senator Kennedy seems appallingly far from recognizing the difference."

He has employed banter shrewdly, both to keep his audiences interested and to appear unruthless. In Tecumseh, Neb., the wind tore a scrap of paper from his hand. "That's my farm program," he said. "Give it back quickly." Are his crowds packed with the young? "I'm going to lower the voting age to seven." What about all that money he's spending? He quotes from Jack: "I have a message from my father: 'I don't mind spending money, but please don't buy one more vote than is necessary.'" To keep the crowds' attention, Kennedy employs a variety of tactics. At the proper moment, he orders: "Clap!" They do, and they laugh.

NIXON'S STEPPINGSTONES: In 1964, Republican candidates searched across the land for the "mainstream." This year again the cliché is liquid. For the moment, the only one who can see solid ground ahead is Richard Nixon. And, indeed, he has found some sturdy steppingstones on the road to the Miami Beach convention. Nebraska Republicans gave him 70% of their vote and 16 delegates in last week's primary. And Maryland's Governor Spiro Agnew, until two months ago one of Rocky's most effusive rooters, made it clear that Nelson no longer commanded his loyalty and that Nixon, who is dropping hints that he might look to Annapolis for a running mate, was looking handsomer than ever.

JNE 7 **HAVEN:** Oregon is haven to the maverick and uplifter of the underdog. In last week's primary, Oregon Democrats allowed Eugene McCarthy to check Robert Kennedy's drive (McCarthy got 45% of the votes, Kennedy 39%), while the Republicans gave new velocity to Richard Nixon's bid for the nomination by giving him 73% of the Republican vote, compared with 23% for Reagan and a write-in vote of 4% for Rockefeller. By so doing, Oregonians made it more likely than ever that the post-convention contest would be between Nixon and Hubert Humphrey, the two ostensible traditionalists in the crowd. [Kennedy came back strongly to win the California primary over McCarthy eight days later, but was shot on the night of his victory. See page 31.]

THE QUIXOTE CANDIDATE: For a while he had one pledged delegate, 666 short of the total he would need to win the Republican presidential nomination. Then he released the one he had. His national campaign staff numbers seven. After Robert Kennedy's murder, he was assigned a few Secret Service guards, which prompted a Congressman's quip: "It's the biggest crowd he's had this campaign." Yet he persists. He is Harold Stassen, who quadrennially offers up his obsession on the public altar—where it is scorned.

Once Stassen was the boy wonder—a county attorney at 23, Governor of Minnesota at 31, Republican Convention keynoter (in 1940) at 33, and floor manager for Wendell Willkie. His own cause peaked in 1948 when he scored impressive victories in the Wisconsin and Nebraska presidential primaries, only to be overwhelmed in Oregon by New York's Governor Tom Dewey. Since then, his course has been downhill. Now 61, he wears an unconvincing toupee and a sadly forced smile. His current slogan is STASSEN '68—WHY NOT? A better question is: WHY?

CORNY BUT EFFECTIVE: In the aftermath of their Miami convention, the Republicans are united. Now what will they do with their unity? The G.O.P. nominee, Richard Nixon, is clearly in tune with his party. Will he be in tune with the country? These are the chief questions that will dominate the political scene for the next 2½ months.

The convention offered mixed portents. Symbols of unity and progress flapped like so many ensigns at fleet review. The platform, the keynote address, and Nixon's acceptance speech were on the whole impeccably progressive in tone, promising jobs, justice, education and a "piece of the action" to the poor, peace in Viet Nam, honorable conciliation with the Communists. Yet those who wanted to could find less obvious signals bearing a slightly different message. Somehow Nixon managed to sound more forceful and specific in emphasizing the need for law and order than in pleading for social justice.

At the end, he took the podium the way he had taken the convention—as if it belonged to him. He stretched out his arms to gather it all in. The fingers on both hands wigwagged victory Vs at the clapping, stamping, shouting, pulsing heart of the Republican Party. He had worked for two weeks on his acceptance speech, writing it out himself on yellow legal pads. It was a mixture of carefully balanced political calculations and genuine personal warmth. It was, by any reasonable standard, corny, but it also was one of Nixon's most effective speeches in years. He was curiously touching in describing the son of the slums who "dreams the dreams of a child. And yet when he awakens, he awakens to a living nightmare." He was rather embarrassing in the sketch of another child, Nixon himself, who hears a train go by and dreams of faraway places. "It seems like an impossible dream." But a self-sacrificing father, a "gentle Quaker mother," a dedicated teacher, a minister, a courageous wife, loyal offspring, devoted followers—plus a cast of millions of voters—combine to put that boy on the train that stopped last week in Miami Beach, possibly on the way to the White House.

Presidential Candidate Richard Nixon serenades the press. A talent for accommodation brings him back from limbo.

The fact that Nixon spoke of himself as the hero of this American dream seemed cloying to some. And the reference to a train whistle was an oddly old-fashioned note: trains do not symbolize escape and movement to today's young. Yet his ability to evoke the good old days and look eagerly to the year 2000, and to make the mix sound coherent, points up his talent for accommodation, which is one explanation for Nixon's return from political limbo.

"A SORT OF NONENTITY": "I'm going to mention two words to you," a TV reporter told pedestrians in downtown Atlanta. "You tell me what they mean. The words are: Spiro Agnew."

"It's some kind of disease," said one man.

"It's some kind of egg," ventured another.

"He's a Greek who owns that shipbuilding firm," declared a third.

Richard Nixon's choice as running mate would not have batted an eye. "Spiro Agnew," admitted Spiro T. Agnew last week, "is not a household word." Elected in 1966 after a Democratic split, Agnew, now 49, quickly gained a reputation as a competent, if not brilliant Governor. The Baltimore riots last April were a traumatic experience for Agnew, who had to call out some 5,700 National Guardsmen and ask for nearly 4,800 federal troops to restore order. Agnew suspected a conspiracy, citing a visit to Baltimore by Stokely Carmichael several days before the trouble—and King's murder—as evidence. Within hours after the shooting stopped, he called 100 moderate Negro leaders into his office and gave them a tongue-lashing for not having counteracted Carmichael's fulminations. Before he had finished, 70 of the 100 had walked out, insulted by his top-sergeant tone. Today he is anathema to Maryland Negroes.

The Marylander's credentials as a potential President and an expert on urban affairs—two of Nixon's stated criteria in making his choice—are not convincing. He has no background at all in foreign affairs and little experience in city problems, which Nixon has said would be a prime concern of his Vice President. Until 1962, Agnew had held no elective office—other than the presidency of the local P.T.A.—and had never proceeded much further in politics than the Baltimore county zoning board. He is therefore something of an unknown quantity even in Maryland. "Agnew," says Roy Innis, national director of the Congress of Racial Equality, "is the kind of guy who can't be described in terms of good or bad. He is sort of a nonentity."

A tall, heavy-set man (6 ft. 2 in., 192 lbs.), whose grooming has won him the accolade of the *Men's Hairstylist & Barber's Journal,* "Ted" Agnew is humorless and cautious, often inflexible. Though Agnew's father was born in the Peloponnesian village of Gargalianoi, he took on most of the ways of the new country after he moved to the U.S in 1897. He changed the family name from Anagnostopoulos to Agnew, and married a Virginian with the un-Hellenic name of Akers. His son went further, converting from Greek Orthodoxy to Episcopalianism. To his embarrassment, Agnew cannot speak any Greek—though that will probably not lose him many of the votes of an estimated 600,000 fellow Greek Americans. Some people indeed were already referring to him last week as "Zorba the Veep."

23 **STALAG '68:** On the site of Chicago's International Amphitheatre, all manholes have been sealed with tar. A chain-link fence, seven feet high and topped with barbed wire, is going into place west of the arena. Secret Service men are checking every pipe, seat and rafter against bombs or snipers' hiding places. Taking antiwar demonstrators at their word, Chicago officials are preparing for every possible disruption at next week's Democratic National Convention. In the process, the nation's second largest city is beginning to take on the appearance of a city under siege—or a kind of Stalag '68. The city's 11,500-man police force will be put on twelve-hour shifts during the week of the convention; 5,500 riot-trained members of the Illinois National Guard are being alerted for duty and have been given permission to bivouac in parks near the hall and in public high schools. Arrayed against this impressive show of official strength will be one of the oddest, least cohesive armies in history—an uncoordinated alliance of hippies, yippies, antiwar militants, unhappy liberals and far-out radicals. Goals vary from outright disruption of the convention proceedings to a ribald mockery of the electoral system. Already the demonstrators have achieved the feat of forcing a major party to pick a candidate for President behind barbed wire, in a charged atmosphere reminiscent of a police state.

SURVIVAL AT THE STOCKYARDS: Schism, bitterness, demands s
for violent solution, disenchantment with the way things are,
fear of what may be—these are the forces, some would say
the demons, that are loose in the U.S. in 1968. The demons
accompanied the Democrats last week to their convention at
Chicago.

The most bruising fight was waged over the Viet Nam plank
of the platform. Practically everybody agreed that the war
should be ended, and the dispute centered on the mechanics
of settlement. Initially, the Platform Committee approved a
plan urging the U.S. to "stop all remaining bombing of North
Viet Nam in the expectation of restraint and reasonable response from Hanoi." Lyndon Johnson did not like the business
about "expectation." Soon the text was changed to read that
the bombing would stop "when this action would not endanger
the lives of our troops in the field." No one was quite sure
what that meant. McCarthy was determined to use the Viet
Nam plank as his springboard to the nomination. By sponsoring a floor fight over the minority proposal, which called
for "an unconditional end to all bombing," he hoped to split
the party and attract enough support to put him over. At
first, the convention's managers sought to schedule debate on
the issue in the early-morning hours when practically nobody
would be watching TV. But the dissidents raised a tremendous
ruckus. "Let's go home, let's go home!" they roared. Convention Chairman Carl Albert seemed at a loss. Finally,
Chicago's Mayor Richard Daley drew a finger across his throat
and Albert got the message. He cut the fuss off by adjourning
the meeting.

When the debate got under way next afternoon, it led to an
unusually free and searching exchange of views. And when Albert read the final tally, it stood at 1,567¾ delegate votes for
the majority or Administration plank, 1,041¼ votes for the minority. Even before he finished reading the results, a chant of lament began in the New York delegation: "We shall overcome,
we shall overcome. . . ." From the galleries: "Stop the war!
Stop the war!"

As happened often during the week in such situations, an official on the podium flashed a signal to the 50-piece orchestra
to strike up some noisy numbers to drown out the chants. In
this case, with stunning inappropriateness after a debate on

bombing, it was the Air Force's song, *Off We Go into the Wild Blue Yonder.*

After the turbulent Viet Nam debate, the delegates took a two-hour break, then began drifting back to the amphitheatre to vote on the presidential nomination. But at that very moment, Chicago's lake front was turning into a battleground. All week, the antiwar demonstrators and Chicago's police had engaged in minor, but sometimes bloody skirmishes. On the night of the presidential balloting, the skirmishes turned into a major battle.

The assault was furious and bizarre. Yet the Chicago police department responded in a way that could only be characterized as sanctioned mayhem. With billy clubs, tear gas and Mace, the blue-shirted, blue-helmeted cops violated the civil rights of countless innocent citizens and contravened every accepted code of professional police discipline. They savagely attacked hippies, yippies, revolutionaries, dissident Democrats, newsmen, photographers, passers-by, clergymen and at least one cripple. *Playboy's* Hugh Hefner took a whack on the backside. The police even victimized a member of the British Parliament, Mrs. Anne Kerr, a vacationing Laborite who was Maced outside the Conrad Hilton and hustled off to the lock-up.

"The force used was the force that was necessary," insisted Police Superintendent James Conlisk Jr. He could point to the fortunate fact that no one was killed. Yet the cops' excesses during the Democratic Convention were not basically Conlisk's doing. Chicago is Mayor Richard J. Daley's satrapy. Daley takes a fierce, eccentric pride in Chicago. For 13 years, he has ruled his province like a Chinese warlord. The last of America's big-city bosses, the jowly, irascible mayor has on the whole been a creative autocrat. But he had virtually invited trouble in his preparations for the convention. He refused the protesters permission to sleep on the grass of Chicago's Lincoln Park, a 1,185-acre expanse on the North Side. Critics of the cops pointed out that the site would have been ideal for the police, who could have left the kids alone and stood guard on the fringes of the park until the soldiers of dissent got bored and left or until the convention was over. It might not have worked out that way, since many of the protesters were fiercely determined to find trouble, but at least the notion offered a better chance of avoiding violence. In some of the wilder fighting, the demonstrators hurled bricks, bottles and nail-studded golf balls at the police lines. During the first three days, the cops generally reacted only with tear gas and occasional beatings. But on Wednesday night, as the convention gathered to nominate Hubert Humphrey, the police had a cathartic bloodletting. Outraged when the protesters lowered a U.S. flag during a rally, the cops hurled tear gas into the crowd. The demonstrators, bent upon parading to the convention hall (Daley had refused a permit), regrouped in front of the Hilton, where they were surrounded by phalanxes of cops. Police warned the demonstrators to clear the streets, waited for five minutes for several busloads of reinforcements to arrive. And then the order was given.

Chicago cops are built like beer trucks. They flailed blindly into the crowd of some 3,000, then ranged onto the sidewalks to attack onlookers. At the amphitheatre, taped scenes of flailing police batons were played over scores of television screens. The delegates were appalled. Standing at the podium to nominate McGovern, Connecticut's Senator Abe Ribicoff looked down at the Illinois delegation 15 feet in front of him, and denounced "Gestapo tactics in the streets of Chicago." Mayor Daley's lieutenants leaped up, shaking their fists. "How hard it is to accept the truth," said Ribicoff calmly, looking straight at Daley. Now Daley was on his feet too, waving his arms, cupping one hand to his mouth and shouting, among other things, "Get out, go home!" at Ribicoff. Speaker after speaker referred to the scene at the Hilton, and each set off a rumbling chorus of boos aimed at Daley. Several delegates demanded that the convention be transferred to another city. Finally, beet-red with anger, Richard Daley stood up and walked out of the hall.

The night after "Bloody Wednesday," as it came to be called, a cordon of plainclothesmen ringed the Illinois delegation, and the galleries were packed with the mayor's henchmen waving freshly printed banners: WE LOVE DALEY.

Humphrey's nomination was almost an anticlimax. It went very much as his aides had anticipated: a first-ballot victory with 1,761¾ votes to 601 for McCarthy, 146½ for McGovern, 67½ for Negro Minister Channing Phillips, of Washington, D.C.

AT LAST!: The nomination had eluded Hubert Humphrey so long—he was first considered a presidential possibility in 1952 —that he had finally despaired of winning it. Thanks to the convulsive events of 1968, it came within his reach. Yet on the day that he finally grasped it, he sat glumly in his suite in Chicago's Conrad Hilton Hotel while young demonstrators and angry police fought in the streets below. He tasted not victory but the acrid fumes of tear gas that wafted through an open window. What was to have been the happiest of days turned out to be an occasion for doubt and depression.

In his acceptance speech the following night, Humphrey faced a difficult task in striking the right tone. He was blatantly corny at times, and he used the device, also employed by Richard Nixon, of giving a point in one sentence and taking it back in the next; social justice balanced by the need for law enforcement, peace, but not forgetting the need for firmness. One of Humphrey's thorniest problems was how to invoke Johnson's name without setting off a deafening—and damaging—chorus of catcalls. He did so by first mentioning the name of every Democratic presidential candidate, beginning with Franklin Roosevelt and only then paying tremulous tribute to Johnson's achievements. ("And tonight, to you, Mr. President, I say thank you. Thank you, Mr. President.") Having done his duty, and drawn boos as well as heavy applause, Humphrey then moved to cut the umbilical. It was now "the end of an era—the beginning of a new day," he said. To ensure that nobody missed the point, he used the "new day" phrase half a dozen more times. In a Humphrey Administration—if there is one—he later told reporters, "I may turn to 'new dawn.' The dawn comes slowly, but it illuminates."

HUMPHREY'S POLISH YANKEE: Maine Senator Edmund Sixtus Muskie looks and sounds like the prototype of the ancestral Down-Easter. Craggy-faced, big-boned and monumentally tall (6 ft. 4 in.), he displays the New England legislator's characteristic attention to detail and distaste for florid rhetoric. It was hardly foreseeable before last week that the Democratic vice-presidential nominee—who is in fact the son of a Polish-born tailor—would be matched against a Republican opposite number from Maryland with a curiously similar background. Muskie and Spiro Agnew, Richard Nixon's running mate, are both sons of immigrants. Both grew up in straitened circumstances. Both have foreshortened surnames [Muskie's father anglicized the family name from Marciszewski], and both are generally unfamiliar to the American electorate.

Unlike Agnew, who was little known among politicians outside his home state of Maryland until he received the G.O.P. vice-presidential nomination, Ed Muskie has a hard-earned reputation on Capitol Hill as a diligent and imaginative politician. As Maine's first Democratic Governor in 20 years (1954-58) and subsequently the first popularly elected Democratic Senator in the state's history, he cracked the granitic G.O.P. fortress in Maine, creating a new independent-minded breed of voters known as Muskie's Republicans. Since then, Muskie has maintained a stubborn political independence. In Washington, he immediately ran afoul of Senate Majority Leader Lyndon Johnson, who asked the freshman to join him in a fight against Senate liberals who were seeking to make it easier to break filibusters. Muskie refused, and Johnson retaliated by denying him his first three choices for committee assignments. "They tell me that Lyndon trades apples for orchards every day," Muskie said ruefully. Johnson later came to appreciate Muskie as a thorough craftsman who approached his work with quiet diplomacy. In 1964, Johnson even seriously considered naming Muskie as his running mate. At 54, Ed Muskie fishes and hunts in the Maine woods, sails off the coast, and is an amateur carpenter. He enjoys cooking the duck, goose and turkey that he bags on shooting expeditions. He also likes to sew—a talent he picked up from his tailor-father.

THE GOVERNMENT IN EXILE: From his bedroom window on the 23rd floor of the Conrad Hilton, Eugene McCarthy viewed the carnage on Michigan Avenue, turning now and again to the TV screen to watch the dissolution of his own hopes at the convention hall. His main concern was with the young people below. That evening he went down to his staff headquarters on the 15th floor, where his doctor, William Davidson, had opened a makeshift hospital. McCarthy comforted the bruised and bleeding.

Shaken, he returned to his suite. In one final gesture, he telephoned his campaign manager at the International Amphitheatre to tell him to withdraw the name of Eugene McCarthy from the balloting. "It looked," he remarked later, "like the convention might break up in chaos. I thought this might stabilize it." By then it was too late. The balloting in the convention had already started, and the count—and the violence below—went on. Next day, McCarthy crossed the street —still lined with troops and cops—to speak to a rally of the disaffected. "I am happy," he said, "to be here to address the government in exile." Already, some of his followers were wearing black arm bands and a new campaign button. It was blank.

T. 13   **THE POLITICS OF SAFETY:** Certain at last that he had found the formula for victory, Richard Nixon began his campaign last week in a mood of hyper-optimism. Starting his push in Chicago, where the Democratic cause had been staggered by police clubs the week before, Nixon received a warm reception from huge noontime crowds in the Loop.

    Nixon's campaign strategy is already well planned. His schedule will be keyed to the evening TV newscasts, and most big events will take place no later than early afternoon, so that the networks will have time to develop their film. Evening rallies, which are too late for the evening news, will be few and far between. "Why should you hold a rally for 15,000 or 20,000 people," says one top aide, "when with TV you can get the whole state?" Evening banquets will go the way of torchlight parades. "All you get at banquets are drunks and fat cats," adds the adviser. "And banquets are the worst possible kind of TV. At night, Nixon rests." Agnew will be kept mostly out in the boondocks until he is completely sure of himself.

T. 20   **LURCHING OFF TO A SHAKY START:** In his first full week of campaigning, Hubert Humphrey managed to summon up every demon that has beset him this year: his inability to focus on the essential, his failure to re-establish his independence of Lyndon Johnson, his lack of an efficient campaign organization, his troubles with the dissident Democratic left. Though not really prepared to mount a major campaign swing, Humphrey was dispatched willy-nilly to Pennsylvania, Colorado, California, Texas, Louisiana, Michigan, Delaware and New Jersey. Tired when he started, he made as many as nine speeches a day. Advance arrangements were sketchy, crowds at some major stops thin or indifferent. In Philadelphia, the sparse crowd gave a bigger hand to Comedian Joey Bishop, a home-town boy who was traveling with Humphrey, than it gave to the candidate. Hecklers turned up at most stops, toting anti-Viet Nam placards and catcalling. Humphrey gamely quipped that "boo" means "I'm for you" in the Sioux language, "but somehow I don't sense it that way today." Meanwhile, Humphrey seems determined to personalize the campaign as much as possible by drawing Nixon into direct combat. So far, Nixon has rejected the bait. He is consciously playing the statesman, in cool command of his passions and his party.

THE COUNTERPUNCHER: When Richard Nixon lifted the Governor of Maryland from relative obscurity to the second spot on the Republican Party's ticket last month, Spiro Theodore Agnew reacted with becoming modesty. By last week, Nixon's running mate was well on his way to making quite a name for himself. In an extraordinary series of press conferences, speeches and interviews, Agnew conjured up some long-dormant poltergeists of American politics. Hubert Humphrey, he said, was "soft on Communism." In addition, the Vice President was "soft on inflation and soft on law and order over the years" —in fact, "squishy soft."

Editorial writers were quick to accuse Agnew of trying to revive the McCarthyism and "Communist witch hunts" of the early '50s. Senate Minority Leader Everett Dirksen and House Republican Leader Gerald Ford held a joint news conference to repudiate the charge against Humphrey. Within the day, Agnew retreated. "If I'd known I'd be cast as the 'Joe McCarthy of 1968,' " he said contritely, "I would have turned five somersaults. I said 'squishy soft,' and I'm not proud of it." His retreat, however, was not a retraction. He emphasized that in his view, Communism was enjoying "a renewed life" rather than a decline in the U.S. and that he intended to continue playing that theme.

To be sure, the Democrats struck back. "It is apparent," said Humphrey Campaign Manager Larry O'Brien, "that Agnew has been delegated by Mr. Nixon to travel the low road, and with the traditions of Nixon campaigns, the low road is the rock bottom." Said Humphrey: "He just got hold of one of Nixon's old speeches."

*A threat that neither Nixon nor Humphrey could measure ac-
curately was that of a third presidential candidate, George C.
Wallace, ex-Governor of Alabama. Running as the candidate of
his own American Independent Party, he drew most of his
strength from the extreme right.*

NEITHER TWEELEDUM NOR TWEEDLEDEE: The scene possessed
a grotesque impropriety. At the tomb of Abraham Lincoln in
Springfield, Ill., Alabama's George Corley Wallace, symbol
of unregenerate Southern racism, reverently placed a wreath
of red and white flowers. Said Wallace: "It's good to be in the
land of Lincoln." Lincoln land seemed fertile ground indeed
for Wallace's third-party candidacy. About 3,000 people greeted him at the airport in Illinois' capital city, many driving as
far as 100 miles and waiting hours under a hot sun to hear
him take out after "scummy anarchists" and pseudo intellectuals. He put forth a strident defense of the nation's police.
"If they could run this country for about two years," he cried,
"they'd straighten it out."

Wallace asserted that the two major parties are as close as
"Tweedledum and Tweedledee," since both are "owned by
the Eastern Establishment." For 100 years, he said, "both parties have looked down their noses and called us rednecks down
here in this part of the country. I'm sick and tired of it, and
on November 5, they're goin' to find out there are a lot of rednecks in this country." From every indication, Wallace is not
exaggerating. A Gallup poll last week showed that millions of
U.S. union members are turning to Wallace, with 50% de-
claring for him in the South, 12% in the rest of the nation.

T. 27 **THE WALLACE FACTOR:** Even "pointed-headed" newsmen, as
he calls them, now concede Wallace anywhere from four to
nine Southern states in November and a large, though still unpredictable, impact on the vote in much of the rest of the country. His audiences nearly everywhere are as big as or even
bigger than Richard Nixon's or Hubert Humphrey's, and usually twice as enthusiastic. Often they are downright fanatical.
Even in such relatively tranquil and liberal states as Connecticut, Kansas and Washington, Wallace support is abundantly
in evidence.

His biggest supporters are, in almost every case, the discontented, a classification that crosses ethnic, social and income barriers. Many of them are well dressed, well housed and relatively well educated. Though racism is the heart of Wallace's appeal, he also touches a responsive chord with almost anyone who, for one reason or another, is unhappy with the way things are. Bureaucrats have never been popular; Wallace pledges to throw "their briefcases into the Potomac." If a left-wing protester ever lies down in front of his car when he is President, it will be the last time that dissenter "ever lays down" in front of a car.

LOVE TICKET, DAVID AND JULIE: In a year of wee-hour skull sessions, G.O.P. strategists could hardly have cooked up such a promotional coup. The idea would have seemed too cloyingly obvious: the candidate's perky, pretty 20-year-old daughter Julie becoming engaged to the 20-year-old grandson of Dwight Eisenhower on the very eve of the presidential primary race. They would then campaign hand-in-hand toward November victory and a White House wedding.

As it happened, Julie Nixon and David Eisenhower came up with that script on their own. They fell in love during a year-long courtship at Smith and Amherst colleges and became engaged last November. Richard Nixon is personally delighted —not to mention his political gratification. "I always campaign better with an Eisenhower," Nixon winks as he introduces his future son-in-law. Indeed, David has become something of a star attraction. Inheriting both the name and his grandfather's grin, the tousled, sometimes diffident college junior lends a certain symmetry to the Nixon drive in the minds of many Republicans. His very presence recalls calmer times when Ike was in the White House.

As national chairman of Youth for Nixon-Agnew, David will try to recruit collegians for the Nixon campaign. He and Julie probably have their greatest impact, however, among the nation's parents and grandparents. Angered and bewildered by marijuana, campus rebellions and antiwar demonstrations, many older voters dote upon David and Julie.

CONFUSION OVER COLLUSION: A chastened Spiro Agnew set out last week to project the image of philosopher-statesman.

His press conferences, noted one aide, "are guaranteed not to make news." Like all guarantees, however, Agnew's had a time limit. Asked in Las Vegas about the charge that one of the major parties was in "collusion" with George Wallace, Agnew snapped: "That charge is not sufficiently dignified to require a comment. The word 'collusion' has nasty connotations." He added with appropriate disdain: "It's as bad as 'soft on Communism.' " The Maryland Governor may have been right, but he had not, it seemed, read the papers. The party accused of conspiring with Wallace was Democratic. The accuser was Richard Nixon.

OCT. 4 **GIVING 'EM HELL:** Hubert Humphrey began swinging hard—at last, said his friends. When antiwar hecklers interrupted him outside Cleveland, the Vice-President dismissed them as "damn fools." He introduced Emmett Kelly, the clown, as "Nixon's economic adviser." When Humphrey loosed a fusillade at Nixon during an A.F.L.-C.I.O. convention in Minneapolis, a happy worker bellowed: "Give 'em hell, Hubie!" Answered the Vice President: "What do you think I'm doing?"

Humphrey's tone is calculated to evoke memories of Harry Truman's bruising 1948 campaign against Thomas E. Dewey. Whatever ground Humphrey may have gained with it last week, however, the Vice President remained an astonishingly

Spiro Agnew. "It's some kind of disease." "It's some kind of egg."

Hubert Humphrey: "Government of the people is American as apple pie."

inconsistent campaigner. At times on the stump he could be inspiring and almost pithy. Then, in the next paragraph, he could sound again like a political calliope, clichés ablast. "Government of the people, for the people, and by the people," he told one audience, "is as American as apple pie."

SENSE OF HUMOR: Maryland's Governor Spiro Agnew so far has committed so many errors that a picket greeted him in Washington last week with a placard reading: APOLOGIZE NOW, SPIRO. IT WILL SAVE TIME LATER.

Some of Agnew's major miscues have been unintentional ethnic slurs. He jovially referred to a Japanese-American reporter accompanying him as a "fat Jap." In Chicago, where the Congressmen have names like Pucinski, Kluczynski and Rostenkowski, he answered a question about the dearth of Negroes in his audiences by saying: "Very frankly, when I am moving in a crowd I don't look and say, 'Well, there's a Negro, there's an Italian, and there's a Greek and there's a Polack.' " Before newsmen late last week, Agnew sought to make light of the whole thing by referring to himself as "Greek, er, Grecian." And he complained that Americans are now "up so tight that our sense of humor is beginning to disappear." Muskie could not let that one pass. "Mr. Agnew tells us that we lack a national sense of humor," Muskie remarked dryly. "I think he is doing his best to restore it."

NOT SO MANY ROCKS: Buoyed by the response to a speech on OCT. Viet Nam [in which he advocated a bombing halt] and by more than $200,000 in fresh contributions—Humphrey plunged into his first round of genuinely successful campaigning since the convention. Ironically, the Vice President drew his largest and friendliest crowd in the South. On turf that George Wallace considers his own, Humphrey tore into the Alabamian with unmatched savagery—and won applause. "He stands, and he has always stood," cried Humphrey of Wallace, "as the apostle of the politics of fear and racism." Humphrey was just warming up. He called Wallace a demagogue and compared him to Hitler. "He has sought to inflame fear, frustration and prejudice," he said. "He pretends to be the friend of the workingman, but he is the creature of the most reactionary underground forces in American life."

Richard Nixon also ventured into the South last week, but his treatment of Wallace was more restrained than Humphrey's. Wallace, he said, "is against many things Americans are frustrated about; I'm against them too. But that goes beyond saying, 'If someone lies down before a limousine I'd run him over.' Anybody who says that shouldn't be President." Nixon's crowds were uniformly large, but for the moment, it was Humphrey's campaign that seemed livelier—if only in contrast to his dismal showing earlier. "I feel good for the first time," Humphrey told reporters aboard his campaign plane. "We're not stepping on so many rocks or in so many holes as we were at first."

GEORGE'S GENERAL: For months, George Wallace had been casting about for a running mate, often in pretty strange waters. He considered "Colonel" Harland Sanders, the fried-chicken king ("It's finger-lickin' good"). He nearly chose A. B. ("Happy") Chandler, the former Governor and Senator from Kentucky, but Chandler proved too moderate on the race issue. Last week, after jokingly warning reporters that "I'm full of surprises," he announced his decision: retired Air Force General Curtis LeMay.

The choice of LeMay, 61, who had been mentioned as a possibility for weeks, was not all that surprising. The only surprise, in fact, was the look on Wallace's face. Beaming with pleasure and pride, the Alabamian introduced his candidate to a Pittsburgh press conference, then stepped aside to let the general speak. Wallace's expression quickly turned to obvious dismay. Within the space of a minute, LeMay had made even Wallace appear, by contrast, the image of the statesmanlike candidate. It took some doing. The general said that he did not like having to fight in Viet Nam and saw no need to use atomic weapons there at present—although he once advocated destroying "every work of man" in North Viet Nam and bombing its citizens "back to the Stone Age" unless Hanoi ended the war. But in his mind an atomic bomb was just another bomb. "If I found it necessary, I would use anything that we could dream up—including the nuclear weapons."

Wallace's discomfort was understandable. He knew that Barry Goldwater lost countless votes in 1964 because he was considered a bomb rattler. Though he is all bluster and bombast on domestic issues and a 100% hawk on Viet Nam, Wallace has barred nuclear weapons in Viet Nam. At the end of LeMay's press conference, Wallace jumped on reporters for even raising the matter.

Wallace was doing well on his own. In a swing through the East and Midwest last week he continued to draw big crowds. Almost everywhere there were hecklers, brandishing such signs as "If You Liked Hitler, You'll Love Wallace" and "Wallace Is Rosemary's Baby." Though he sometimes appears nettled by the gibes, Wallace generally shows great skill in turning them to his own advantage. "That's all right," he says, "just turn the television on them." Aides joke that if protesters ever fail to appear, Wallace would have to hire some. The candidate quips: "They just got me another 1,000,000 votes."

BOMBER ON THE STUMP: "If you have to go," John Kennedy once said, "you want LeMay in the lead bomber. But you never want LeMay deciding whether or not you have to go." The reason for Kennedy's caveat was that, like many fighting men, Curtis Emerson LeMay tends to view the world in crisp, absolutist terms. Forbidding, heavy-jowled, with a cigar customarily clenched between his teeth, LeMay has unintentionally promoted his own image as a character from *Dr. Strangelove*.

That caricature has tended to obscure what should be remembered as a highly distinguished military career. In World War II, he became something of a legend. In England, LeMay concluded that too many of his B-17s were missing targets because they zigzagged away from antiaircraft fire. He led the next raid over Saint-Nazaire himself, directing his planes in a straight-line block formation right through the flak. Next day he ordered his planes to take no more evasive actions on their final bombing runs. Losses went up, but so did the proficiency of his bombers. LeMay took similar risks in the Pacific. Assigned to run 300-plane B-29 raids against Japan, he removed his bombers' guns and gunners, overloaded them with fire bombs to dump on the enemy from a dangerously low level. Three years later, as chief of the U.S. air forces in Europe, LeMay was an architect of the Berlin airlift. In his years at SAC (1948-57), U.S. bombers were on airborne alert round the clock, and the nation's capacity for devastating retaliation was unquestioned. So was the efficiency of Curt LeMay. His men regarded him with a combination of respect and abject terror. After eight years as Air Force Vice Chief and finally Chief of Staff, LeMay retired to become chairman of the board—at $50,000 a year—of Networks Electronic. Last month he took a leave of absence to join Wallace. The role has brought him criticism. In Columbus last week, students at his old high school demanded that his portrait be removed from a hallway. [Before the campaign was over, LeMay was ousted from his $50,000-a-year job at Networks Electronic on the ground that his connections with Wallace were causing the firm's stock to drop in value.]

CT. 25   **MEANWHILE, SPIRO:** Meanwhile, Spiro T. Agnew veered sharply to the right in a deliberate effort to woo Wallaceites to Nixon. He attacked "phony intellectuals who don't understand what we mean by hard work and patriotism." And probably not even Wallace would have said, as Agnew did in Detroit, that "if you've seen one ghetto area, you've seen them all." Certainly few could have matched his airy defense of the established order. "You may give us your symptoms," he informed dissenters. "We will make the diagnosis. And we the Establishment—for which I make no apologies for being a part of—will implement the cure."

ATTACK, ATTACK, ATTACK: At last Hubert Humphrey's strategy was clear in his mind: Attack, attack, attack. George Wallace, he tells wavering unionists, was a "union-busting Governor and you know it." He brings the same indictment against Nixon, whom he labels "Richard the chicken-hearted" for refusing to debate. Wallace and Curtis LeMay become the "bombsy twins." "I can't afford to sun myself on Key Biscayne," he says in yet another dig at the well-rested Nixon. "I have to take my case to the people."

OV. 15   **PAINFULLY NARROW VICTORY:** Polled and analyzed as never before, accused of indifference toward the candidates and alarm over the issues, the nation's electorate finally got its turn. It spoke quietly. It expressed no overwhelming preference for a personality or a party. But it acted coolly, picking and choosing among candidates for high office and low. And it laid to rest some phantoms that had threatened to haunt the two-party system for years. Yet the nation denied Richard Nixon the massive "mandate to govern" he had pleaded for. Indeed, the voters belatedly warmed to Humphrey's gutsy drive for an upset in such numbers as to make Election Night one of the most suspenseful in memory.

In a record turnout of more than 72 million, Nixon's victory was painfully narrow. With 93% of the unofficial count in, Nixon had 29,565,052 (43%); Hubert Humphrey, 29,539,-500 (43%); and George Wallace, 9,181,466 (13%). [Final vote: Nixon, 31,770,237 (43.4%); Humphrey 31,270,533 (42.7%); Wallace, 9,906,141 (13.5%).] The indicated electoral vote was 290 for Nixon, 203 for Humphrey and 45 for Wallace. Wallace's 13% was impressive in one sense: it was more than twice the combined totals won by Progressive Henry Wallace and Dixiecrat Strom Thurmond in 1948 and was the largest third-party turnout since Robert La Follette garnered nearly 17% in 1924. However, outside the Deep South his showing shrank dramatically below his standing in the polls through the late summer and early fall. He failed to prove his contention that the "rednecks" he bragged about were sufficiently numerous or widely enough distributed to people a national movement. Thus the future of the two-party system seems more secure.

Historically, there is nothing too unusual about minority Presidents. Lincoln, Cleveland, Wilson and Truman all had to make do with less than 50%, as did John F. Kennedy. But not since Wilson's first election in 1912 with 41.9% of the vote has a President received so small a share as Nixon has. And no other modern President has been elected to a first term to confront a Congress controlled by the opposition. Although the G.O.P. gained Senate strength, the 91st Congress will be in Democratic hands.

NIXON'S CHANCE TO LEAD: "I know some of you have been through defeats, as I have, and had your hearts broken. It has been said that a great philosophy is not won without defeat. But a great philosophy is always won without fear."

So said Richard Nixon to his party workers during the campaign. So he said again when he appeared before his followers to accept and savor his victory. Now he could forget the defeats, both the hairbreadth miss of 1960 and the humiliating rebuff of 1962. Now he could put behind him the fear that maybe he was, after all, a born loser. Now he could relish the fruits of unremitting labor for his party, of countless fundraising dinners and victory banquets and formula speeches in remote towns. Now he could demonstrate to the nation—and perhaps to himself—just what his "great philosophy" is. Now, at last, he had achieved a goal that seemed to have eluded him forever.

It has been a desperately long road for the grocer's son from Whittier, Calif., and perhaps the most fascinating stretch now lay before him. Nixon will bring to the office undeniable gifts as an organizer. He has a valuable, no-nonsense appreciation of the presidency as a job that requires the self-discipline of what he calls a spartan life. Though he spent eight years under a man who was wary of the powers of the office, he declared in a speech on the presidency—one of his best—on Sept. 19: "The days of a passive presidency belong to a simpler past. The next President must take an activist view of his office. He must articulate the nation's values, define its goals and marshal its will."

The question about Richard M. Nixon—in fact, the question that would be asked of any man about to be tested in the White House—is whether he is capable of coming close to that ideal. He faces the immensely difficult problem of reconciling an alienated left and an uneasy right, of bringing together Negroes and young people, Wallace followers and middle-class Americans who feel an ever more crushing burden of taxes. He has yet to persuade a great number of citizens that he is wholly to be trusted. Nixon has amply proved that he can improvise, tinker, administer, manage—and think. Now the nation, by its choice, has given him the opportunity to demonstrate whether he can pass the ultimate test of a President in this complex age: Can he lead?

DEC. 20 **GETTING TO KNOW THEM:** The TV Spectacular of the Week was the all-network, prime-time *Richard Nixon Show,* introducing to the nation the twelve men the President-elect has chosen to head the top Government departments. Their debut was telecast live and in color. Nixon made a few minor fluffs during his unrehearsed half-hour stand-up performance at Washington's Shoreham Hotel. He forgot to name Maurice

Stans as he introduced his Secretary of Commerce, and he referred to President Kennedy's "first inaugural"; there was, of course, only one. But he spoke without notes or lectern, in marked contrast to the wrap-around electronic prompters Lyndon Johnson regularly uses. Because of the ease and experience that he gained on camera in the 1968 campaign, he plans to make repeated informal use of TV in his Administration to get even closer to U.S. firesides than Franklin Roosevelt did with his celebrated radio chats. As one aide explains: "How else can you get 50 million people?"

The morning after the telecast, Nixon gathered his Cabinet and their wives at the Shoreham for a day-long briefing on the problems the new Administration will face. The wives were invited, Nixon explained, because "I want them to be there on the takeoffs—so that they may avoid a crash landing a little later." (Some of the wives dutifully took notes.) Beginning this week, the new Cabinet members will meet one by one with President Johnson.

A PARLOR CABINET: The men suggest cool competence rather than passion or brilliance. They are problem solvers rather than idea brokers. There are no blooded patricians in the lot, just strivers who have acted out the middle-class dream. Thus, as much as any dozen individuals can, Richard Nixon's new Cabinet members mirror the qualities of their boss, of the campaign he waged, of the aspirations of the constituency that elected him.

The group is somewhat more homogeneous than the cross section that Nixon sought. Earlier he had promised to put together "a Government drawn from the broadest possible base, an Administration made up of Republicans, Democrats and independents," one comprising "the very best men and women I can find in the country—from business, from government, from labor, from all the areas." Not by choice, he ended up with a group that is all white, all male, all Republican.

The new Cabinet is heavily weighted with men of business backgrounds. Three got rich in the construction industry: Massachusetts Governor John Volpe (Secretary of Transportation), Alaska Governor Walter Hickel (Interior), and Chamber of Commerce President Winton Blount (Postmaster General). The best-known figure in the group, Michigan Governor

George Romney (Housing and Urban Development), was head of American Motors. The two academicians in the Cabinet, Chancellor Clifford Hardin of the University of Nebraska (Agriculture) and George Shultz, dean of the University of Chicago's Graduate School of Business (Labor), made their marks as administrators as much as scholars. David Kennedy (Treasury) is a Chicago banker so well regarded by both parties that Lyndon Johnson, without success, invited him to head the Treasury in 1965.

More than most Presidents-elect, Nixon relied heavily on the supporting cast he has learned to trust from close experience. Maurice Stans (Commerce) is a colleague from the Eisenhower days and a longtime Republican fund raiser. John Mitchell (Attorney General) was Nixon's law partner and campaign manager. Wisconsin Congressman Melvin Laird (Defense) has served Nixon as an adviser. California Lieutenant Governor Robert Finch (Health, Education and Welfare) is an old friend, campaign aide and confidant. In fact, Finch is matched in the boss's personal esteem only by William Pierce Rogers, Attorney General in the Eisenhower Administration, whom Nixon selected to become the 55th Secretary of State. Over the years, Nixon has reserved his friendship for few men. With intimates like Finch, Mitchell and Rogers heading major departments, what in other Administrations would serve as a Kitchen Cabinet will be officially installed in the parlor.

C. 27 **EASING INTO POWER:** "Remember," Richard Nixon admonished Republican congressional leaders last week, "we've got a Democratic Congress and we want to get along with them." After a cautious campaign and a transition period relatively free of friction, Nixon apparently intends to ease through his first months of incumbency in much the same manner. Instead of requesting major legislation, Nixon intends to use executive orders and existing programs whenever possible. His approach was aptly summed up by Robert Finch, who will be the new Administration's Secretary of Health, Education and Welfare. "Our job," Finch told newsmen last week, "is to rationalize and implement the legislation now on the books."

One set of decisions that the new Administration cannot defer is the selection of people to run and represent the Government. Last week Richard Nixon made these appointments:

¶ Charles W. Yost, 61, retired diplomat, became the surprise choice as Ambassador to the United Nations. A Democrat, Yost entered the foreign service in 1930 and rose steadily to the coveted rank of career ambassador.

¶ J. Edgar Hoover accepted Nixon's invitation to remain as FBI chief. Nixon will be Hoover's eighth President (Calvin Coolidge was the first) and almost certainly his last. "The Director" is already four years past the normal mandatory retirement age (he will be 74 on New Year's Day), and it is understood that he will step down at age 75 with 45 years of service as the bureau's chief. Why the extension? Explained a Nixon aide: "You don't begin a law and order campaign by firing J. Edgar Hoover."

The Congress

WILBUR THE WILLFUL: In the midst of Washington's worried deliberations over Viet Nam and Korea last week, Secretary of State Dean Rusk took time out to join Treasury Secretary Henry Fowler on a quiet but urgent mission to Little Rock, Ark. There, in The Coachman's Inn, the two Cabinet members spent a precious two hours and ten minutes with Representative Wilbur Mills in yet another effort to enlist his support for the President's tax bill. Mills, characteristically, was unimpressed. The Rusk-Fowler trip pointed up the immense importance the White House attaches to both the tax increase and Mills's position as chairman of the powerful House Ways and Means Committee. Lyndon Johnson has lined up his whole Cabinet, the Federal Reserve Board and battalions of bankers, businessmen and economists behind the tax bill. But standing against this seemingly irresistible tide is Wilbur the Willful, an immovable sea wall.

A bland, stocky native of Kensett (pop. 905), Democrat Mills, 58, maintains that the tax bill is not languishing in his committee because of his personal opposition. Congressional liaison men from the White House and legislative leaders of both parties agree that the House itself overwhelmingly opposes the tax bill. Says Wisconsin's John Byrnes, the senior Republican on Mills's committee: "This is a lot of malarkey about

Mills's holding up this bill. It isn't the committee or the Congress. It's the people."

The trouble with Mills is that he simply does not like to lose. And he also happens to be completely unconvinced that the tax bill is necessary or desirable. He profoundly disagrees with Johnson's policy of attempting to finance the Viet Nam war and domestic social reforms simultaneously, insists that spending will have to be reduced somewhere. "If I asked the American taxpayer to pull in his belt," Mills said after the Rusk-Fowler visit, "I would expect the Government to do the same thing."

L 19 **OPENING THE DOORS:** If, as Lyndon Johnson intended, the 1964 civil rights bill was a monument to John Kennedy, the measure that became law last week will stand in part as a memorial to Martin Luther King. The 1968 Civil Rights Act, opening some 80% of all the nation's housing to Negroes, should also endure as a major legislative landmark of the Johnson Administration. "The proudest moments of my presidency," said L.B.J. at the bill-signing ceremony in the White House, "have been such times as this when I have signed into law the promises of a century."

NE 7 **WILBUR'S FULL HOUSE:** "All those men have their price," sneered England's 18th century Prime Minister, Sir Robert Walpole, speaking of his opposition. In Wilbur Mills's case, the price came high: $6 billion sliced from the proposed 1968-69 federal budget of $186 billion. Not a cent less, insists the flinty House Ways and Means Committee chairman. With the graven mien of a frontier gambler who has peeked at his opponent's hole card, the Arkansas Democrat has stood pat against Lyndon Johnson—himself the master emeritus of Capitol Hill poker—matching imperturbably the President's wiles, threats and blandishments for 16 weary months. Last week, drawing strength from a majority of like-minded congressional conservatives in both parties, Mills coolly turned up a full house. He defeated handily, by 259 to 137 votes, an attempt to make him abide by the cut of only $4 billion that would be acceptable to the White House. Next day the President capitulated on Mills's terms even though the cut will slash into the bone and sinew of Great Society programs he deems essential to assuage America's social ills. Without increased taxes, Johnson warned, "the gates of economic chaos could open."

The new tax, retroactive to January 1 for corporations and to April 1 for individuals, should garner $10 billion in a calendar year to offset a deficit that could run as high as $25 billion —even after the cutback in expenditures—and bolster sagging international confidence in the dollar.

SHOT DOWN: Both houses of Congress last week virtually shot AUG down any hope of meaningful federal control of guns. The major defeat occurred in the House, where it came in the form —but not the substance—of victory for tighter laws. The House passed and sent to the Senate a bill that would limit interstate mail-order sales of long guns and certain types of ammunition. However, charged the bill's disappointed floor manager, Brooklyn Democrat Emanuel Celler, the measure left loopholes "as wide as the Grand Canyon." Among the 19 amendments adopted was one permitting gun collectors to qualify as "dealers" and thus become exempt from the interstate ban. Another amendment—a clear victory for the National Rifle Association—would exempt long-gun ammunition from the mail-order ban.

Even so, the minimal bill will ban over-the-counter sales of rifles, shotguns, and bigger weapons to most out-of-staters, those under 18, fugitives, mental defectives, felons and anyone under indictment for a crime. Neither the House bill nor a similar Senate bill, cleared by the Judiciary Committee the same day, provides for licensing gun owners or federal registration of firearms. In the House, New Jersey Democrat Charles S. Joelson was not heartened when told that gun-control foes "could live with" the watered-down bill. "I suggest," he chided his colleagues, "that tens of thousands of Americans can die with it."

CLOSING THE BOOKS ON THE 90TH: Careening toward adjourn- OCT ment, Congress last week approved the largest defense appropriation in history ($72 billion) and the stingiest foreign-aid appropriation ($1.75 billion). Those two figures told much about the week on Capitol Hill, and indeed about the entire contentious, niggardly 90th. The week began with a slapstick squabble over a bill to waive the requirement that radio and television grant equal time to all candidates. The waiver would have cleared the way for presidential debates among the major candidates—something that Hubert Humphrey wants and Richard Nixon, as the man with a big lead to preserve, does not. In their maneuvering over the bill, the Democrats staged a lock-in in the House, and the Republicans held a sit-out in the Senate. When House Republicans conducted a 27-hour filibuster by insisting on time-consuming roll calls, Speaker John McCormack finally locked the doors for the first time since 1917. With a captive quorum, Democrats were able to ram the measure through. In the Senate, however, wily Minority Leader Everett Dirksen reversed the procedure by stationing a page outside the doors to send Republicans away. Lacking a quorum, the Senate was stymied, and Majority Leader Mike Mansfield finally signaled defeat for the TV debates.

The Supreme Court

For more than a decade, reflecting the philosophy of Chief Justice Earl Warren, the Supreme Court had been a center of controversy because of its decisions on such issues as desegregation, free speech, pornography and the rights of criminals. This libertarian trend continued in 1968.

RIL 5 **SHARP LINE ON FREE SPEECH:** Just what does free speech include? How obscene must a book or film be to lose the First Amendment protection? When can a soldier speak without fear of being punished for his words? Last week the question being argued before the U.S. Supreme Court was whether or not a teacher can be fired by a public-school board for criticizing the superintendent of schools. In light of the continual immediacy of the problem, court watchers were looking carefully at Justice Hugo Black's Carpentier Lectures delivered at Columbia University, in which Black dwelled on picketing and other forms of so-called symbolic speech. Black reiterated his oft-expressed opinion that the free-speech guarantee includes every sort of speech, no matter how obscene. "All I am doing," he said, "is following what to me is the clear wording of the First Amendment that 'Congress shall make no law . . . abridging the freedom of speech or of the press.' As I have said innumerable times before, I simply believe that 'no law' means no law. I think the Supreme Court is about the most inappropriate supreme board of censors that could be found. The plain language of the Constitution recognizes that censorship is the deadly enemy of freedom and progress and forbids it." In short, free speech is an "absolute command" in Black's mind.

But he draws a sharp line between speech and action. "I believe, with Jefferson," he says, "that it is time enough for government to step in to regulate people when they *do* something, not when they *say* something." Recently, "many loose words have been spoken and written about an alleged First Amendment right to picket, demonstrate or march, usually accompanied by singing, shouting or loud praying, along the public streets, or in and around government-owned buildings, or in and around other people's property, including their homes, without the owners' consent. I do not believe that the First Amendment grants a constitutional right" in this area. "Marching back and forth, though utilized to communicate ideas, is not speech and therefore is not protected by the First Amendment." Nor, by that reasoning, is there any free speech protection for those who burn draft cards or desecrate the flag. Black went on to make clear, however, that while the Government may, if it wishes, make laws to restrict demonstrations and pickets, it must apply such laws equally. Concluded he: "These laws must never be used as a guise to suppress particular views which the Government dislikes."

MINOR OBSCENITY: Lately, the Supreme Court has regularly MAY been finding anti-obscenity laws unconstitutional. But it has also hinted that it would find no objection to laws specifically aimed at the protection of juveniles. Last week, by a vote of 6 to 3, the court fulfilled the hints by holding that states may make it a crime knowingly to sell "to minors under 17 years of age material defined to be obscene to them whether or not it would be obscene to adults."

In 1965, a 16-year-old boy bought a few girlie magazines from Sam Ginsberg at his Bellmore, L.I., stationery store and luncheonette. Ginsberg was tried and convicted under New

York's new juvenile obscenity law; he appealed. His contention was that the right of a person to read or see material "cannot be made to depend upon whether the citizen is an adult or a minor." But the contention does not wash, said Justice William Brennan. For one thing, the court held that "the power of the state to control the conduct of children reaches beyond the scope of its authority over adults." As to whether or not girlie magazines and similar material actually impair—in the words of New York's law—"the ethical and moral development of youth," Brennan concluded that scientific evidence had neither proved nor disproved that point.

Dissenting, Justice Abe Fortas pointed out that the boy had been directed to make the purchase by his mother in an effort to get Ginsberg convicted. "Bookselling," said Fortas, "should not be a hazardous profession." The magazines that Sam Ginsberg sold were admittedly not obscene for adults; how was he to know that they were obscene for children? The court must define "the extent to which literature or pictures may be less offensive in order to be 'obscene' for purposes of a statute confined to youth."

E 7 **DESEGREGATION NOW:** It has been 14 years since the Supreme Court ruled Southern school segregation unconstitutional, 13 years since the court ordered desegregation "with all deliberate speed," and four years since it ruled that "the time for mere 'deliberate speed' has run out." Last week, on behalf of an impatient and unanimous court, Justice William Brennan wrote: "The burden on the school board today is to come forward with a plan that promises realistically to work, and promises realistically to work *now.*"

Bluntly, Brennan spelled out the court's dissatisfaction with the so-called "freedom of choice" plans that have been adopted in more than 1,300 Southern school districts. The trouble with the plans is that they simply do not work. In New Kent County, Va., and Gould, Ark.—the two areas specifically examined by the court—schools remain largely segregated because the responsibility for action has been placed on the Negro students: they must take it upon themselves to request a transfer. And all too few of them make the effort. But they should not have to, said the court. It is the school boards, not the students, who are "clearly charged with the affirmative duty to take whatever steps might be necessary to convert to a unitary system in which racial discrimination would be eliminated root and branch." Unless a freedom-of-choice plan achieves that goal, it is unacceptable.

Georgia Governor Lester Maddox understood full well what the court's decision meant for the South. He ordered all flags on state property flown at half-mast, and in an official proclamation announced that it had been "another black and tragic Monday, when the United States Supreme Court again ruled in support of the demands of the Communist Party."

ACTIVIST FORTAS: When newly sworn Supreme Court Justice Abe Fortas wrote his first dissent at the end of 1965, the issue involved a minor dispute over a Small Business Administration contract. With characteristic energy, Fortas prepared a meticulously reasoned draft. When it was circulated among his colleagues, two members of the five-man majority found it so persuasive that their view shifted. Fortas' dissent became the majority opinion.

It was a fitting beginning. In the three years that Fortas has been on the court, his incisive reasoning has propelled him past some of the more senior Justices to a position as one of the court's most brilliant and intriguing members. Last week the public at large got a clearer view of Fortas' mind at work as a publisher brought out his 64-page pamphlet *Concerning Dissent and Civil Disobedience*, a compact discussion of the issues that have been raised by what he calls "the most profound and pervasive revolution ever achieved by substantially peaceful means."

Fortas, 58, wrote the booklet during and after a series of speaking trips to college campuses last year. Those trips "got me scared," he explained. Sympathetic to the aspirations of rebellious Negroes, Viet Nam war protesters and students, he fully endorses their right to dissent; yet he points out that "the motive of civil disobedience, whatever its type, does not confer immunity for law violation. Just as we expect the government to be bound by all laws, so each individual is bound by all of the laws under the Constitution. He cannot pick and choose."

Whether as public servant or private counsel, Fortas has never been an easy, friendly man. In his hugely successful

Washington law firm of Arnold, Fortas & Porter, his younger associates found him machine-like, testy and hard-boiled. Said one when asked for a brief description: "Unpleasant." Fortas' high-powered intellect, combined with a legendary ability as a problem-fixer and a penchant for never repeating a confidence made him one of Washington's most influential private citizens long before his court appointment. It also made him a trusted adviser to President Johnson on everything from the Walter Jenkins scandal to the Dominican crisis. When Arthur Goldberg resigned from the court to move to the U.N., Johnson's first choice to replace him was inevitably Fortas. It was a political convenience that Fortas also happened to be Jewish and it was the court's "Jewish seat" that was open.

E 21   **APPROVAL TO "STOP & FRISK":** It happens almost every day: a policeman catches sight of a suspicious character, stops him and frisks him. But doesn't the Fourth Amendment specifically bar "unreasonable searches and seizures"? It does indeed, said the Supreme Court last week, but the operative word is "unreasonable." Speaking for an 8-to-1 majority, Chief Justice Warren held that the Constitution permits a policeman to accost an individual if there is good reason to suspect that he is up to no good, and to search him for weapons if there is good reason to suspect that he may be armed.

E 28   **WARREN, OUT OF THE STORM CENTER:** Americans, enthralled by the personality of their President and the power of his office, tend to talk about their political history in terms of presidential administrations. Yet last week, when it was learned that Earl Warren, the 14th Chief Justice of the United States, would soon retire from the Supreme Court, it was clear that another branch of government can define a historic period just as sharply—if not more so. For the past 15 years, the extraordinary "Warren court," spanning all but a few months of the terms of three Presidents, has had no less an impact on American life than the Eisenhower, Kennedy and Johnson administrations combined. Under Warren, the court has addressed itself principally to three great areas: civil rights, reapportionment under the one-man, one-vote doctrine, and criminal justice. As earlier courts have been dominated by such concerns as property rights, the building of the central

Chief Justice Warren. He put his stamp on an era; now he wants to retire.

Associate Justice Fortas. His nomination for the top job is talked to death.

government and slavery, Warren's court confronted, in an unusual number of cases, one overriding problem—the rights of the individual. In so doing, the court guaranteed that it would spark controversy. As Oliver Wendell Holmes said of the court in one of his celebrated remarks: "We are very quiet there, but it is the quiet of the storm center."

There is no compulsory retirement for a Supreme Court Justice, and Warren, at 77, could have remained active as long as health and spirit lasted. But Warren apparently wanted to retire while his physical and mental abilities were still keen. Moreover, he was eager to enable President Johnson, a personal friend, to name a new Chief Justice who would follow in the liberal, activist tradition. And the Chief Justice was also worried, according to friends, that Richard Nixon, a man he heartily dislikes, would be elected President in November and fill the spot with a conservative.

All through the Warren years, criticism of the court rarely ceased. White Southerners dubbed May 17, 1954—the day that *Brown v. Board of Education* (which outlawed public school segregation) was announced—"Black Monday." The title was subsequently applied to many another Monday, the traditional day for issuing decisions, as the court bit by bit chipped away the legal basis of white supremacy. When the court later handed down its decisions outlawing the daily recitation of prayers in public schools, Alabama's Representative George Andrews cried: "They put the Negroes in the schools, and now they've driven God out."

Throughout, Earl Warren was both symbol and target. Bumper stickers reading IMPEACH EARL WARREN—or in California, FLUORIDATE EARL WARREN—festooned countless autos, and the Chief Justice was long No. 1 on the far right's hate list. In 1954, Mississippi's Senator James Eastland denounced Warren's court as "the greatest single threat to our Constitution"; last week George Wallace declared that "he's done more to destroy constitutional government in this country than any one man." Even Dwight Eisenhower, who thought of Warren as a mildly progressive Republican when he named him Chief Justice, reportedly described the appointment years afterward as the "biggest damfool mistake I ever made." "I wasn't close to him when I appointed him," Eisenhower later declared, "didn't really know him. But I liked his family, and I'd been told he'd been a good Governor."

Actually, the critics have not been exactly on target in attacking Warren, for the Chief Justice is only one of nine men, with only one of nine votes. Still, the "Warren court" is not merely a title of convenience. The 14th Chief Justice has all along given the court his own stamp and subtly molded the shape of its decisions. In choosing Justices to write the majority opinion—a power that Warren used most astutely—he could usually determine, within broad guidelines, the direction the opinion would take. Warren's forte—unlike that of Holmes, Brandeis, Frankfurter or Abe Fortas of today's court—was not legal analysis. One law professor who admires him says that "he doesn't have the intellectual qualities for the faculty of any good law school." While other Justices never let on what they are thinking when they hear oral arguments, Warren's feelings, says Berkeley Professor David Feller, "are right there on his shirtsleeves. You can see right through the robe." Impatient when lawyers cited obscure legal precedents to buttress their cases, the pragmatic Chief Justice would often ask simply: "Yes, but is it fair?"

LY 5   **CHIEF CONFIDANT TO CHIEF JUSTICE:** The Supreme Court's decisions affect every American, living and unborn. And it is the final, irrevocable judge of every President and Congress. Thus last week, when Lyndon Johnson nominated Associate Justice Abe Fortas to be the 15th Chief Justice of the United States, his selection was almost as significant as the election of a new President in November.

In view of President Johnson's fondness for unexpected appointments, the nomination of Fortas to succeed Earl Warren was surprising only in its predictability. And yet the nomination provoked unexpectedly strong opposition in the Senate. The appointment of the President's close friend and confidant smacked of "cronyism at its worst," said Michigan's Robert Griffin, "and everybody knows it." The charge of cronyism was reinforced by the fact that to fill the vacancy left by Earl Warren's retirement and Fortas' move up, Lyndon Johnson appointed his old friend and fellow Texan, Homer Thornberry.

FORTAS AT THE BAR: For congressional opponents of the Supreme Court, it was a moment of high satisfaction. Never before had a Chief Justice-designate been grilled by a Senate committee. Never before had there been so dramatic an opportunity to voice criticism of the Warren court. For Abe Fortas, the confrontation must have been an occasion of particular pain. After four days of hearings before James Eastland's Senate Judiciary Committee, it was plain that the most serious impediment to his confirmation as 15th Chief Justice of the United States may prove to be his friendship with Lyndon Johnson. The issue of "cronyism" seemed to overshadow all others. As Fortas described it, his role as presidential adviser has been grossly exaggerated. While he was indeed called in on "a few critical matters," most notably Viet Nam and the Detroit riots, he said that his role was not to shape policy but to synthesize the arguments of others in clear legal style. "My function," he noted, "has been to listen to what is said . . . then to sum up the arguments on the one side, the considerations on the other."

But Fortas' friendship with the President was not the only objection raised to his confirmation. For some, it was merely a screen to hide their real concern. Many Southerners dislike the activist trend of the court altogether and see Fortas as a too liberal successor to Warren. As Mississippi's John Stennis complained: "He has clearly shown his alignment with the liberal bloc and has often provided the fifth vote in the all too numerous 5-to-4 decisions by which the court has asserted its assumed role of rewriting the Constitution." Pursuing that line with unrelenting tenacity, South Carolina's Strom Thurmond spent more than four hours denouncing decisions that have guaranteed the rights of criminal defendants. Claiming that the court's guarantees of defendants' rights sometimes permitted the guilty to go free along with the innocent, Thurmond rasped, "What difference does it make if there is a lawyer present or not? What difference does it make if you get the truth?" Fortas replied that the difference might be the Constitution. With "the greatest regret," Fortas refused to answer more than 50 of Thurmond's 100-odd questions, on the ground that the legislative branch must not interfere with the judiciary. Only once did Fortas show anger. That was when Thurmond asked whether Fortas agreed that the Supreme Court was "the principal reason for the turmoil and air of revolutionary conditions that prevailed in Washington." After a long pause in which he was obviously trying to contain himself, Fortas merely said "No."

THE FORTAS FILM FESTIVAL: Berating the U.S. Supreme Court used to be the fairly exclusive pastime of racists and other right-wing extremists. Now it has become a more popular preoccupation. Many people who think that U.S. society is somehow sick tend to blame the court for much of the rise in crime, the loosening of morals, the racial conflict and the general air of permissiveness. Most of those complaints have welled up in the acrimonious debate in the Senate over Lyndon Johnson's nomination of Abe Fortas to become the nation's 15th Chief Justice.

The fight against Fortas was stepped up on two fronts. One was being carefully led on the Senate floor by Michigan Republican Robert P. Griffin. The other was pressed within the Senate Judiciary Committee by Republican Strom Thurmond, the gentleman Torquemada from South Carolina. Thurmond continued to hammer at an emotional, if elusive issue: pornography. He condemned the fact that Fortas had voted with the court majority in a 5-to-4 decision holding that a Los Angeles exhibitor did not violate the law with his raunchy films. The ruling made it easier for other U.S. exhibitors to show films featuring total male and female nudity.

Day after day last week, Thurmond buttonholed his colleagues to watch the films in darkened Senate offices. One aide called it "the Fortas Film Festival." It mattered little that nobody really knew what Fortas thought about the films. The court judgment involving them was one of the many decisions which do not require Justices to write their opinions. In an obscenity case, what is often at issue is not the merits or demerits of the film itself but the manner in which it was seized, the legality of the prior court action, and the definition of obscenity in the individual situation.

Fortas' own interpretations vary, depending on the case. In 1966, he voted with the 5-to-4 majority to uphold the conviction of *Eros* Publisher Ralph Ginzburg on grounds that he pandered to prurient interests by using overly suggestive advertising. But that did not make much of an impression upon Eastland, Thurmond and other critics even farther to the right. In a large mailing, the fanatically right-wing Liberty Lobby accused Fortas of being a convinced revolutionary and a supporter of the pornography industry. More doubts about Fortas' chances were raised by a disclosure last week that he had accepted $15,000 for 18 hours of summer-school teaching at American University's law school. Though some other Justices accept fees, there is an ethical question about whether they should. What aggravates the question of Fortas' particularly generous fee is that it was donated by five big businessmen who some day may well have matters of interest come before the court.

Congressional opposition to Fortas continued to mount, and finally crystallized in a Senate filibuster.

THE FORTAS DEFEAT: "Never in our history," cried Michigan's OCT Democratic Senator Philip Hart, "has a matter of the nomination of a Justice to the Supreme Court been resolved by a filibuster." But shortly after Hart spoke, the Senate refused to cut off debate on whether it should even take up the Fortas nomination, thereby killing his chances. The vote was 43 against cloture to 45 in favor—14 short of the two-thirds needed to stop the anti-Fortas filibuster. Next day, at Fortas' request, Lyndon Johnson withdrew the nomination. It was a profound humiliation for the President. Said Johnson: "The action of the Senate, a body I revere and to which I devoted a dozen years of my life, is historically and constitutionally tragic." Johnson was referring to the fact that the Senate had never actually voted on the merits of the nomination, only on the procedural question of giving it formal consideration. All but forgotten was another loser in the affair: Homer Thornberry, who was to have replaced Fortas as an Associate Justice on the court. Since Fortas will now keep his own seat, there is now no room for Thornberry; his nomination lies in a legal limbo.

Races

1   **THE BEATIFICATION OF MALCOLM X:** Across the land last week, disciples of Malcolm X marked the third anniversary of the Negro militant's assassination by turning the event—just one day before Washington's Birthday—into what they hope will be a series of black holidays. "We need our days," said a Boston celebrant, "just as Jewish people have days to express their identity. At the time Washington was very busy being the father of our country, we were very busy being slaves. He doesn't have much relevance for us. We hope to celebrate other days that are relevant—Nat Turner Day or Marcus Garvey Day."

The apostles of Malcolm X made their prophet's own speeches seem restrained by comparison. In New York City's Harlem, nearly 600 people packed an ultramodern public school building to celebrate a program attended by Malcolm's widow. Also on hand: Writer James Baldwin who capped the program by calling the U.S. "the Fourth Reich."

BLACK POCKETBOOK POWER: Black Power sentiment is fed, among other things, by the urban Negro's pent-up resentment of the white businessmen who make their living from the slum's daily needs. These white-run enterprises, blacks complain, not only batten on the ghetto's misery by overcharging for shoddy goods but also siphon off their profits from Negro neighborhoods and seldom employ black workers. But black animosity can breed an antidote to its own racial poison. In Chicago, where the white community dismissed Martin Luther King's 1966 civil rights crusade with a hatful of vapid promises, black pocketbook power has become an effective, constructive force. In less than two years, the Rev. Jesse Jackson, 26, a burly King lieutenant who praises the Lord and believes in the might of economics, has wrested work from ghetto businessmen for 3,000 of his flock and boosted South Side Negroes' annual income by $22 million.

Running his Operation Breadbasket from a dingy cubicle on the second floor of King's dilapidated South Side headquarters, Jackson fixed his strategy in April 1966 in his first campaign against a dairy with 104 outlets in Negro neighborhoods. Jackson's request to examine the company's employment rolls was refused. Next Sunday, pastors from 100 Negro pulpits urged a boycott of the dairy's products; by Thursday, the company had capitulated, offering ghetto dwellers 44 new or upgraded jobs—20% of its total employment. A 54-store grocery chain proved tougher. Platoons of housewife picketers mobilized by Jesse Jackson's cadre marched for ten days until the chain hired 183 Negroes in jobs ranging from department managers to delivery boys; today it employs 309 Negroes. After testing Operation Breadbasket's strength,

The Rev. Jesse Jackson: "Where big money stays, big decisions are made."

Roy Innis of CORE. If it's to be suicide, he favors kamikaze over harakiri.

A. & P. stores in Chicago found 970 jobs for Jackson, and Jewel Tea has hired 661 Negroes. Dozens of other white employers did not wait for a boycott. "You can't calculate the number of jobs made available because they hear those footsteps coming," says Jackson.

Casting around for opportunities to promote Negro-owned businesses, Jackson and his aides have organized service companies and matched them with customers. Trash from 40 A. & P. stores is now collected by a Jackson-organized sanitation firm ("What's more grass-rootsy than garbage?"), and the chain has also taken on Negro janitors and exterminators. "Up until then," Jackson snorts, "we didn't even control our own rats and roaches." Jackson is convinced that a new political order will eventually emerge as Negro economic power and pride increase. To make doubly sure, Operation Breadbasket pressure has persuaded ghetto firms to open accounts in two Negro banks, thus boosting deposits from $5,000,000 to $22 million. "Where big money stays," the pastor preaches, "big decisions are made."

5 **MEMPHIS BLUES:** For seven weeks racial tensions had mounted in Memphis, as the city's garbage strike escalated into a showdown between Mayor Henry Loeb and more than 200,000 Negroes seeking economic parity with whites. Last week black blues erupted into violence when militants got the opportunity they had been seeking. It was given to them by Dr. Martin Luther King. The explosion was as senseless as it was inevitable, once King took his 4,500 marchers onto historic Beale Street. A band of young Negroes called the Invaders had been waiting for the event. "We been making plans to tear this town up for a long time," an Invader chieftain said. "But we didn't dare do it on our own. We needed a crowd. We knew he'd turn out a crowd, and with a crowd the cops would have a hard time laying hands on us." One hundred strong, the Invaders infiltrated the marchers' flanks, planning to disperse in flying squads and riot on cue.

Hardly had King, the apostle of nonviolence, led the way out onto the street than the rocks began to fly. Glass shards sprayed from splintered windows. Rioters galloped from downtown store to store. The parade faltered, halted, turned upon itself to retrace its steps. Police fired tear gas at random, as King beat a prudent retreat to his motel, leaving local civil rights leaders to herd the marchers back to their headquarters church. Looting began, and the police lost their cherished reputation for restraint. Cops thwacked away with clubs, and Negroes turned savagely upon isolated officers. By the end of the day—the tenth anniversary of Memphis Blues-smith W. C. Handy's death—there were 282 arrests, 62 injuries and one fatality: a 16-year-old Negro shotgunned by police. Nightfall brought double the usual number of fires, most of them in uncollected garbage piled along curbs.

Though relatively mild, the rampage panicked authorities. Mayor Loeb slapped down a curfew, shuttered liquor stores, bars and entertainment places, and stopped the buses. Governor Buford Ellington rushed in 250 state troopers and 4,000 Tennessee National Guardsmen. King has heard himself dubbed a rabble-rouser before; now, for leaving the march, he was called a coward as well. Undismayed, though his nonviolent mantle was in shreds, King vowed to lead another march on Memphis this week. [Before he could do so King was slain by a gunman. See page 24.]

BLACK SEPARATIST: Integration has been the aim of the Congress of Racial Equality since CORE was born in 1942. Its intramural squabbles have never been concerned with the principle of desegregation but with its pace. Two years ago, Floyd McKissick replaced Founder James Farmer because he was not moving fast enough. Last week McKissick, in turn, was supplanted by a more aggressive lieutenant. CORE's new chief, however, advocates rigid separation of the races.

Roy Innis, 34, a Harlem-honed black nationalist, who will formally replace McKissick next month, is a bearded manifesto maker who professes a fear of genocide, not "by the gas chamber but by the slow taking away of our existence" through racial amalgamation. Appealing to Negroes to improve their own lot rather than die in all-out conflict with the white man, Innis adds nonetheless: "We believe that if we must die, it will not be by harakiri but by kamikaze—take as many with us as we can." By accepting Innis' incendiary view, CORE alienates not only whites but black moderates. Thus it joins the Student Nonviolent Coordinating Committee and the Southern Christian Leadership Conference in a militant shift to the left.

13   **SCORECARD:** In the first few days after the assassination of Martin Luther King last April, the rioting that swept American cities was almost as widespread and destructive as in all of 1967. Last year, 233 racial upheavals in 168 cities and towns caused 82 deaths, 3,400 injuries and 18,800 arrests. By comparison, in April alone this year, 202 racial disturbances hit 172 cities, resulting in 43 deaths, 3,500 injuries and 27,000 arrests. Leaders among both blacks and whites feared that the emotional orgy of those few days would prove to be only a prelude to the nation's longest, hottest summer of urban mayhem. So far, those fears have not been realized. Last week, as millions of youngsters left the ghetto streets to return to school, the usual riot season more or less ended. During the summer there have been no disorders as big or bad as the holocausts that gutted Watts, Newark or Detroit in previous years. The U.S. had 286 racial disturbances from May through the end of August, but most were relatively small and short. Though practically any city could still blow, the summer of 1968 now ranks as the most tranquil since 1964.

Part of the reason is that many angry Negroes spent their steam in the cathartic aftermath of the King murder. More deeply, Negroes have discovered that they are the worst-hurt victims of ghetto violence. Along with their desire for self-preservation goes a strong drive for self-determination. Instead of incinerating their neighborhoods, many have begun concentrating on building them up. Dr. Hiawatha Harris, head of a psychiatric clinic in Watts, echoes the common belief that "the rioting phase, where we burn down businesses in our own areas, is over now. The whole movement is in another direction —toward implementing black power and finding our dignity as a people." In Boston, Washington, Los Angeles and many other cities, ghetto community groups have opened black-run shops and factories, with big white-run companies providing the capital, training or markets. Significantly, both presidential candidates have pledged major Government help for this movement. Nixon began promoting the cause of "Black Capitalism," and Humphrey called for "Black Entrepreneurship."

There is, however, another ominous trend in the land. Violence as a form of Negro protest appears to be changing from the spontaneous combustion of a mob to the premeditated shootouts of a far-out few. Many battles have started with well-planned sniping at police. The summer's bloodiest confrontation occurred last July in Cleveland, where an ambush of police by black extremists led to an uprising that took eleven lives. Since then, groups of policemen have been wounded by Negro guerrillas in Seattle and Peoria, Ill., and lesser sniping skirmishes have been reported in a dozen other cities. But this has apparently been the work of a handful of fanatics, and they have failed to rally much of a following. While the extremists speak loudly, and often gain the headlines, they do not come near to representing the peaceful and constructive majority of the rapidly changing American Negro community.

THE PANTHERS' BITE: "If Huey goes, the sky's the limit." For almost a year now, the black and white communities of Oakland, Calif., arrayed against each other in uneasy enmity, have heard the words with grim fascination. The threat was made by the friends of Huey P. Newton, the 26-year-old ex-convict who heads the Black Panther Party for Self-Defense which has caught the public eye as the most extreme of the black extremist groups. Newton was accused of killing a cop in a gunfight, for which he could have gone to the gas chamber. Last week, instead, he was found guilty of manslaughter, and now he faces two to 15 years in prison. Though there were only a few racial outbursts to mark the court's finding, no one in Oakland was taking threats by Black Panthers with anything but seriousness.

In the two years since the first tiny pack of Panthers emerged in Oakland, they have seized pre-eminence in the Black Power movement. They are not only militant but also militaristic. They have guns, determination, discipline and the makings of a nationwide organization. In a dozen black ghettos, Panthers prowl in uniform: black jackets, black berets, tight black trousers. They proclaim their right to bear arms, and they have an affinity for violence. Committed to revolution, devoted to some hard-line Chinese Communist double-talk, they are gathering notoriety as an American Mao-Mao. The Panthers are the largest and fastest growing of the ultraradical Negro groups. Lately, Panthers have been opening dingy storefront headquarters in Los Angeles, Seattle, Newark and Washington, D.C. Chapters are rapidly being established by Stokely Carmichael, who, along with some other former members of the

Student Nonviolent Coordinating Committee, has switched to the Panthers. Their appeal is to bravado. A state of war exists between them and the police, whom the Panthers always call "pigs." In Seattle and Brooklyn, police have been ambushed by snipers close to Panther hangouts. Federal law officers have a strong hunch that some Panthers augment their membership dues with burglaries. Not surprisingly, police get tough with Panthers. In April the group's 17-year-old treasurer was shot dead by Oakland police after a gun battle. In August, three other members were killed in a shooting match with Los Angeles police.

In the group's hierarchy, Newton is flanked by his minister of information, Eldridge Cleaver, the ex-convict author of *Soul on Ice,* who is the presidential candidate of the multiracial Peace and Freedom Party. The code of the Panthers is a ten-point manifesto, written by Newton in 1966, that calls for complete black control of the businesses, police and courts in Negro areas. Newton also demands freedom for all Negroes in prison and draft exemption for Negroes. Last week Herman B. Ferguson, who is under indictment for a conspiracy to assassinate moderate Negro leaders, advised an audience of 200 Brooklyn slum dwellers on how to handle arguments with white merchants about overdue bills. His admonition: take a Panther along as a convincer.

CT. 4   **PENNING THE PANTHERS:** Huey P. Newton, the handsome, lightskinned leader of the hypermilitant Black Panther Party for Self-Defense, stood impassively as the sentence was handed down. He had been convicted of manslaughter in the shooting of an Oakland, Calif., patrolman during a wild gun battle in October 1967, which left another policeman injured and Newton grievously wounded with a bullet through his stomach. It was one of the acts of war between police and Panthers that have bloodied the streets of Oakland for almost two years. Now, as Newton's black-uniformed followers looked on in silent anger, County Judge Monroe Friedman ordered him imprisoned for two to 15 years. Friedman denied a motion to free Newton on bail, glanced only cursorily at a 15-inch stack of petitions signed by 29,301 people testifying to Huey's character as "an honest, dedicated, loyal and selfless human being." During the trial, Newton's Panthers promised violent vengeance if he were convicted. Lengthy appeals planned by Newton's defense attorney, however, helped mute their wrath. There were no demonstrations as Newton, 26, was manacled and driven away.

Another Panther was still having his problems with the law last week. The Panthers' "minister of information," Author Eldridge Cleaver, was ordered back to prison for violating his parole from an assault conviction. Cleaver became involved last April in a firefight during which the Panthers' 17-year-old treasurer was shot by Oakland policemen. Cleaver himself was wounded. As a result, his parole was revoked, and he was accused of assault with intent to commit murder. A lower court later freed him, ruling that Cleaver was being held because of his extremist political opinions. Last week, however, the California Court of Appeals reversed that ruling, granting Cleaver 60 days at liberty for appeals. For Cleaver, a jail-educated militant of abrasive eloquence, the court order for his imprisonment comes at an embarrassing moment. He is the presidential candidate for the antiwar Peace and Freedom Party, and is also scheduled to appear as a guest lecturer at the University of California's Berkeley campus. For the Panthers, with two of their leaders on ice, it was a time of barely throttled fury. [Cleaver disappeared in late November when his parole was revoked, and at the end of the year was still in hiding.]

The Draft

DOCTOR'S DILEMMA: Dandling a copy of his bestselling baby JAN book on one knee, Dr. Benjamin Spock, 64, attempted to define himself before the television cameras in his Manhattan apartment. "I'm not a pacifist," declared the man who was once more concerned with diaper rash than diatribes. "I was very much for the war against Hitler and I supported the intervention in Korea. But in this war, we went in to steal Viet Nam." Spock's efforts to foil that imagined attempt at grand larceny led last week to his indictment by a federal Grand Jury on charges that could lead to five years in prison and a $10,000 fine.

Named with the baby doctor for "conspiring to counsel,

aid and abet" young men to evade service in the armed forces were four other anti-warriors: Yale University Chaplain William Sloane Coffin Jr., 43, long an activist in civil rights and antiwar causes; Brooklyn-born Novelist-Polemicist Mitchell Goodman, 44, who interrupted last year's National Book Awards ceremony by shouting: "We are burning children in Viet Nam"; former White House Disarmament Aide Marcus Raskin, 33, who now serves as co-director of a Washington research organization; and Michael Ferber, 23, Harvard graduate student and peace preacher.

H 15 **HOW TO BEAT IT WITHOUT REALLY TRYING:** For a generation and more, many a hale male has dreamed of beating the draft by persuading the psychiatrist at the induction center that he was some kind of nut. That, however, is going about it the hard way. Men are rejected if they are hypersensitive to bee stings, have a severe ingrown toenail, or even if they have too many—or too obscene—tattoos. In a study of 1,500,000 men called for examinations between 1960 and 1962, Col. Robert A. Bier, chief medical officer for the national Selective Service System, found that 382,000 (or 25.4%) were granted medical deferments. Chief causes were musculoskeletal complaints (14.9%) such as stiff arms, trick knees, flat feet or the loss of an index, middle or ring finger from at least the mid-portion (slicing off the first joint will not do). Cardiovascular diseases and psychiatric disorders—including homosexuality and bedwetting—each accounted for 11%. So did being 20% overweight or underweight. Bad eyesight claimed 6%, while 11,400 beat the system by being either too tall or too short (the upper limit is now 6 ft. 8 in., the lower limit 5 ft.). A surprisingly large number—22,800—were kept out by bad cases of acne.

Y 31 **FREE SPEECH OR CONSPIRACY?:** On the screen in black and white with the soundtrack of Bach's "Sheep May Safely Graze," the line of young men one after another touched their draft cards to a flickering candle. After watching the cards blaze down to finger-burning remains, they dropped the charred stubs in a silver bowl and shook hands with the Rev. William Sloane Coffin. Shown in a darkened Boston federal courtroom last week, the TV newsreel was offered by a federal prosecutor as part of the evidence against Yale Chaplain

Coffin, 43, Pediatrician Benjamin Spock, 65, and three co-defendants, all charged with conspiracy. In presenting its case to the all-male jury, the prosecution charged that the five conspired "to unlawfully, knowingly and wilfully counsel, aid and abet" young Americans in evading the draft. Lawyers for the defense answered the charges with the argument that the free-speech guarantee of the First Amendment shielded their clients from prosecution.

The Government's massive evidence was presented to the jury by Assistant U.S. Attorney John Wall, 32, a former paratrooper and Army intelligence officer. In addition to showing several film clips, Wall read militant handbills and news releases issued by the defendants, bearing such titles as "A Call to Resist Illegitimate Authority." Wall challenged the defendants' not-guilty pleas by quoting Dr. Spock, who in December had told FBI men: "I'm well aware that I could wind up in jail because of my illegal activities."

STANDING IN THE DRAFT: If a young man's opposition to in- JUN duction and a trip to Viet Nam is strong enough, he should have little trouble getting his day in court. He need only refuse to be drafted or burn his draft card. But what of the average draftee who feels he should be either reclassified or excused from service, yet shies away from deliberate violation of the law?

He stands before his local draft board very much like a man on trial. But unlike an ordinary defendant, he is, in effect, guilty until proved innocent—that is, he is 1A until he can demonstrate that he deserves to be deferred. Moreover, draft boards, made up of well-intentioned but often legally untrained pillars of the community, are not courts of law. They are federal administrative agencies charged with producing a quota of inductees each month, and they have wide latitude in deciding when, why and who shall go. A man claiming conscientious-objector status usually has a particularly hard time. Relatively few boards seem to know or care that the Supreme Court significantly broadened the qualifications three years ago. Now a man need only possess beliefs that prompt his objection to all wars and that "occupy the same place in his life as the belief in a traditional deity." But even if he knows how to raise that argument legally, home-town board members may well pay no attention because they think that such a test is much too easy.

A Selective Service rule bars lawyers from accompanying a draftee before the local board. San Francisco Attorney Malcolm Burnstein, who often represents registrants, objects: "When you can take away a man's liberty for two years, you've got to provide him with counsel if he wants it." Lieut. General Lewis Hershey, Selective Service director, strongly opposes lawyers. Testifying recently before a Senate committee, Hershey insisted that diligent attorneys could bog down the swift provision of men for the armed services. Repeal of the ban on lawyers was roundly defeated in the Senate last month. And civil libertarians' tempers have still not cooled over Hershey's written suggestion to all boards that those who impede the draft be classified as delinquents, thereby hastening their induction. This use of draft boards to impose punishment has already prompted at least 49 cases that are climbing through the court system.

E 21   **SPOCK GUILTY:** Last week at Boston's Federal District Court, an all-male jury pronounced Pediatrician Benjamin Spock, 65, guilty of conspiring to counsel and abet young men in evading the draft. Also found guilty: Yale Chaplain William Sloane Coffin Jr., 44, Harvard Graduate Student Michael Ferber, 23, and Writer Mitchell Goodman, 44. The fifth member of "the Boston Five," Marcus Raskin, 34, a former White House disarmament aide, was acquitted.

PT. 20   **HOW THE RESISTERS FARE:** "The food is very good, much better than the food at the University of Chicago. The beds are clean, and you are given a change of linen once a week. You can change your underwear and socks daily if you're the fastidious sort. A lot of hardened cons are, strange to relate."

Except for the last sentence, Terry Sullivan, 30, could have been writing home about graduate school. Instead, his words appeared in a recent issue of *Win*, a magazine devoted to the Nonviolent Movement against the Viet Nam war. Sullivan's observations were intended to reassure fledgling draft resisters, to tell them that the ordeal of prison is not as terrifying as it seems. A draft resister who spent ten months at Danbury Correctional Institution in Connecticut, Sullivan was released a year ago. He recommends prison as "a great experience— you'll love it."

At present, almost 800 draft resisters and evaders are locked up in federal prisons throughout the country. Whether they opposed war in general or the Viet Nam war in particular, whether they burned their draft cards or simply refused to go, each was convicted under the same clause of the Selective Service Act. Yet sentences vary enormously, depending upon the attitudes of the federal district judges. Some defendants are put on probation and will probably never go to prison at all; others draw the maximum sentence of five years and a $10,000 fine. Last year the average sentence was 32.1 months.

The conditions of imprisonment vary just as widely. The Government tries to put each resister into the federal prison in his area, and also takes into account his age and education when assigning him. College Dropout Sullivan notes that at Danbury he had the company of "a couple of lawyers, at least one doctor and three railroad presidents." In Allenwood, Pa., resisters make up almost half the prison population of 300. But elsewhere they are a minority among bootleggers, forgers and robbers. A few have even been tossed in with murderers and other hardened criminals at such maximum-security prisons as Leavenworth. For most of the resisters, the biggest enemies are boredom, lack of privacy, separation from friends and loved ones, and petty harassment by guards. They work as prison-library clerks, auto-shop mechanics, gardeners, dishwashers or launderers. Some of them find the repressive atmosphere of prison just one more reflection of an authoritarian society outside the walls.

However easy or unpleasant his prison stay, the draft evader who has served his time soon finds that his problems are not over. As felons, draft resisters cannot vote in some states, drive cars, own property, work for a government agency or get licenses for certain businesses and professions.

Veterans

"OH, YOU'RE BACK?": When Jim Sloan, 23, returned to Harvard JAN. after service as an Army sergeant in Viet Nam, he was laughingly labeled "the resident fascist pig of Adams House." Richard Parish, 22, was an Air Cav rifleman when a chunk of Communist shrapnel ripped his right shoulder to the joint; back in Michigan as a civilian, the Negro high school graduate was unable to pass physical examinations at either Cadillac Motors or Detroit Edison, and reluctantly began drawing disability pay. First Lieut. Leo Glover, 26, won a Silver Star and a Purple Heart near the DMZ as a Marine air controller, then turned his aerial expertise into a job as a flight engineer for Trans World Airlines in Kansas City, Mo.—but nearly busted up a cocktail lounge one night when some drunks refused to be quiet during a televised speech by General William Westmoreland.

Sloan, Parish and Glover are three of some 1,700,000 veterans who have made the painful transition from service to civilian life since the Viet Nam war became a major military effort in 1964. This year, at least 900,000 more will muster out— all of them to face an adjustment problem unique among U.S. war vets.

The men who fought in World Wars I and II and Korea found gratitude and the traditional heroes' welcome awaiting them at home; the Vietvet returns with no fanfare to a nation whose response ranges from a noncommittal "Oh, you're back?" to—in some cases—downright hostility.

For black G.I.s, coming home can be hell. San Francisco's Carl Witherspoon, 21, was a track star and scholastic achiever before he joined the Marines. In Viet Nam he collected a Bronze Star and two bullets in the gut. After nine months in hospitals, Witherspoon mustered out and began looking for a job and a home for himself and his pretty wife Paulette. Frequently rebuffed and insulted, Witherspoon finally landed work with the telephone company and an apartment in a good neighborhood. Though he and his wife are rarely even at home in the evenings (they work), white neighbors are already complaining about "too much noise between 6 and 9." "Sometimes I feel it was all for nothing," he says of Viet Nam. "You know, we go over there and tell them their house is dirty before we got our own house clean."

EB. 9 **HOMECOMING:** James Edward Johnson, 23, a Marine veteran of Viet Nam, went home to West Virginia 17 months ago with a Purple Heart and a dream: he wanted to become a state trooper. But Johnson had two problems. One was his right ankle, shattered by a Viet Cong machine-gun slug in April 1966, when he was a sergeant with the 4th Marine Division. With regular exercise, he was able to get into good enough shape to pass the physical. His other problem was less easily solved. Johnson is a Negro, and there were no Negroes— Vietvets or otherwise—among West Virginia's 322 troopers.

Nonetheless, the state was eager to integrate its force and readily accepted Johnson's application. Last July, after voluntarily giving up $140 a month in disability pay, Johnson joined white recruits in a 20-week training course at the state-police academy near Charleston. It was, almost from the beginning, as psychologically trying as anything he had known in Viet Nam. All but one of the recruits—Michael Blasher, 24, a friend since their teens—either ignored or insulted him, says Johnson. When the men sat down at mess, there was a scramble to avoid Johnson's table. When they went into the field, seven or eight trainees would pile into one car, leaving Johnson and Blasher alone in another. When lessons were given in mouth-to-mouth resuscitation, the instructor showed how a handkerchief could be used—in case anyone was ever called upon to save a Negro. The word nigger was used freely, and because of their friendship, Blasher and Johnson were called "salt and pepper."

Something had to give. Blasher was forced out because of his "attitude"—though he was first in the class scholastically. Impulsively, Johnson resigned in protest, charging that Blasher had been bounced because of his friendship for him. Blasher, who had spent a year on the Los Angeles city force, had no trouble finding another police job in Maryland's Montgomery County, next door to Washington.

The Cities

FRAGRANT DAYS IN FUN CITY: For New York City's 8,000,000 FEB. adversity-tempered citizens, the sanitation workers' strike was merely a nuisance at first. By the end of last week, it had turned into a genuine crisis. Nearly 100,000 tons of uncollected garbage lay in noisome heaps on sidewalks and in doorways.

Trash fires flared all over town. Rats rummaged through pyramidal piles of refuse. Public-health authorities, warning of the danger of typhoid and other diseases, proclaimed the city's first general health emergency since a 1931 polio epidemic. The confrontation between Mayor John Lindsay and the Teamster-affiliated Uniformed Sanitationmen's Association had been abuilding for months. The mayor thought that he had a tacit understanding with Union President John DeLury for a reasonable settlement. The city was willing to give an annual increase of $350, plus fringe improvements, to the 10,000 workers who now receive $7,956 after three years' service. But DeLury, apparently unable to sell those terms to his men, demanded $600. After sporadic negotiations, the union staged a wild rally at City Hall two weeks ago, virtually forced DeLury to call a strike. Said he, ducking an egg thrown at him: "I accept the motion to go-go-go."

Next day, the strike was on. Refusing to knuckle under to what he called "blackmail, brute force and muscle," Lindsay fought back as best he could with legal action and calls for unity. "Now is the time and here is the place," he declared, "for the city to determine what it is made of."

Lindsay had DeLury jailed for ignoring a court injunction issued under a new state law, but this merely solidified the union. The mayor's pleas for help from other city employees were immediately rebuffed. On the strike's seventh day, Lindsay was forced to turn to his fellow liberal Republican, Governor Nelson Rockefeller. The mayor wanted the National Guard called in to clean up the city, and Rockefeller was the only man who could do it. Rockefeller's relationship with Lindsay has never been more than coldly cordial, but even if it were warm, it is doubtful whether Rockefeller would have agreed to mobilize the Guard. The Governor has considerable rapport with labor and he was loath to become a strikebreaking Governor.

Rockefeller seized the initiative from Lindsay by taking over the negotiations. He named his own mediation panel to supplant the mayor's and treated the outlaw union with unwonted deference. Rockefeller's mediators proposed a pay increase of $425. The union accepted immediately, and the Governor hailed the proposal as "fair and reasonable." Lindsay rejected it out of hand. Though the difference over wages had become seemingly insignificant, Lindsay was determined not to reward the strikers with a figure above what the union leadership had been willing to accept earlier. "A little blackmail," he said, was still blackmail. Even the New York Times, normally a Rockefeller supporter, flayed the Governor in uncharacteristically harsh terms, indicting him for "sabotage," "appeasement," "bad politics and bad government."

By the weekend, the fight was clearly lost. Parts of the city were reeking, and Lindsay could do nothing except stand on principle. Rockefeller announced a settlement that was really an ultimatum to Lindsay. The union agreed to send its men back to work immediately in exchange for the $425 pay raise that Lindsay had earlier rejected. As written by Rockefeller, the moral of New York's latest step toward chaos seemed to be that it pays to strike.

IS IT GOVERNABLE?: On Fifth Avenue an unending parade of NOV shoppers canvassed the world's most elegant bazaar. The Broadway marquees touted yet another hectic season. From the Battery to The Bronx, the thud of dynamite and the roar of drills accompanied probably the greatest construction boom in the history of cities. No other metropolis in the world offered its inhabitants greater hope of material success or a wider variety of cultural rewards. Yet for all its dynamism and glamour, New York City, day by day, little by little, was sliding toward chaos. "The question now," said its handsome young Mayor, John Lindsay, "is whether we can continue to survive as a city."

Many New Yorkers shared that somber view. The city's plight, of course, was not one of physical survival—though some cynics argued that New York's complex ills could only be cured if the metropolis were razed and rebuilt. Its breakdown this fall was one of spirit and nerve, a malaise that most responsible citizens concede to be one of the ugliest situations in memory, in which strikes and the threat of strikes pitted not only union against employer—the city—but, worse, black against white, Jew against Gentile, middle class against poor.

In front of City Hall, 2,000 picketing policemen yelled "Blue power!" and carried signs exhorting "Dump Lindsay" and "We Want Daley." Until their union ended the practice as many as 3,000 men, one-fifth of the force scheduled for duty, reported "sick" each day with a fictitious strain of Asian flu.

Cops on duty watched benignly as motorists left their cars in bus stops and no-parking zones. Minor complaints were simply ignored, and traffic became badly snarled. Firemen refused housekeeping duties, such as checking fire hydrants and inspecting buildings, and the head of the firemen's union warned that the slowdown "could escalate into a full-scale strike" that would leave alarms unanswered and homes in danger.

The least dangerous breakdown in public services was the most serious. For the third time since September [see Education, page 233], the majority of the city's 58,000 teachers defied state law to go out on strike, and more than a million students were denied the vital right of education. Teachers marched outside their schools and children watched as picketers traded insults and obscenities with non-strikers and parents.

Only three months ago a prime candidate for the Republican vice-presidential nomination, John Vliet Lindsay, 46, the 103rd Mayor of New York and the holder of the second toughest political post in the U.S., was faced with the distinct prospect of political repudiation. The city's 2,000,000 Jews, once a cornerstone of his constituency, had turned cool and often hostile. Jeers greeted his name at synagogues; "hate mail" came into his office. City Hall became a fortress against an angry city, and Lindsay spent more and more time at Gracie Mansion, the city's elegant mayoral residence overlooking the East River. Only a short time ago, it had looked as if Lindsay could charm the whole city, which is about as charmproof as any in the world; now the whole community seemed to have turned against him. Says one City Hall acquaintance: "The birds have started circling around, as they watch the animal falter."

But far more than the career of John Lindsay—or even the stability of the nation's largest city—was at stake. The same forces of race and poverty, fear and instability that transfix New York now are present in scores of other U.S. cities, large and small. In cutting through the tangles that choke his city, Lindsay has done better than just about anyone else could have. Not always appreciated in New York—or in Nelson Rockefeller's Albany—he is generally regarded in Washington offices that handle urban programs as the best big-city mayor in the country. One of his biggest accomplishments has been to restore some measure of grace to a city not noted for its civility, and to slow, if only by a fraction, the numerous forces that make New York an increasingly unlivable city. Under Lindsay, the parks have been made into attractive recreational centers, with cafés and musicales and bicycling on roadways that are closed to cars on weekends and holidays. Air pollution has been cut slightly, and advanced techniques of systems analysis are being applied to bureaucratic procedures that had not changed by more than a jot in a century. Still in dire need of money, the city's budget has been brought in line with income. And the police department has been humanized. But for all this, the question that is always asked about New York can be asked about any other metropolis in the U.S. today: Is it governable? Under its present antique structure, the answer is quickly becoming obvious: it is not.

Aviation

THE SKYJACKERS: For growing numbers of airline passengers, JUL flights almost anywhere in the Southern U.S. have become dubious adventures in serendipity. The unsought—and usually unwanted—dividend is a side trip to Havana. Since 1961, 15 aircraft have been hijacked in U.S. skies and forced to land in Cuba. This year alone, gunmen have commandeered nine U.S. planes; all but one made compulsory stopovers at Havana. The problem has grown so epidemic that one airline servicing Miami and other Southern cities in the U.S. has decided to equip pilots with approach charts for Havana's José Martí Airport and written instructions on dealing with hijackers ("Do as they say").

Last week in Los Angeles, a young Cuban who identified himself as R. Hernandez boarded National Airlines Flight 1064 bound for Miami. After a stop at Houston, the Cuban confronted Stewardess Kathleen Dickinson with a pistol and a handkerchief-wrapped object that he indicated was a grenade. "Fidel ordered me back to Havana, dead or alive," he said in Spanish. Though Pilot Sidney Oliver convinced the hijacker of the need for a refueling stop at New Orleans, lawmen there could not attempt to retake the plane without risking the lives of the 57 passengers and seven crew members aboard. Only when Hernandez was safely on the ground in Havana did he reveal, with some glee, that his "grenade" was a bottle of Old Spice after-shave lotion.

G. 2 **SATURATED SKY:** Although Government and industry groped for ways to alleviate America's aerial arteriosclerosis, the traffic jam in the skies has suddenly shifted from acute to chronic. The glut that has all but congealed the New York City metropolitan area's "Bird Cage"—Kennedy, La Guardia and Newark airports—now spreads confusion across the country and abroad, shredding connecting schedules in Los Angeles and squeezing service in Miami. Fortnight ago, "Black Friday" choked the Golden Triangle between New York City, Chicago and Washington with 2,079 delays. Chicago's O'Hare, the world's busiest commercial airport, was logging two-hour tie-ups. One frustrated Detroit-bound passenger decided to drive instead—and almost beat the plane.

C. 6 **WHAT TO DO WHEN THE HIJACKER COMES:** They were headed for Miami, or San Juan or Houston, but a funny thing happened. Over the past eleven months, more than 1,000 Americans have visited Cuba unexpectedly; their airplanes were hijacked. In all, 17 U.S. planes have been diverted to Cuba since January, and a record of sorts was set last week when three jets carrying 238 people made forced landings in Havana within eight days. So far, nobody has been hurt—mainly because airline crews are carefully briefed for such an emergency. But nobody has yet thought to brief the poor passengers. The following orders might well be added to the "Important Information" cards commonly stuffed into the seat pockets of airliners:

¶ Don't be aggressive; hijackers are usually armed, and they tend to be nervous. (The penalty for hijacking is death, or 20 years in prison.) Their choice of weapons varies. Guns and knives are common.

¶ Don't panic. Hijackers, although unwelcome, can be congenial. One of the three men who took over Pan American's San Juan-bound Flight 281 in November passed out .32-cal. bullets as souvenirs and chatted amicably with passengers.

¶ Don't push the call button. The sudden *ping* in the cockpit

might startle the felon and provoke him to fire his pistol.
¶ Don't call aloud for the stewardess. If you require assistance or must go to the lavatory, raise your hand.
¶ No matter where you think you are headed when you prepare for a trip, pack a bathing suit, because Cuba's Varadero Beach, a 15-mile-long ribbon of white sand, is magnificent. Passengers on Eastern Flight 73 were taken here and allowed to go swimming.

Disaster

DEATH IN CONSOL NO. 9: At 5:25 one morning last week, 99 coal miners on the midnight-to-8 a.m. "cat-eye" shift were working the rich bituminous veins of the Consolidation Coal Co.'s No. 9 mine in northern West Virginia. Suddenly, deep in the earth, an explosion thundered through the eight-mile-long labyrinth of shafts and tunnels. At daybreak, thick clouds of greasy black smoke billowed 150 ft. into the grey morning air. Before the day was over, 21 men had made it to the frozen surface; but 78 others still remained trapped, some of them 600 ft. below the ground. As hope diminished for their rescue, the disaster looked to be the worst mining accident in the U.S. since 119 men died in a 1951 explosion in West Frankfort, Ill. (The worst ever in the U.S.: a 1907 explosion which killed 361 at Monongah, W. Va., a mere dozen miles from the site of last week's blast. Since that year, 87,850 U.S. miners have died in accidents on the job.) Muffled explosions shook Consol No. 9 for three days, preventing rescue workers from going in after possible survivors. NOV

TOO LATE FOR 78: After ten days during which 16 explosions rocked the mine and turned its tunnels into blast furnaces of flame, gas and smoke, Consolidation Coal Company's Number 9 was sealed last week. DEC.

That somber decision made the mine a tomb for the 78 men missing in its depths. But company, government and union officials agreed that there was no other way to save the burning mine—and that the trapped men below were almost certainly dead from fire or gas, or both.

Weddings

¶ 25 **THE END OF CAMELOT:** From practically every capital and every level of society the guests and members of the wedding came, by jetliner, shuttle plane and helicopter, to Aristotle Onassis' mountainous island of Skorpiós in the sunny Ionian Sea. From Holland an elaborate airlift brought in mountains of tulips, and lemon buds to be woven into garlands for the bridal pair. From the mainland came Father Polykarpos Athanassion. *Bouzouki* bandsmen were on hand to play the haunting melodies so dear to Jacqueline Kennedy's heart. Argosies of viands and wines were lightered in and unloaded while the white-hulled honeymoon yacht, *Christina,* creaked at her quay.

In a cypress grove above the harbor, workmen labored on the task of refurbishing the tiny, neoclassic chapel. Everything, from sugared almonds to the waiting yacht, was ready to celebrate the new life of Mr. and Mrs. Aristotle Onassis. Everything, that is, except what is known as "the world," which seemed unable to comprehend or accept the match.

Reaction in the U.S. and abroad ranged from dismay to a kind of shocked ribaldry. JACKIE, HOW COULD YOU? headlined Stockholm's Expressen. "Nixon has a Greek running mate," cracked Bob Hope, "and now everyone wants one." Said a former Kennedy aide: "She's gone from Prince Charming to Caliban." To most Americans, Jackie's marriage symbolized her goodbye to an era and a hero. "It's the end of Camelot," was a common reaction. In choosing "Ari" Onassis, a man of 62 (or 68), a divorcee, a centimillionaire little known for generosity and very well known for his flamboyant mode of life, Jacqueline Kennedy seemed brusquely to abdicate the throne that Americans had made for her.

On her public pedestal, under 24-hour surveillance by Secret Service agents, Jackie had heretofore been extremely circumspect with her male acquaintances. Quite often, she borrowed husbands as safe escorts: Roswell Gilpatric, 61, former Deputy Defense Secretary; Arthur Schlesinger Jr., 51; Composer-Conductor Leonard Bernstein, 50; even Robert McNamara, 52, of whom one observer noted: "When Jackie's around, the computer turns into a puppy dog wagging its tail." More fascinating was the speculation on the eligible bachelors whom Jackie dated. In the forefront was Britain's Lord Harlech, 50, the former David Ormsby-Gore, who was British ambassador to Washington during John Kennedy's presidency. It fell to a few movie magazines to suggest strongly that Onassis was a possible spouse for Jackie—which suggests that perhaps movie magazines should be considered more seriously. At the urging of her sister Princess Lee Radziwill, a close friend of Ari's, Jackie had cruised on his yacht in 1963, shortly after the death of her infant son, Patrick Bouvier Kennedy. Onassis was one of the first non-clan visitors she received after J.F.K.'s death later that year. But Onassis appeared too rough-edged ("He's not a man of the salon," says one detractor. "He's a man of the pier") and too old to rate as a suitor.

He was, after all, a notorious collector. He collected status symbols like his 325-foot yacht; art works ranging from a bejeweled Buddha to a $250,000 El Greco; and important people. Winston Churchill, Greta Garbo, Cary Grant—all the famed and beautiful cruised on Onassis' yacht. In Opera Singer Maria Callas, whom Onassis lured away from a dull but decent Italian businessman-husband, he collected the "richest voice in the world," as one intimate puts it, "while hating opera." When he made a special effort to squire Jackie about, it seemed nothing more than another example of his inveterate collection mania.

But Jackie, too, is an avid collector—of paintings, personages and new impressions. And her choice of Onassis may well represent a distillation of many desires. Onassis is a man of considerable magnetism. He is iron-willed, infinitely considerate of his women, vain of his limitless ability to charm, entertain and protect those whom he likes or loves.

Indeed, there is no doubt that on Skorpiós, Jacqueline Kennedy will be queen of far more than she can survey: mistress of a private empire sustained by 200 servants, wafted wherever she desires in her choice of two amphibians, a helicopter, the entire Olympic Airways system (which her husband owns), or the *Christina*. Beyond this island and its pleasure domes there is the whole domain of international life and amusements, which she patently enjoys. Having stepped down from an uncomfortable American pedestal, she may find precisely the sort of life she has long sought. Romantics, after getting over their first shock of vicarious loss, will simply have to accept that fact. For when she was asked once to decide where and in what era she would have preferred to live, Jacqueline Kennedy picked 18th century France. And the unfettered universe of Aristotle Socrates Onassis comes closer to the kingdom of Louis XV—if not of Camelot—than any other around.

THE WEDDING: The ceremony that joined the pair was almost self-consciously modest. Rain, considered a blessing by the Greeks, had descended like a grey benediction across the Onassis-owned island of Skorpiós. In the tiny chapel, Jackie stood quietly—almost in a daze—in her beige chiffon-and-lace dress. Ari in his dark blue business suit, John and Caroline, each carrying a single tall white candle, flanked them. As Archimandrite Polykarpos Athanassion intoned the solemn Greek of the nuptial liturgy, Jackie and Ari exchanged rings and wreaths of lemon blossoms, and drank wine from a single chalice. Then the priest led them round a table three times in the ritual dance of Isaiah.

Traditionally in the dance, one of the newlyweds steps on his (or her) partner's foot to signify who will command in the marriage. None of the 25 guests admitted seeing such one-foot-upmanship.

Afternoon modesty inevitably yielded to evening pomp. First came the semi-official merrymaking, amid champagne toasts, flowers and *bouzoukis,* on the afterdeck of the Onassis yacht *Christina.* Later, reported the Washington Post's Maxine Cheshire, came the real show: Ari's wedding gift to Jackie. Already, a Chicago newsman had tendered a few suggestions for those who might not know what to give a couple who had everything: the Taj Mahal, the Boston Pops, the S.S. *Queen Elizabeth II,* the De Beers diamond mines, the New York Stock Exchange—or the Richard Burtons. Onassis' actual gift to Jackie was nearly as awesome. When she came into the yacht's lounge for the wedding dinner, Jackie was wearing it: on her left hand, a ring with a huge ruby surrounded by large diamonds; on her ears, matching ruby-and-diamond earrings. Caroline broke the stunned silence: "Mummy, Mummy, Mummy! They're so pretty. You're so pretty." Laughing, Jackie removed the ring to let Caroline play with it. The jewels reportedly cost Onassis $1.2 million.

Not everything was so impressively heart-shaped for the newlyweds. The shrill criticism of their marriage finally provoked a response from Jackie's old friend and spiritual adviser, Richard Cardinal Cushing of Boston. In the anguished days of the assassination five years ago, it was Cushing's cracked, gravel-voiced prayer for "dear Jack" that suffused the austere ritual of J.F.K.'s requiem with a warm humanity. Last week, sounding another note of humanity, the cardinal told a Boston audience that the only way to view Jackie's marriage was with charity. He pleaded for "love, mutual respect and esteem." What he got in response was a mountain of mail so overwhelmingly critical that he decided to resign by the end of the year. The Vatican's canon lawyers found themselves unable to share Cushing's generous view of the marriage. By marrying the divorced Onassis, they said, the woman who had met the Pope in at least five private audiences had cut herself off from Roman Catholic sacraments and had become, at least technically, a "public sinner."

MILESTONES

BORN: To Ethel Kennedy, 40, widow of Senator Robert F. Kennedy: her eleventh child, fourth daughter; in Washington, D.C. After eight weeks in bed since she suffered false labor pains Ethel was delivered by caesarean section in a 40-minute operation. It was her fifth caesarean.

MARRIED: Julie Nixon, 20, President-elect Richard M. Nixon's younger daughter; and Dwight David Eisenhower II, 20, only grandson of former President Dwight Eisenhower; in a 15-minute ceremony performed at Manhattan's Marble Collegiate Church by the Rev. Dr. Norman Vincent Peale. Julie wanted the wedding to be quiet, private and as small as possible. Only 500 family and friends were at the church, while Ike and Mamie watched over closed-circuit TV from his suite at Walter Reed Army Medical Center in Washington, D.C.

DIED: Edna Ferber, 80, *grande dame* of the big, romantic American novel, whose 32 books included *So Big, Show Boat, Cimarron, Saratoga Trunk, Giant* and *Ice Palace*.

DIED: Marcel Duchamp, 81, France's Grand Dada of art, whose iconoclastic paintings, "readymades" and other assemblages of the early 1900s became cryptic formulas for the future; in Neuilly, France. Guards had to restrain angry art lovers when Duchamp's disjointed *Nude Descending a Staircase* went on view at Manhattan's 1913 Armory Show. The gaunt, enigmatic Frenchman painted a mustache and goatee on a *Mona Lisa* reproduction, submitted a urinal titled *Fountain* to a 1917 salon, made reviewers dizzy with swiveling patterns driven by electric motors. After ten years, his nihilism reached its logical conclusion—he retired.

THE WORLD

War in Viet Nam

The conflict between North and South Viet Nam seemed to be reaching a point of military stalemate early in 1968. Despite the presence of nearly 500,000 U.S. troops in South Viet Nam, the effort at pacification was still lagging, and the Communists continued to bring combat units and supplies down from the north.

B. 2 **SHOWDOWN AT KHE SANH:** A battle is now shaping up around the U.S. Marine base of Khe Sanh in South Viet Nam's northwest corner, could be the biggest of the war. Khe Sanh has been dug out of the red clay of a plateau that is ringed by high hills thick with trees and bamboo. Some 15 miles south of the DMZ and only ten miles east of the Laotian border, the Marine base lies directly athwart the easiest infiltration routes into South Viet Nam. To eliminate the roadblock, the North Vietnamese have ranged an estimated 20,000 men directly around Khe Sanh, have at least another 20,000 in reserve in Laos and immediately north of the DMZ, all located within 20 miles of the post. Together, they constitute the largest and best-equipped military force that North Viet Nam has ever concentrated on a single battleground. Khe Sanh, moreover, lies within range of Hanoi's big Russian-made 152-mm. howitzers emplaced in North Viet Nam and Laos.

To meet the threat, General William Westmoreland has built up the base's garrison to more than 5,000 Marines in a hasty airlift of troops and equipment that suspended all civilian air traffic throughout Viet Nam. Other allied units shifted nearer the scene of the impending battle to be ready if needed until Westmoreland had deployed some 45,000 men to meet the 40,-000 North Vietnamese closing in.

Khe Sanh bears some topographical resemblance to Dien-bienphu, where the French were surrounded and defeated in

1954. Sitting at the bottom of its bowl of hills, it is vulnerable to artillery and machine-gun fire from the heights. Some of the hills are controlled by Marines. But one Communist-held hill, numbered 950 (all are named after their height in meters), runs parallel to Khe Sanh's runway only three miles away and commands a view of the entire camp. The North Vietnamese have dug antiaircraft and machine guns into it and have already succeeded in shooting down three U.S. fighter-bombers and three helicopters over the airstrip. Every plane that lands at Khe Sanh now expects to do so under fire, and more and more equipment is being parachuted in. Khe Sanh's weather this time of year may also aid the Communists. Fog rolls in at night and sometimes does not burn off until midday or later, making air support all but impossible.

Inside the base, Marines wait shoulder to shoulder in their trenches, bunkers and fighting holes all around the half-mile-wide perimeter. Everything in Khe Sanh is dug in, even the trucks. Each day, as they wait, the Marines dig in deeper, filling shiny grey sandbags and adding more layers atop their bunkers, preparing for the inevitable moment when the enemy makes the ultimate test of Khe Sanh's defenses.

CORRUPTION: Among his major campaign promises, South Viet Nam's President Nguyen Van Thieu pledged himself to root out government corruption at the national and provincial levels. Last week Senator Edward Kennedy, a recent visitor to Viet Nam, delivered his own progress report on Thieu's efforts. He painted a grim picture. "The government of South Viet Nam is infested with corruption," Kennedy said. "Government jobs are bought and paid for. Police accept bribes. Officials and their wives run operations in the black market."

Recently, officials caught a South Vietnamese army unit that was actually running hot goods to Saigon's black market in an ambulance, complete with blaring siren. Even the chief of staff of a South Vietnamese division was caught using government trucks to transport U.S. rice to areas where it could be sold to the Viet Cong.

THE "TET" OFFENSIVE: Though ominous harbingers of trouble FEB had been in the air for days, most of South Viet Nam lazed in uneasy truce, savoring the happiest and holiest holiday of the

Vietnamese year. All but a few Americans retired to their compounds to leave the feast of *Tet* to the Vietnamese celebrators filling the streets. Vietnamese soldiers made a special effort to rejoin their families. The Year of the Monkey had begun, and every Vietnamese knew that it was wise to make merry while there was yet time; for in the Buddhist lunar cycle, 1968 is a grimly inauspicious year.

Wounded Marines being evacuated in Viet Nam. The Communists celebrate the Year of the Monkey with the war's wildest offensive.

Through the streets of Saigon, and in the dark approaches to dozens of towns and military installations throughout South Viet Nam, other Vietnamese made their furtive way, intent on celebrating only death. After the merrymakers had retired and the last firecrackers had sputtered out on the ground, the intruders struck with a fierceness and bloody destructiveness that Viet Nam has not seen even in 30 years of nearly continuous warfare. The Communists hit in a hundred places from one end of the country to the other. No target was too big or too impossible, including Saigon itself and General William Westmoreland's headquarters. South Viet Nam's capital, which even in the worst days of the Indo-China war had never been hit so hard, was turned into a city besieged by house-to-house fighting. In Hué, the ancient imperial city of Viet Nam and the architectural and spiritual repository of Vietnamese history, the Communists seized large parts of the city—and only grudgingly yielded them block by block under heavy allied counterattacks at week's end.

ON THE DEFENSIVE: A full 25 days after the Communists first launched their general offensive, South Viet Nam was still a country taut with terror and riven by fire. In Hué, South Vietnamese and U.S. Marines were still engaged in the most desperate fighting of the war to drive the last of the North Vietnamese out of the ancient Citadel. At Khe Sanh, the pressure mounted on the waiting U.S. Marines, who underwent one of the most concentrated barrages of the war—1,307 rounds of shells in one five-hour stretch. By pulling in their forces to defend the cities, the allies have been forced to cede large areas of the countryside to the Communists. Except for the largest population centers, the rich Delta is now almost entirely in Viet Cong hands. There is not a Delta road safe to drive on, by day or night.

SAIGON UNDER SIEGE: In many ways Saigon is only half alive. The public-transportation system operates only sporadically or not at all. Mail has piled up undelivered in the post offices, weeks late. The city's hospitals are so crowded that only emergency cases are accepted, and even then the newcomer may have to sleep on the floor. Coffins lie unburied for days because of a lack of gravediggers. And the government's twelve-hour curfew (7 p.m. to 7 a.m.), intended to hamper the Viet Cong terrorists, has hampered the average Saigonese even more. Having in the past moonlighted on one or two extra jobs in order to make ends meet, he now is able to hold only one job—if he is lucky enough to still have one.

VICTORY AT KHE SANH: Wincing in the unaccustomed sunlight, U.S. Marines of the 6,000-man Khe Sanh garrison tumbled out of their bunkers into the open air. Amid shell craters and the wreckage of destroyed Jeeps, helicopters and buildings, they washed grimy clothes and gamboled in makeshift showers. Three Marines dug out baseball gloves and began playing catch. There was no enemy to be seen, though an occasional artillery or mortar round still whistled in on the camp. For Operation Pegasus, a relief force of 30,000 Marines, Army troopers and South Vietnamese soldiers, was on its way to the beleaguered outpost and the enemy had pulled back. Thus, after 76 harrowing days, the siege of Khe Sanh last week came to an ironic end. What had loomed as the great set-piece battle of the war—the ultimate test of Hanoi's military menace and the grand symbol of U.S. determination—dissolved at last almost without a shot being fired.

Communist sources claimed that Hanoi had voluntarily lifted the siege of Khe Sanh as a gesture of good will toward peace talks. But the U.S. command is convinced that North Viet Nam's General Vo Nguyen Giap, if he ever intended to attack Khe Sanh, was forced to abandon the idea and the siege because of his losses under relentless allied air attacks. The bombardment was the most intensive in the history of aerial warfare. All told, more than 110,000 tons of explosives rained down during the siege, breaking up formations, destroying supplies and setting off thousands of secondary explosions. Said General William Westmoreland, who spiraled in by helicopter for a quick visit to the base: "We took 220 killed at Khe Sanh and about 800 wounded and evacuated. The enemy by my count has suffered at least 15,000 dead in the area."

19 **CHANGING OF THE GUARD:** Even as Washington and Hanoi conducted the delicate diplomatic exchanges that could lead to negotiations, the U.S. last week announced a major shift in the strategy of the Viet Nam war and named a new commander to carry it out. The strategy, set forth in his first press conference by Defense Secretary Clark Clifford, is a decision by the U.S. to turn the war gradually over to the South Vietnamese and to give them the firepower and backing to wage it effectively. The new man in Viet Nam is General Creighton W. ("Abe") Abrams, 53, who will succeed General William C. Westmoreland, soon to return to Washington as Army Chief of Staff. As Westmoreland's deputy commander, Abrams has spent the past ten months working with ARVN (the Army of the Republic of Viet Nam) to shape up its structure, stiffen its spine and improve its performance. In their extremely violent *Tet* offensive, the Communists unwittingly showed that Abrams has had some success: to the surprise of many Americans and the consternation of the Communists, ARVN bore the brunt of the early fighting with bravery and élan, performing better than almost anyone would have expected.

General Westmoreland. He turns to the battle of Washington.

General Abrams. A believer in violence takes over.

The new general is a tough, plain-speaking New Englander and onetime tank commander who could inspire aggressiveness in a begonia. As one of General George Patton's top armor commanders in World War II Abrams developed a distinctive combat style that other military men characterize as "careful planning and violent execution." Abrams articulated it himself. "We don't want the Germans to fall back," he said during the war. "We want them to try to defend their positions so we can destroy them and their equipment. We've got to set our minds to destroying them—that's the only way to get this job done and done fast. Our operations are all based on violence."

THE LONGEST: As of midnight on Sunday, June 23, the Viet JUN Nam conflict became the longest war ever fought by Americans. It was 2,376 days since Dec. 22, 1961, when Viet Cong bullets killed the first American soldier. The U.S. death toll to date: 25,068. The previous longest U.S. conflict: the War of Independence, which lasted 2,375 days and, according to the Revolutionary Army's records, cost 4,435 American dead.

SYMBOL NO MORE: The U.S. last week began to abandon Khe JUL Sanh, the once idyllic valley in South Viet Nam's northwest corner that early this year became the scene of the war's biggest and bitterest siege. The news could hardly have been more startling. For months, the American people had been told that the base was indispensable to U.S. strategy and prestige. Khe Sanh became a symbol of U.S. determination to stick it out under heavy pressure. And yet, scarcely half a year later, the U.S. Marines were filling the red clay scars that trenches had cut into the once verdant plateau. Demolition men destroyed bunker after bunker, the single bit of protection against the rain of North Vietnamese steel that had lashed the base for almost half a year.

Why the change of heart? The U.S. command explained that the tactical situation had been altered dramatically. Whereas the North Vietnamese had the equivalent of only six divisions below the Demilitarized Zone last January, they now had eight. To counter that increased threat, U.S. commanders reasoned, the 271,000 allied forces in the area would have to be highly mobile. A fixed and exposed base like Khe Sanh would no longer make sense.

EC. 6   **THE SECOND PHASE IN PARIS:** Saigon's announcement that it would send a delegation to Paris came nearly four weeks after Lyndon Johnson announced that he was extending his limited bombing halt to cover all of North Viet Nam. U.S. Ambassador Ellsworth Bunker went to work on President Nguyen Van Thieu, who had been under pressure from hard-liners within his own government and wanted guarantees that there would be no recognition in Paris of the Viet Cong and no attempt to impose a coalition regime on Saigon. The final 750-word statement offered explicit assurances to Saigon that Washington:

¶ Does not recognize the National Liberation Front, the Viet Cong's political agency, even though the N.L.F. will attend the talks. "We will regard all the persons on the other side of the table as members of a single side, that of Hanoi," said the statement.

¶ Will not give in to Hanoi's demands for enforced Viet Cong representation in any government of South Viet Nam.

¶ Expects Saigon to "take the lead and be the main spokesman on all matters which are of principal concern to South Viet Nam." In such matters of "hardware" as troop withdrawals and a cease-fire, the U.S. will continue to speak for the allies.

Thieu quickly began assembling a 100-man team to attend

the talks, and announced that Vice President Nguyen Cao Ky, while not actually heading the delegation, would be "supervising, controlling, directing, going between Saigon and Paris to receive instructions."

Czechoslovakia

The eyes of the world were riveted on this Iron Curtain country in 1968 as a conflict arose between hard-line Communist leaders loyal to Moscow and liberal leaders determined to bring about an increasing amount of self-determination for their nation.

DUBČEK TO THE FORE: Czechoslovakia's Communist Party JAN Boss Antonin Novotný rose to the top in 1953—the year of Stalin's death—but never quite adjusted to the Kremlin's new softer line or Eastern Europe's post-Stalin era of liberalization. Only a few months ago, he warned the country's intellectuals that he would never tolerate "the spread of liberalism" or any other contaminating Western ideology. In turn, Czechoslovakia never really adjusted to Novotný. Recently, an increasingly vocal opposition to his hard-lining ways percolated right up to the innermost circles of the Communist Party. Last month the ruling Presidium voted to fire Novotný as party chief, and only a hasty trip to Prague by Soviet Party Boss Leonid Brezhnev saved his skin.

It was only a temporary save. Last week the party's Central Committee met and declared the end for Novotný. Though its communiqué allowed him to "resign" and mechanically praised his accomplishments, the committee fired Novotný as party leader, the country's most powerful post, leaving him only in the figurehead role of President. Into Novotný's place stepped the man who engineered the ouster. He is Alexander Dubček, 46, a leader of the Slovak wing of the Czechoslovak Communist Party, and the first member of the country's 5,000,000 Slovak minority to hold the reins of power.

OUTCRY IN PURGATORY: Suddenly, Czechs have been snatching MAF up newspapers as if they were priceless manuscripts. The nor-

A TRIP IN TIME

Some years make more than their share of headlines.

Take 1959. Fidel Castro conquered Cuba. Khrushchev pounded his shoe on a U.N. desk. China crushed Tibet.

Or 1956, 1950, 1945, 1944, 1943, 1942, 1941, 1940, 1939, 1933, 1932, 1929, 1927, 1923. They were all headline makers. Important years to know about.

That's why TIME-LIFE BOOKS has published TIME CAPSULES, the entertaining books condensed from TIME, with all the immediacy and freshness for which TIME, The Weekly News Magazine, is famous.

TIME CAPSULES follow the big stories (and the fascinating small ones behind the headlines) with a style that has no relationship to the usual historical treatise. That's because you see the past exactly as it looked to perceptive editors while it was happening.

There's documentation of World War II in TIME CAPSULES/1939-1945, with all its drama and emotion and urgency plus, of course, TIME's famous reviews of books, films, Broadway shows...In TIME CAPSULE/ 1927 you'll find out what TIME's critics thought of Ezra Pound, Sinclair Lewis, Ernest Hemingway, Thomas Mann, Thornton Wilder (all published that year)...

Just turn the page to find out what other TIME CAPSULES review.

TIME CAPSULES are on sale wherever books and magazines are sold. $1.65 each.

Or, if you prefer, you may order directly. Just write TIME-LIFE BOOKS, 540 North Michigan, Chicago, Illinois 60611, enclosing a check or money order.

TIME
LIFE
BOOKS

THE HEADLINE YEARS

TIME CAPSULE/1923: President Harding's sudden death; Hitler's abortive beer-hall putsch; the murder of Pancho Villa; Dempsey downs Firpo.

TIME CAPSULE/1925: The Tennessee "monkey" trial; the Billy Mitchell court-martial; Stalin demotes Trotsky; Charlie Chaplin in *"The Gold Rush."*

TIME CAPSULE/1927: Lindbergh flies to Paris; the execution of Sacco and Vanzetti; year's authors include Ezra Pound, Sinclair Lewis, Ernest Hemingway, Thomas Mann, Thornton Wilder.

TIME CAPSULE/1929: St. Valentine's Day massacre; the stock market crash; Gandhi starts passive resistance; Hemingway's *"A Farewell to Arms."*

TIME CAPSULE/1932: FDR elected; the Lindbergh kidnapping; Japan captures Shanghai; Gandhi goes to jail; mysterious death of Stalin's wife.

TIME CAPSULE/1933: Roosevelt escapes assassination; the New Deal begins; Nazi persecution of the Jews; Max Baer vs. Max Schmeling.

TIME CAPSULE/1939: World War II begins; Germany invades Poland; France and Britain declare war; Pope Pius XI dies; movies include *"The Wizard of Oz," "Gone with the Wind."*

TIME CAPSULE/1940: FDR wins third term; Germany invades Norway; Denmark, Lowland; Dunkirk and the fall of France; Trotsky assassinated; Hemingway's *"For Whom the Bell Toll"*

TIME CAPSULE/1941: The Japanese attack Pearl Harbor; Hitler declares war on Russia; Sister Kenny's polio treatment.

TIME CAPSULE/1942: U.S. troops invade North Africa; Montgomery vs. Rommel at El Alamein and the battle of Midway.

TIME CAPSULE/1943: FDR, Churchill and Stalin meet in Teheran; Allies land in Italy; *"Oklahoma"* begins its Broadway run.

TIME CAPSULE/1944: D-Day in Normandy; Paris and Rome liberated; buzz bombs fall on London; MacArthur returns to the Philippines.

TIME CAPSULE/1945: World War II ends; FDR dies; Hitler commits suicide; A-bomb dropped on Hiroshima; the U.N. is born.

TIME CAPSULE/1950: War breaks out in Korea; Senator Joseph McCarthy begins anti-Communist drive; television sweeps the country.

TIME CAPSULE/1956: The thwarted revolt in Hungary; Khrushchev de-Stalinizes Communism; the great Suez crisis; Ike defeats Adlai.

TIME CAPSULE/1959: Castro conquers Cuba; Russia hits the moon; Khrushchev visits the U.S.; the Dalai Lama flees Tibet.

mally routine and propagandistic Rudé Právo is usually sold out by midmorning; people regularly besiege kiosks for the livelier afternoon papers. The cause of the excitement is the transformation that is occurring in Czechoslovakia under Alexander Dubček, who is swiftly putting into action a program that his supporters promise will bring a semblance of democracy to Czechoslovak public life. As proof of his intentions, Dubček has removed almost every restraint on the press and other media. He has banished the party censors who oversee the printing of everything from books to streetcar tickets. He has released for production four movie scripts that had been gathering dust in the censors' office. With the floodgates thus open, the long-dammed tides are rushing in every direction. Trade unions are agitating for an end to party interference in their affairs. Officials in the Justice Ministry are demanding greater independence for judges. Professor Ota Sik, architect of the country's economic reform, has taken to making TV appearances, insisting that the reform cannot be really effective until the oldtime conservatives are cleaned out of the top ministries.

12 **WHIRLWIND:** The whirlwind liberalization continued to buffet the country, bringing joy to most people but guilt and grief to others. Josef Břeštanský, 42, deputy president of the Czechoslovak Supreme Court and the man in charge of reviewing the trials of the Stalinist purge victims of the 1950s, apparently took his own life after learning of a newspaper article denouncing his role in a rigged trial during that decade. His body was found hanging from a hornbeam tree in the woods south of Prague, an empty bottle of cheap wine at his feet. On an island in the Vltava River, more than 3,000 people imprisoned and tortured when the Communists first came to power met to praise Dubček and unfurl a white banner that read: "Never let it happen again."

The reforms were moving so fast that at week's end the party felt obliged to sound a note of caution. Conscious of the apprehension of the Soviet Union and other Communist neighbors, the Central Committee passed a resolution warning of the dangers of two extremes. On the one hand, the resolution declared the party's firm intention of preventing a return to the era before Dubček's takeover; on the other, it cautioned the people against trying to go back to the days before Communism.

PUTTING THE SQUEEZE ON: Czechoslovakia, the little country JULY that is trying the difficult and perhaps impossible task of combining Communism with freedom, is stirring up resentment and alarm in its Communist neighbors. Two of the men who rule the Soviet Union, Communist Party Boss Leonid Brezhnev and President Nikolai Podgorny, flew into Warsaw last week for an emergency conference. Their troika partner, Aleksei Kosygin, cut short a state visit to Sweden to join them there for talks with party leaders from Hungary, Poland, Bulgaria and East Germany. The Communist summit, the third of its kind in four months, was the Soviet response to the onrush of reform in Czechoslovakia.

The Russians apparently decided that matters had got out of hand when Prague newspapers printed a manifesto demanding that hard-line Communists be driven from high government and party posts, and urging the public to use strikes, boycotts and demonstrations to force them out. Known as "the 2,000 words," the manifesto was originally signed by 70 members of the country's elite, including artists, film directors and athletes; later, more than 30,000 more Czechoslovaks signed up.

SHOWDOWN: Czechoslovakia has twice been in need of the JULY world's help when threatened by the aggressiveness of its neighbors. Help did not come when Hitler dismembered the country in 1938 or when the Russians organized a Communist coup in 1948. Last week Czechoslovakia's 14,300,000 citizens found themselves in a desperate situation once again, as Russia did everything that it could, short of sending tanks to halt and reverse the reform program led by Party Boss Alexander Dubček.

Soviet Party Boss Leonid Brezhnev had imperiously summoned Dubček to the Soviet Union for a face-to-face meeting. Radio Prague reported that Dubček would not go until some 16,000 Soviet troops remaining on Czechoslovak soil after recent "maneuvers" leave the country. Besieged all week by threats from the Soviet Union and pressured further by the continued presence of the Russian troops, Dubček took to national TV to rally his people around him. He talked as no Communist leader had ever dared to do before. Czechoslovakia, he pledged, would "not make the slightest retreat from the path that we took up in January." Then he made an open plea to the people: "What we need most now is the support of all of you at this critical moment."

There was little doubt among Dubček's reformers that a recent swing toward them in almost every region of Czechoslovakia was the reason behind the panic summit in Warsaw. And though the communiqué from the Warsaw conference was unremarkable enough, a letter sent to Prague 48 hours after the meeting ended was a shocker.

"This is no longer your affair alone," said the letter ominously. "We are convinced that a situation has arisen that endangers the foundations of socialism in Czechoslovakia and threatens the vital common interests of other socialist countries. The people of other countries would never forgive us our indifference and carelessness in the face of such danger."

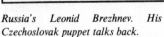

Russia's Leonid Brezhnev. His Czechoslovak puppet talks back.

Alexander Dubček. He calls it liberalization; Russia calls it revolt.

G. 9 **A KISS FOR DUBČEK:** The scene in the Czechoslovak city of Bratislava seemed an unlikely end to the long weeks of crisis and confrontation. As soon as the train arriving from the Soviet Union came to a stop, the leaders of the Kremlin bounced out of their coaches and began effusively embracing the leaders of Czechoslovakia. Soviet Party Boss Leonid Brezhnev planted smacking kisses on both the country's President, Ludvík Svoboda, and its First Party Secretary, Alexander Dubček. Judged by their ebullient mood, the Russians seemed to be celebrating a victory of their own. But the victory last week clearly went to the Czechoslovaks. Earlier in the week, the largest delegation of the Soviet Politburo ever to travel abroad together went to the tiny railroad junction of Cierna in Czechoslovakia to try to force the regime in Prague to back down and reimpose many of the old restrictions on freedom that Dubček has removed. When the confrontation ended, however, the Czechoslovaks had successfully stared down the Russians, stuck to their reforms, and emerged with their program virtually intact.

"We promised you that we would stand firm," Dubček told his people in a radio message after the Cierna summit. "I will tell you frankly that you can be well satisfied with the results of this meeting. We have kept the promises that we gave you."

"RUSSIANS GO HOME!": It had been a lilting summer day AUC throughout Eastern Europe. In the cool of a starry evening in the Czechoslovak capital of Prague, vast Wenceslas Square was alive with couples strolling arm in arm, tourists and Czechoslovaks bustling homeward. Then, just before midnight, telephones began to jangle as friends and relatives living in border towns frantically put in calls to the capital. The alert was spread by taxi drivers and owners of private cars, who raced through the medieval streets with their horns wailing warning. Soon the roar of jet engines reverberated through the night skies; Russian planes were flying ominously low. At 1:10 a.m., Radio Prague interrupted a program of music to confirm the worst: "Yesterday, on August 20, about 11 p.m., troops of the Soviet Union, the Polish People's Republic and the Hungarian People's Republic, the German Democratic People's Republic and the Bulgarian People's Republic crossed the frontiers of the Czechoslovak Socialist Republic."

Striking with stunning speed and surprise, some 200,000 soldiers of the five Warsaw Pact countries punched across the Czechoslovak border to snuff out the eight-month-old experiment by Alexander Dubček's regime in humanizing Communism. Some 250 Soviet T-54 tanks raced from Hungary into the Slovak capital of Bratislava. They hit the city at an awesome speed of 35 m.p.h., their smoking treads churning up the asphalt as they knocked down lampposts, street signs, even automobiles that stood in their way.

"How could they do this to me?" asked a dazed Dubček. "I have served the cause of the Soviet Union and Communism all of my life." Dubček refused to try to escape and, with other Presidium members, waited for the Russian troops to ring the building; he was seized by 15 Soviet officers and plainclothesmen in his office. It was morning before most Czechoslovaks came face to face with the reality of the invasion, and by then the entire country lay in the vise of Soviet power. Everywhere, paratroops in purple berets stood guard alongside tank crews in full battle dress, cradling automatic rifles in their laps.

After the invasion young Czechs demonstrate in Prague, crying "Russians go home!" and "Long live Dubček!"

On the first day of the occupation, Czechoslovak crowds surged around the alien tankers and Czech youths shouted "Long live Dubček!" and "Russians go home!" Whenever the tanks stopped, the interrogations began—surely some of history's most curious confrontations between conqueror and conquered. Hounded by questions, many of the Russians— some of whom were youths no older than 18—looked nervous and stared blankly into the distance to avoid further embarrassment. Then, the Czechoslovaks' mood began to change.

Mobs of youths mounted squat tanks, forcing their crews to disappear inside the hatch. Like elephant trunks swatting at flies, their gun turrets swung around eerily in an effort to knock off the screaming, chanting Czechoslovaks, who also bombarded the tanks with bricks, painted their flanks with swastikas, and dumped garbage on their hot engine covers to create a stench. Daring youths set a few tanks afire with flaming pieces of carpet and bottles of gasoline. In response, the tanks chased the youths into alleys and side streets with volleys of machine-gun fire. In a scene recalling fiercer battles in the streets of Budapest in 1956, a Russian tank and two armored ammunition carriers soon burned in the streets.

The struggle grew more and more coordinated and cunning as the Czechoslovaks mobilized all their resources to baffle, stymie and frustrate their occupiers. The campaign was directed and inspired by radio stations that continued to operate secretly throughout the country—reportedly with transmitters provided by the Czechoslovak army—after the Russians had shut down the regular government transmitters. "We have no weapons, but our contempt is stronger than tanks," proclaimed one such station near Bratislava. The station suggested that its listeners "switch around street signs, take house numbers from the doors, remove nameplates from public buildings and, when a Soviet soldier asks you something, say that you don't understand Russian." The people did just that.

While the Soviets tried in vain to create at least a modicum of government over the recalcitrant Czechoslovaks, the destiny of the nation was being debated behind closed doors in both Prague and Moscow.

Dubček and Premier Cerník were flown off to Moscow in a Soviet military jet. The Russians were also negotiating in Prague with President Ludvík Svoboda, who commands immense popular prestige in both Czechoslovakia and Russia as a World War II leader of the Czechoslovak army that fought with the Soviets against Hitler. But though troops ringed his residence in Hradčany Castle, Svoboda was able to broadcast over the free radio in Prague, and from the first his words attempted to reassure. "There is no way back from freedom and democracy. The troops must leave."

Svoboda soon decided that he wanted to talk directly with the Kremlin leaders: Moscow agreed that he could come. But when Svoboda sat down with Brezhnev in the Kremlin, he discovered that the Russians wanted to talk only with him and the handful of men who had come with him from Prague. Svoboda threatened to break off all negotiations unless Dubček was included, and at last Brezhnev gave in.

Back home, the Czechoslovak people continued to show the same sort of solidarity with Dubček that Svoboda had shown. They burned propaganda leaflets dropped from Soviet helicopters. Radio Prague began broadcasting the license-plate numbers of secret police cars so that people could slash their tires. In this frustrating atmosphere, some Russian soldiers were getting trigger-happy and tough. Retaliating against lone snipers who took potshots at them during the night, they raked whole neighborhoods with small-arms fire.

T. 6 **BACK INTO THE DARKNESS:** One by one, Czechoslovakia's faint remaining hopes for freedom last week flickered up, then died in the darkness of a new Soviet tyranny. Party Leader Alexander Dubček and his government returned from Moscow alive and intact, only to be forced to dismantle their democratic reforms. The tanks pulled back out of sight from the centers of Czechoslovakia's cities, only to be replaced by hundreds of grim, brutal KGB (secret police) agents flown in from Moscow to monitor the country's life. The freed radio stations that had sustained the Czechoslovaks in the first days of invasion and uncertainty faded out, and state censorship was reimposed. A great exodus began, as thousands of the country's ablest professors, artists, writers and journalists fled to freedom in the West. Gradually, the little country that for eight months gave promise of showing Communism the way into the modern world—and for eight days dared defy its oppressors—slipped back into the dark age of a Stalinist-style police state.

T. 13 **LIVING WITH RUSSIANS:** After ten days of work stoppages, with drastic losses for Czechoslovakia's already ailing economy, factory laborers relit blast furnaces and returned to their work benches. The curfew was lifted. Nightclubs and cinemas reopened. The juggler was even back in action at Prague's Tetran club, though he tended to drop more plates than usual.

The switch from defiance to docility was a conscious and uncomfortable act of a people who by and large are not collaborators but simply captives. On Dubček's instructions, Czechoslovaks scraped away anti-Soviet posters from walls and windows. Women in billowing peasant skirts moved down miles of highway painting out the anti-Soviet graffiti that had been lettered on the roads. At highway intersections, farmers readjusted the directional markers that had been turned the wrong way in hopes of confusing the invaders.

THE CAPTIVES FORGE THEIR OWN CHAINS: In quick succession, SEP the National Assembly reimposed censorship on Czechoslovakia's press, revoked the right of assembly and association, and reaffirmed the total and irrevocable supremacy of the Communist Party. By afternoon, it was all over and the captives had forged their own chains. Another important shackle was riveted onto Czechoslovakia in Moscow. Journeying to the Soviet capital, Czechoslovak Premier Oldřich Cerníck put his signature on a new seven-year economic agreement that abolishes any hope that Czechoslovakia might be able to seek funds and know-how in the West to revitalize its disastrously outmoded industry. The agreement was another barter deal, similar to earlier ones that ruinously shortchanged the Czechoslovaks; they must deliver trucks and other manufactured goods to the Russians in return for raw materials. Meanwhile, newspapers, radio and television spewed forth daily drivel about happy factory workers, joyous farmers and the blessings of Marxism.

France

COMPLIMENT: Cows don't sing, whales don't fly, and Charles JAN. de Gaulle doesn't take back anything he's said in all his 77 years. Except this time, maybe. Evidently alarmed by the angry charges of anti-Semitism that followed his attack on Israel at last month's press conference, De Gaulle wrote a three-page justification of his remarks to former Israeli Premier David Ben-Gurion. He had really meant it as a compliment, said *le grand Charles,* when he described the Jews as "an elite, sure of themselves and domineering." De Gaulle likes people who fit that description.

CH 8 **DE GAULLE ON L.B.J.:** In a new biography to be published in France next month and in the U.S. in the fall, Charles de Gaulle, quoted in an unguarded moment, delivers his private opinion of Lyndon Johnson:

"He's a cowboy, and that's saying everything. If he had been born in Europe, he would have gone to Africa to hunt water buffaloes or to America to search for gold. But born in the land of the ranch and the Colt, he shot his way up to sheriff. He's a legionnaire, a regular army noncom who earns his stripes, one after the other. An efficient man without any style. I rather like Johnson. He doesn't even take the trouble to pretend he's thinking. Roosevelt and Kennedy were masks over the real face of America. Johnson is the very portrait of America. He reveals the country to us as it is, rough and raw. If he didn't exist, we'd have to invent him."

Y 17 **BATTLE OF THE SORBONNE:** "This is real guerrilla action," said Paris Police Chief Maurice Grimaud. Indeed it was. In a year that has been marked almost everywhere by student upheaval, Paris last week captured the record for the largest student riots so far in 1968. While the city prepared for the opening of Vietnamese peace talks [see page 18], students staged the sharpest street fighting since the end of World War II. By week's end, the gulf between the government and students—

French police storm student barricades in Paris—now a city of uprooted paving stones, splintered trees, bloody streets.

who were joined by France's major unions—had widened into a serious anarchical challenge to Charles de Gaulle's government.

The trouble began two weeks ago, when authorities abruptly closed the Nanterre College of Letters, a suburban branch of the 150,000-student University of Paris, because a small band of Maoist, Marxist, Trotskyite and Guevarist militants had thrown the campus into a turmoil with strikes and threats of gang war. Next day the Nanterre leftists streamed into Paris' Latin Quarter, began demonstrating in the Sorbonne campus quadrangle. After the university called in police to eject them, bloody clashes brought 600 arrests and forced the Sorbonne, France's oldest university, to close. That served only to rally broad support for the troublemakers. Massing by the thousands along the Boulevard St. Germain and cross streets, students ripped up paving stones and steel posts, bombarded steel-helmeted police from behind barricades of overturned and burning cars.

The seeds of the student revolt have long existed in France's archaic system of higher education. Overcrowded to a point that stifles learning, lamentably short of professors, and managed by a mammoth but mediocre bureaucracy that resists change, French universities annually flunk some 20% of their 550,000 students while another 50% give up and quit. Resentment against the system erupted in the rioting.

THE SPREADING REVOLT: The spirit of revolution, whose modern roots were struck in France nearly two centuries ago, reappeared with a vengeance again last week and shook the Fifth Republic of Charles de Gaulle. It began with rebellious students, but it spread with ominous speed through the ranks of France's workers, creating such a tempestuous alliance that Charles de Gaulle, in what must have been one of the most humiliating moments of his career, cut short a visit to Rumania and returned home to face the greatest challenge of his ten years in power.

The convulsion was part carnival, part anarchist spree— but, more than anything, it was a spontaneous spark of national temper. Inspired by the students' example and glad of the chance to vent their own grievances, striking workers seized scores of factories in the worst epidemic of wildcat work stoppages in thirty years. By the weekend, the fast-spreading wave of strikes had squeezed transportation to a crawl, crippled mail service and both Paris airports, and spread into dozens of manufacturing industries.

Among the student strike leaders last week, few were more in evidence than a chubby, confident sociology major named Daniel Cohn-Bendit, 23, a self-styled anarchist who says he aims for "the suppression of capitalist society." At Nanterre, it was "Danny the Red" who stirred up so much trouble among its 12,000 students that authorities panicked and closed the place down. That lifted Cohn-Bendit from obscurity to notoriety, and all week long he moved from rally to rally, haranguing the Left Bank students as they groped for a sense of direction in their revolt against the government.

By last weekend, strikes engulfed the whole country. Most trains halted, as did Paris subway traffic. Air France canceled all flights. Police demanded immediate pay increases.

Y 31 **BATTLE FOR SURVIVAL:** For ten years, the aspirations of France and the dictates of Charles de Gaulle have appeared to be inseparable—a tribute to both his undeniable greatness and his penchant for saying it so often that people believed it. Last week the myth that France and De Gaulle are one lay shattered forever amid the garbage festering in the streets of Paris, the litter of uprooted paving stones, the splinters of chestnut trees hacked down to make barricades, the blood spilled on the capital's boulevards. France was a nation in angry rebellion —at times, it seemed, not far removed from civil war. Half of the nation's 16 million workers were on strike, and most of the rest were idled by a massive transportation shutdown. Students barricaded themselves in their universities. Farmers defiantly parked their tractors across the nation's highways. Protesters surged through Paris streets by the thousands each night, battling police and riot troopers.

For nearly three weeks, as revolt spread, De Gaulle said nothing in public. The universities have failed, he conceded. He promised that they would be overhauled. But there was a bigger problem: "All the indications show the necessity of a mutation of our society." But, he warned, that mutation must be orderly. For nearly 30 years, said De Gaulle, he had led France toward its destiny; "I am ready to do it again." But, he added, "this time, especially this time, I need—yes, I need—the French people to tell me that this is their wish." It was an extraordinary and almost touching admission from De Gaulle. Then he explained that he intended to submit some time in June a referendum to the voters in which he would spell out his proposals for modifying French life.

ONCE MORE THE MYSTIQUE: Charles de Gaulle has always laid claim to an extraordinary, almost mystical empathy with the French people. As France lay gripped by the worst economic paralysis in its peacetime history and cries for his resignation echoed in the streets of every major French city and town, De Gaulle flew to French military headquarters at Taverny. There he used the secret communications net to sound out his senior military officers. Then he climbed into the presidential Caravelle and jetted to Baden-Baden, the location of French army headquarters in Germany, for a face-to-face talk with two combat-division commanders there. Then he sped on to Mulhouse, near the German border, where his son-in-law, General Alain de Boissieu, commands the French army's 7th Division. During the meeting, at which twelve other generals were present, De Gaulle asked how the army would react if there were a showdown with the French left. The generals first told him in no uncertain terms that the army would never fire on students or coerce striking workers into resuming production. But, they added, in the event that the Communists made a determined effort to overthrow the regime through street fighting and guerrilla warfare, the army was prepared to intervene with its elite tank and paratroop units. That was all De Gaulle needed to know.

Next morning, after spending the night at his hilltop estate in Colombey, De Gaulle returned to Paris in a fighting mood. Emerging from a quickly convened Cabinet meeting at the palace, his Ministers wore the grim visages of men preparing to enter combat. What had been De Gaulle's message? asked newsmen. "Vigor," replied a Minister. "Vigor." Inside, in clipped, angry phrases, De Gaulle was shouting into a tape recorder his speech to the nation. Within a quarter-hour, his words were relayed throughout France.

"I shall not withdraw," said De Gaulle. "I have a mandate from the people. I shall fulfill it." Because of the widespread

President Charles de Gaulle on French television. "I shall not withdraw. I have a mandate. I shall fulfill it."

disorders, De Gaulle was postponing his referendum in which he had hoped to win a *oui* for his proposed social and university reforms. Instead, he planned to dissolve the National Assembly and call new parliamentary elections.

"France is indeed threatened by dictatorship," cried De Gaulle. The "totalitarian Communists," he warned, were waiting to ride to power on France's despair. Alluding to his new alliance with the army, he warned that he would use force to crush any further insurrection. "The republic will not abdicate!" he shouted hoarsely. "The people will collect themselves. Progress, independence and peace will prevail along with liberty. *Vive la France!*"

The speech lasted a bare three minutes, but it galvanized France. In an outpouring of emotion, some 600,000 to 1,000,000 Frenchmen marched up the Champs-Elysées in the biggest parade in the capital since Parisians triumphantly walked behind De Gaulle as he liberated the city 24 years ago. Businessmen in impeccable grey suits linked arms with shopkeepers and clerks. World War II Resistance fighters broke out tattered arm bands, and old parachutists wore their red berets. "We are the silent majority!" shouted the marchers. "Liberate the Sorbonne! Down with anarchy!"

As the demonstration unfolded on the streets, the National Assembly met to hear itself dissolved. Though De Gaulle had moved a tank regiment into the vicinity of Paris and alerted a few reserve units, there was no fresh rush to the barricades by his opponents, the workers and the anarchical students. Shoring up his government, De Gaulle fired eight Ministers, including just about everyone identified with his old social and labor policies, and switched two important portfolios: Foreign Minister Maurice Couve de Murville went to the Treasury, while Finance Minister Michel Debré moved over to the Quai d'Orsay to take Couve's place. France, which had fallen apart with such appalling rapidity, now seemed to coalesce with the same amazing speed.

A SUDDEN PARTING: "There cannot be a couple at the head of JUL state. Only one man can be in charge. Otherwise, the people get the impression that the No. 2 man is doing the steering."

—De Gaulle (1967)

Last week, in what was perhaps the most ungracious ouster of a head of government since Germany's Wilhelm II fired Bismarck in 1890, De Gaulle dropped his old friend and loyal helper, Georges Pompidou, as Premier. As his replacement, De Gaulle tapped his longtime Foreign Minister, Maurice Couve de Murville, a suave aristocrat who has no personal political ambitions. The dismissal was all the more ironic because, in all likelihood, De Gaulle would no longer be in the Elysée Palace if it were not for Pompidou. At the height of the May riots, it was Pompidou who kept the government running, cooled the strife between the security forces and the rebellious students, and got the workers back to their jobs. After that, he masterminded the amazingly successful election campaign that won for Gaullists the largest parliamentary majority that any government has held in nearly 100 years. Most people felt that it was simply a case of an old man canning a younger potential rival who, in the words of one of Pompidou's aides, "had gotten too big too soon."

JOINING THE CLUB: France's first hydrogen bomb exploded AUG last week over the Fangataufa atoll in the South Pacific, forming a huge exclamation mark to punctuate the difficulties of nonproliferation. The U.S. exploded its first H-bomb in 1952, the Soviet Union in 1953, the British in 1957, and the Chinese in 1967. Though it has become the fifth member of the hydrogen club, France is at least four years away from having a missile system capable of giving its big new bang the proper ride. Still, despite his recent troubles at home, Charles de Gaulle is determined to press ahead with his nuclear-weapon development program as the premier proof of his restoration of *la gloire* to France.

. 22 **"ABSURDITY"**: New tremors shook world money markets last week, with a flight from the French franc causing the greatest alarm. Forced to perform a major rescue job, the French government announced a series of tight credit restrictions designed to ease the pressures on the country's currency. That done, President Charles de Gaulle went to the trouble of personally denying rumors that the franc was about to be devalued. Such a move, the General told his cabinet, "would be the worst possible absurdity."

Absurd or not, the possibility of the franc's devaluation has flared intermittently ever since last spring's general strike, which led to a wave of staggering wage hikes for French labor and soaring price increases.

v. 29 **FIGHT FOR THE FRANC:** Speculation against the franc continued to mount last week until it neared crisis proportions, threatening to unbalance the entire, delicate mobile of the Western monetary system.

In the days before De Gaulle made his decision, Frenchmen streamed across the borders carrying suitcases filled with francs. Confidence in France's money continued to sink. Cab drivers in Geneva refused to accept French francs. London hotels took them only at a humiliating discount. Meanwhile, the West German mark, bloated by the franc inflow, gained in value and the Germans refused to try and stop the trend. As Chancellor Kurt Kiesinger publicly declared, "The ills of the sick should not be cured at the expense of the healthy."

Finally, the money managers and bankers of Europe and the U.S. assembled in Bonn in an emergency session, and solemnly rendered collective judgment that the franc must be devalued. The French braced for the worst. De Gaulle's critics could scarcely contain their glee that, at last, the oracle of the Elysée would be found fallible.

It all counted for nought with the President of France. Last week, in a stunning act of defiance against the world's financial experts and the seeming necessity of events, he refused to devalue the franc by one centime.

Actually, the French economy is essentially sound. In food and industrial resources, France is largely self-sufficient. It is not yet in real balance of payments difficulties. And the crisis of the franc was primarily created by the lure of capital funds into the mark by speculators who believed it was about to be revalued. In strict and narrow economic terms, France does not need a devaluation. That is why De Gaulle's gamble is essentially a psychological one. He does not need to reform the French economy so much as he needs to re-create confidence in the idea of the franc itself.

CRISIS EASED: As Charles de Gaulle imposed a severe economic DEC. squeeze on France last week, the money speculators retreated. An uneasy quiet took hold in Europe's reopened currency markets, and in contrast with the acrimonious debate that preceded their decision to lend France $2 billion to fight speculative runs on its currency, the world's industrial powers chorused assurances of support.

In a personal message to the President of France, Lyndon Johnson pledged that the U.S. would cooperate "in any way we can." Such backing was understandable. France's hard choice spared other countries painful repercussions—at least for the moment. Devaluation of the franc very likely would have started speculation first against the British pound, then against the U.S. dollar.

France began its save-the-franc austerity by imposing its tightest money controls since the early postwar years. The government decreed a $140 limit on the amount of French and foreign cash that tourists of any nationality may take out of the country. Police reinforced customs officers along all French borders. At Paris' Orly airport, international flights were delayed while customs officials and police poked through every outgoing suitcase.

To the humiliation of many a traveler, they counted money in every purse and wallet, and any excess was seized, to be held until the traveler's return. On the first day alone, the customs take totaled $3,000,000, spoiling the vacations of countless Frenchmen.

The Middle East

After a six-day war between Israel and the Arab states in 1967, Israeli forces had occupied large areas of Jordan, Syria and Egypt, including the east bank of the Suez Canal, which was now blocked to traffic by ships sunk during the battle. Arab military forces were crippled in the fighting, but commandos continued to carry out guerrilla attacks.

FEB. 9 IMPASSE AT SUEZ: After the worst flare-up of shooting across its placid waters since last October, the Suez Canal last week seemed more than ever a permanent casualty of the Arab-Israeli war. And the brief hopes that 15 trapped freighters might finally be freed after eight months of captivity flickered rapidly away in a three-hour gun duel between Egyptian and Israeli forces. By the time the truce was restored by the U.N.'s blue-helmeted observers, the Egyptians had not only suspended their efforts to release the rusting ships but declared that they would do nothing at all to reopen the canal until a complete Middle East settlement is reached.

Aside from the grief over the dozen or so casualties, no one seemed overly distressed by the new impasse. The U.S. seems quite content to watch Soviet ships bound for North Viet Nam having to take a wearying 14,000-mile trip around Africa (*v.* 7,000 miles through Suez). But the longer the canal stays shut, the harder it will be to open. Silt is piling up so fast that five feet of navigable depth have already been lost. "If the canal stays closed another year," said an American engineer last week, "it will be in such bad shape that they might as well turn it into an irrigation ditch and plant potatoes around it."

FEB. 23 ISRAEL STRIKES BACK: Israel and Jordan became involved last week in the heaviest fighting since the cease-fire last June. Sporadic artillery duels sent kibbutz dwellers in Galilee scurrying for cover and killed 17 Arabs in a refugee camp. After a few days' lull, the Israelis struck back. Along a 60-mile front howitzers, heavy mortars and tanks pounded Jordanian positions with merciless accuracy. Then the Israelis called out their air force. For nearly seven hours, squadrons of jet fighter-bombers dumped rockets, phosphorus bombs and napalm on the east bank. They destroyed a guerrilla base, damaged several towns, terrorized Arab refugee tent-camps and knocked out gun emplacements. Finally, with much of his army again in ruins—and with Radio Amman broadcasting appeals for blood donors—Jordan's King Hussein called it quits and asked the U.S. for help in arranging a cease-fire.

SKYWAY ROBBERY: The hijacking of U.S. airliners for unsched- AUG. uled trips to Cuba has become so commonplace that a virtually automatic routine has evolved for the prompt release of planes and passengers. The matter was far more serious last week when three well-dressed Arab passengers seized Israel's El Al Flight 426 an hour out of Rome and forced it to divert its course from Tel Aviv to Algiers. What the Arabs wanted from their skyway robbery was not a free trip but bounty and hostages to use against Israel.

One of the hijackers, a swarthy man who had evidently had flying experience, opened the unlocked door to the flight deck, clubbed Copilot Maoz Poraz with the butt of his pistol, and slid into a seat behind Captain Oded Abarbanel, ordering a change of course to Algiers. Back in the cabin, his two accomplices brandished pistols and hand grenades in order to keep the frightened passengers in their seats. When the big Boeing 707 touched down at Algiers' Dar-el-Beida airport, Algerian authorities impounded it. Next day they sent all passengers identified as non-Israelis to France after giving them a sightseeing trip. Twelve Israeli passengers and the Israeli crew of ten were held, possibly as hostages for hundreds of Arab guerrillas currently in Israeli custody. The hijackers were quickly identified as Palestinian Arab commandos.

LIFE OR DEATH: When Israeli jets whooshed low over the Jor- AUG. danian town of Salt one midmorning last week, the townspeople paid scant heed. For Jordan's air force was destroyed in last year's Six-Day War, and Israel has had the virtual freedom of Jordanian skies ever since. This time, however, the Israeli overflight was far from routine. Angered by daily raids on Israeli-occupied territory by Jordan-based Arab commandos, Israel had decided to make use of its air superiority to strike back. El Fatah, the largest and most aggressive of the commando groups, had its operations headquarters in a half-acre grove of fig and olive trees just outside Salt. The Israeli jets were out to destroy it in the heaviest Israeli air raid against the Arabs since the war began. When the planes let up briefly, the people of Salt streamed out to survey the damage and were hit by a second wave of planes that caught Arab ambulances in the open. Altogether, the Jordanians claimed, 34 people died and 82 were wounded. Leaflets dropped from the planes made clear the lesson Israel intended: "Death for those who ask for death. Life for those who want to live in peace."

T. 13 **TERRORISM IN TEL AVIV:** The announced goal of El Fatah, the Arab terrorist organization, is to provoke Israelis into a pogrom of Arabs living in Israel and thereby shatter all Israeli hopes for peaceful coexistence in their occupied territories. Last week, in the latest of a series of attacks, Arab terrorists struck for the first time in Tel Aviv and succeeded in rousing an angry Jewish response. The attack came at noon, in the form of three time bombs wrapped in plastic bags and dropped in litter baskets in downtown Tel Aviv. All three detonated within 20 minutes. One Israeli was killed, and 50 others were wounded, most of them by flying fragments of metal. As El Fatah had evidently hoped, a crowd of angry Israelis pounced on and beat every Arab it could find in the vicinity. As police rushed to protect Arab passers-by, the mob surged into neighboring Jaffa's Arab quarter, smashing Arab shops.

Temperatures cooled when police announced that they had rounded up 23 Arab suspects, two of whom confessed and said that they were members of a terrorist gang that set off three bombs in Jerusalem last month, one of which had sparked a similar Israeli rampage against Arabs. Meanwhile, Israeli Foreign Minister Abba Eban scored a diplomatic success of sorts by gaining the release of the Israeli Boeing 707 that had been skyjacked by El Fatah agents and held in Algiers with twelve passengers since July. Because Israel had little bargaining leverage in this case, it had to make a reciprocal gesture: the release of 16 imprisoned Arab terrorists.

V. 15 **DEEPEST YET:** The fresh hostilities between the Arabs and Israel flared, as usual, in the name of retaliation—that modern word for the Biblical "eye for an eye" that both sides have employed to justify repeated violations of the 17-month-old cease-fire. Last week it was Israel's turn to retaliate. A few days earlier, the Egyptians had unleashed a sudden Sabbath rocket and artillery barrage that killed 15 Israeli soldiers guarding the right bank of the Suez Canal. Israel's spectacular riposte came on the Nile River, deep in Egypt's heartland. By the light of a nearly full moon, a band of airborne Israeli commandos penetrated farther into enemy territory (140 miles) than they had ventured even during last year's war. Splitting into three groups, the force attacked a bridge-dam whose lock controls the flow of water for irrigating sugar-cane fields, and hit one of the four major electric relay stations between Cairo and the Aswan Dam. A short time later, all three units disappeared back into Israel. They left behind deep holes in the bridge and dam, and roaring fires in eight of the nine transformers built by Russia at a cost of $15 million. About all Egypt's shaken President Gamal Nasser could do was call an emergency Cabinet meeting to discuss ways "to put the United Arab Republic on a war footing," including formation of a popular defense force.

THE DIALECTIC OF BOMBS: On a Friday morning, the busiest NOV place in Jerusalem is the Mahaneh Yehuda (Camp of Judah) market. Last week, a crowd of 3,000 filled its narrow lanes and open stalls as housewives shopped for the Sabbath. No one noticed a small blue delivery van parked on Agrippas Street, nor could they know that it carried 450 lbs. of explosives and a timing device. At precisely 9:28 a.m., the van blew up. The enormous explosion killed twelve shoppers and shopkeepers, seriously wounded 17, and sent another 36 to the hospital. In the panicked crowd, a nine-year-old boy screamed: "I saw a hand flying in the air. I saw a head rolling in the street." So fierce was the blast that it shattered windows half a mile away. It was the worst Arab terrorist bombing since 1948 and the latest in a series of thrusts by Arab commandos. In the Middle East's familiar dialectic of attack and reprisal, that verdict seemed to leave in doubt only the time and place of Israel's retaliation.

ATTACK ON BEIRUT: Alone among the Arab states sharing borders with Israel, tiny cosmopolitan Lebanon had escaped direct involvement in the Middle East's frequent outbursts of hostility. Like Arabs everywhere else, the Lebanese had paid lip service and tithes to the Arab cause against Israel, but they were far more interested in commerce than in aggressive politics. But last week violence came to Lebanon with a vengeance. In perhaps the single most audacious military exploit in their already spectacular history, Israeli forces swept down in helicopters on Beirut's busy international airport, through which thousands of Arab and Western tourists and businessmen pass each day. In 45 minutes, a dozen Lebanese civilian planes were destroyed or damaged, hangars and fuel dumps set afire, all apparently without loss of life to either side. Damage was estimated at $100 million. It was a swift, surgical and devastating raid—and it once again raised the stakes in the Middle East, edging the area closer to another full-scale war.

The action was in reprisal for an Arab act of terrorism that had taken place only two days before at Athens' international airport. There, a New York-bound Boeing 707 belonging to El Al, the Israeli airline, had just moved away from its loading ramp when two men dashed onto the runway and fired a fusillade of bullets at the fuselage. They killed one passenger. In accordance with a policy of holding Arab governments responsible for fedayeen terrorism, Israel quickly blamed Lebanon. The terrorists, said a Tel Aviv statement, had flown to Athens from Beirut's airport, and belong to a group of Arab saboteurs that was based in Lebanon. "The mark of Cain is on the heads of the perpetrators," declared Israeli Prime Minister Levi Eshkol. The Middle East has learned to take such Israeli warnings seriously, and Lebanon braced for some sort of reprisal. The raid on Beirut came within 48 hours.

Brazil

EC. 20   **CRACKDOWN:** Three months ago, after police stormed the campus of Brasília University, Congressman Márcio Moreira Alves rose in Brazil's Chamber of Deputies and urged his countrymen to boycott Independence Day military parades to show their disapproval. Last week that seemingly insignificant act led to some startlingly drastic consequences for South America's biggest, most populous nation. The government imposed censorship on the country's radio and press, put the armed forces on alert and, finally, suspended Brazil's constitution and shut down its Congress—both indefinitely.

Alves, 32, is the chief parliamentary critic of the military strongmen behind Brazil's President Arthur da Costa e Silva. Last year, he wrote *Tortures and the Tortured,* a study of the brutal manner in which Brazil's military deal with their political opponents. The book was banned temporarily. After his September speech, in which he assailed the military as a "nest of torturers," the generals decided that it was time to ban Alves himself. They insisted that he be arrested, tried by the Supreme Court and stripped of his political rights for ten years. Before he could be brought to trial, however, the normally compliant Congress had to agree to suspend his immunity. The government foresaw little trouble. But last week, the government suffered a stunning defeat as the deputies quashed a motion to lift Alves' parliamentary immunity and permit his conviction for "publicly inciting animosity." A handful of spectators in the galleries jumped to their feet cheering, then began to sing the national anthem. After a moment's hesitation, most of the deputies in the chamber joined in.

Their joy was short-lived. Brazil's military leaders wasted no time in acting. Having failed to remove Alves by legal parliamentary procedures, they decided to do away with the procedures themselves. Radio stations were ordered to stop broadcasting the result of the Alves vote. Censors and policemen invaded newspapers and press-agency offices. One respected daily was ordered to kill its morning edition because a critical editorial warned Costa e Silva: "You can't run a country of 80 million people like an army division."

The next day, just before midnight, a solemn-faced justice minister interrupted radio and television broadcasts to announce that the President had signed the Fifth Institutional Act, giving him full dictatorial powers in "defense of the necessary interests of the nation." The act, the fifth of its kind in the last four years, gave Costa e Silva the right to close Congress, rule by decree, cancel the political rights of any person, declare a state of siege, dismiss public officials, waive writs of habeas corpus. One of the first to be arrested under the new decree was former President Juscelino Kubitschek, whose popularity has consistently gained as that of Costa has waned.

Britain

26 **SAD SALUTE TO FACT:** Almost down to the last dread detail, it was the speech that had been forecast for weeks by diplomats, economists and the British press corps. Still, as Prime Minister Harold Wilson rose before Parliament last week and methodically ticked off his program "to make devaluation work," the import of his words made the occasion historic. [Still suffering from the economic effects of World War II, Britain had carried out its second devaluation of the pound since the war in November 1967.] "We have come to terms with our role in the world," announced Wilson. "Our security lies fundamentally in Europe." But even the world's hardened realists seemed to cringe at Chancellor of the Exchequer Roy Jenkins' sad salute to fact. "We are recognizing," he told the House of Commons, "that we are no longer a superpower."

Tethering British defense to Europe to save money will permit Wilson to hasten the withdrawal of 35,000 troops stationed in the Far East and to clear out of Persian Gulf bases as well—all within three years. Thus by the end of 1971, except for the 10,000-man Hong Kong garrison and a few other colonial police details, British arms will be deployed no farther from home than the Mediterranean. Britain's up-to-date nuclear-delivery muscle will be reduced to four Polaris submarines. A post-1971 phase-out of all aircraft carriers will drastically cut Britain's fighting mobility. Spared by Wilson's ax were two expensive investments in the future being undertaken jointly with France: the Concorde supersonic airliner, due for its test flight this spring, and the Dover-to-Calais Channel tunnel, which is scheduled to go under construction in the next decade.

CH 8 **CLOSING THE GATE:** The kaleidoscopic colors of an oriental bazaar swirled through London's normally drab Heathrow Airport. Clutching bundles bulging with everything from jars of curry powder to television sets, turbaned men, sari-clad women and coffee-tinted youngsters stepped off planes from such diverse points as Cairo and Athens. Most of their journeys began in Kenya, where they had sold their businesses at panic prices, paid scalpers' ransom rates for airline tickets and grabbed planes to any place that offered hope of a connecting flight to Britain. Thus last week, in a final, frantic stampede,

6,200 of Kenya's Asians descended on London before Britain finally slammed the gate on one of its major sources of colored immigrants. Until then, any of the more than 125,000 Asians in Kenya who opted for British citizenship when the colony became independent in 1963 were free to enter Britain whenever they wished.

Unwelcome in the cradle of the British Commonwealth, the immigrants have turned to their own kind, formed large colored communities across England's Midlands and in London slums. Against the background of white resentment, the colored communities are growing restive. Much of their bitterness is justified. Colored doctors and nurses are a mainstay of Britain's nationalized medicine, and bus services throughout Britain would grind to a halt without colored crews. Even though non-whites account for only 2% of Britain's population, Prime Minister Harold Wilson's Laborites bowed to mounting public pressure and rammed emergency legislation through Parliament to shut off the flood. Despite the overwhelming 372-to-62 vote in the House of Commons, many Britons were deeply disturbed by the racist implications of the bill and by the first restrictions on the unchallenged right, tracing back to Magna Carta, of all British citizens to enter the home country at will. As many as 180 M.P.s either abstained or absented themselves during the ballot. Many newspapers bitterly

"Punch" views the British exclusion act, which closes the gates of the homeland to nonwhite citizens. Says the London Times: *"A wretched affair."*

branded the bill as a betrayal. The London Times declared: "It has been a wretched affair."

3 **EXPLOSION OF RACISM:** Like the gunpowder concealed in the cellar of Parliament by Guy Fawkes, an explosive issue has long lain hidden beneath the even fabric of British life. Last week it exploded into the open—and presented Britain with an ugly, gnawing and virulent problem. The man who sparked the explosion was only saying what a great many Britons think: that non-whites are not welcome in Britain. But before the week was out, race had become the most heated and controversial subject of the year—and an issue that may well influence the next election.

The furor began when Enoch Powell, 55, a right-wing Tory M.P. from the industrial Midlands, launched an attack on an antidiscrimination bill introduced by the Labor government to protect the 1,000,000 coloreds—a term that covers shades from light tan to dark black—who are already legally in Britain or are still allowed, despite recent restrictions, to enter.

"Those whom the gods wish to destroy, they first make mad," said Powell, borrowing from Euripides. Britain "must be mad as a nation, literally mad," he went on, to continue letting in colored immigrants, who have made Britons "feel like strangers in their own country." Powell demanded a virtual end to immigration and payments of cash bonuses to immigrants willing to leave. Predicting a 250% rise in the colored population within two decades, he declared: "As I look ahead, I am filled with much foreboding. Like the Roman, I seem to see 'the River Tiber foaming with much blood.'"

Shocked by the speech, Tory Leader Edward Heath fired Powell as Minister of Defense in his shadow Cabinet. But the speech produced an outpouring of support for Powell's position. More than 2,000 tough Limehouse dockworkers walked off their jobs and marched on Parliament with signs that read BACK BRITAIN, NOT BLACK BRITAIN. They were followed by butchers from Smithfield Market, still dressed in their bloodied smocks. At one point, the longshoremen's protest tied up London's docks. The London Times called Powell's speech "evil" and "disgraceful." But from the length and breadth of Britain came more than 85,000 letters to Powell himself, all but 30 or so, by his reckoning, reacting favorably to his speech.

Canada

SWINGING PRIME MINISTER: He is an attractive, wealthy intellectual and *bon vivant* who zips around in a Mercedes 300 SL sports car and favors a far-out wardrobe that includes pastel shirts, trilby hats and green leather overcoats. Considering these attributes, the last thing one would expect him to be is a politician, especially in Canada. AP

And yet, after only three years in Parliament and one year as Minister of Justice, Pierre Elliott Trudeau, 48, is about to become Canada's new Prime Minister. At first, Trudeau was only one of several strong contenders but he quickly drew ahead of the field. After waging a tireless cross-country campaign, he came to last week's Liberal Party convention in Ottawa as a front runner.

Canada's Prime Minister Trudeau (left). He is attractive, wealthy, impatient and an intellectual man on the go.

At week's end Trudeau was elected party leader. Thus he will formally succeed Pearson as Prime Minister some time later this month.

Trudeau's toughest problem is Canada's constitutional crisis. Though Trudeau is a French Canadian and personally popular in Quebec, he is ideologically at odds with those who want a quasi-independent status for the French-speaking province. Trudeau strongly opposes French separatism and argues persuasively for a genuinely federal system. As he sees it, Quebec should surrender its demands for special status, and English Canada should give up its vision of Canada as an essentially English-dominated country.

But the big difference between Trudeau and Pearson is style. While Pearson is a largely unadventurous politician, Trudeau is an intellectual man on the go, impatient with old ideas and restless for results. Zoologist Desmond Morris, author of *The Naked Ape,* says that Trudeau has "animal qualities" that "bring him to the top of the heap." The son of a millionaire land and oil investor, he studied law at the University of Montreal, political economics at Harvard, went on to the London School of Economics. When he arrived back in Canada, Trudeau drifted from job to job, editing a political science magazine, teaching constitutional law at the University of Montreal and acting as a labor lawyer. Then, three years ago, he entered politics and won a parliamentary seat from an English-speaking constituency in Montreal. "After 15 years in the role of critic," he explained, "I think it's time to go out and try to do the job myself."

China

5 **BANG NO. 7:** In the seventh Chinese atomic test since Peking joined the nuclear club three years ago, the flash of a fireball last week lit up the desert around Lop Nor in northwestern China. It was the first test since last spring, when a Maoist mushroom cloud proved to the world that the Chinese had succeeded in the *summa* of atomic arts—building a hydrogen bomb. Bang No. 7 was far, far smaller, probably in the Hiroshima-bomb range of 20 kilotons. But its improved miniaturization indicated that China has advanced well along in its countdown toward bombs tidy enough to ride missiles to their targets. The Chinese, who claim to have invented the rocket 700 years ago, already have short- and medium-range (1,500 miles) missiles perfected, and this year are expected to begin building emplacements for them along China's coast, thus bringing a large part of Asia within the arc of their nuclear capability.

PRICE OF REVOLUTION: "There can be no construction without M destruction."—Mao Tse-tung

Two years ago this week, Mao launched the Great Proletarian Cultural Revolution, and the first wall poster, dripping with vitriol, blossomed on the east wall of Peking University's dining hall. Fearful that China was losing the purity of its first revolution and sliding down "the capitalist road" taken by "bourgeois" Russia, Mao set out to purge his vast nation, which has a population of 750 million people. His weapons were the People's Liberation Army and the youth of the Red Guards, whom he mobilized by closing down the schools. His targets were the party and governmental structures of China, the handiwork of President Liu Shao-chi, who became the all-purpose symbol of everything "revisionist" in China that Mao aimed to destroy.

Mao's purge is still in progress. Radio Shanghai recently announced that seven "renegades and active counter-revolutionary criminals" had been executed while 10,000 Maoist onlookers "shouted slogans at the top of their voices, rejoicing and clapping their hands." Despite such salutary lessons, however, Mao has been unable to stifle his opposition. The Cultural Revolution Bulletin reported, in fact, that he narrowly escaped being captured by rebellious troops last July when he went to Wuhan, China's transportation hub and fifth-largest city, to bring a revolting commander to heel. Nor is Mao's dream of a China holding hands in a single, beatific chanting chain any nearer. The many months of character assassination, chaos, instigated lawlessness and near civil war have taken a terrible toll on nearly every human, political and economic resource in China.

The result has been the creation of a leadership vacuum so great that China today is less a nation governed than a nation harangued. Despite Mao's order to reopen the schools last year, many are still closed. China's cultural life has been brought to a dreary standstill; not a single book of any major value has been published for two years, and the only new play that showed promise, *The Madman of the New Age*, was condemned by the critics as an oblique attack on Mao himself.

The economy, too, has suffered ruinously. In February, Premier Chou En-lai warned that China's vital coal production had fallen off alarmingly. Transportation has been totally disrupted, and sabotage of trains is common as the Maoists and anti-Maoists fight. Trucks are often idle for lack of fuel. China's biggest oil refinery at Taching was partly destroyed by sabotage. Shortage of oil left Peking without heat for much of the winter. Steel and textile production are also down, and only the best weather in a decade last year prevented a fall-off in grain production that would have meant famine in many areas.

5 **THE PEARL'S GRISLY FLOTSAM:** Swollen to flood stage by recent rainstorms, the muddy Pearl River last week washed some grisly flotsam onto the shores of the islands that hug South China. On Hong Kong and Macao, 43 bodies drifted to shore —many brutally slashed and six of them trussed, their arms and legs roped to their necks. The Pearl's cargo confirmed, in dramatic fashion, reports from the mainland by travelers, press and radio that the worst factional fighting in a year is spreading throughout much of China. Armed with everything from bamboo poles to rifles, thousands of workers and students have clashed in bloody battles. In the countryside, some peasants have torn up roads leading to their villages to keep out marauding bands of fighters.

6 **WHO STOLE THE LOCOMOTIVE?:** Only rarely does the world have an opportunity to catch glimpses of the confused reality behind Communist China's façade, and last week Chinawatchers were poring over a Red Guard pamphlet that purports to be the minutes of a meeting of the Peking leadership with rival Red Guard factions who had been curtailing rail shipment of aid to Hanoi. Exasperated officials summoned Red Guard leaders to an acrimonious conference in Peking, where the rebels were interrogated by the leadership, including Premier Chou En-lai.

Chou: "Is it true that your men took away the locomotive of Train No. 45?"

Red Guard: "Only once."

Chou: "Once is serious enough. You threatened the driver with a machine gun and took away the locomotive. It was only after I called directly over long-distance telephone and gave up a good night's sleep that you returned it. *(Turning to another leader):* You took part in the looting of ammunition destined for Viet Nam. You have seized 11,800 cases of ammunition. That is no small matter. How can you tell lies to us and try to get away with it?"

It was a farewell performance for the young Red Guards. Within two weeks, thousands of them were on their way to corrective labor, their part in Mao Tse-tung's campaign to revive revolutionary ardor at an end.

West Germany

EMULATION: Violence flared in Europe last week. An assassin picked as his target Rudi Dutschke, 28, a self-avowed revolutionary, leader of Germany's student unrest and author of fierce tirades against "repressive" European society. As Dutschke wheeled his bicycle along West Berlin's Kurfürstendamm, a young man who had been lying in wait fired three shots at him from a pistol. The bullets hit "Red Rudi" at close range in the chest and head. After a sharp firefight, police wounded the assailant and dragged him from a nearby cellar. He was identified as a 23-year-old Munich house painter named Josef Bachmann, who had traveled to Berlin expressly to kill Dutschke. "I read about Martin Luther King and thought, 'You too must do something like this,' " he explained to police. Even as Dutschke underwent a successful five-hour operation for the removal of a bullet from his skull, the news of the attempted assassination caused Germany's most widespread civil disturbances since the early 1930s.

Chanting their war cry, "Ho-Ho-Ho Chi Minh!", students, many of whom wore protective helmets and carried heavy clubs, went on rampages in virtually every major German city. Almost everywhere they went, they blockaded and sometimes stoned the local printing plants of conservative Publisher Axel Springer, whose newspapers, notably the mass-circulation Bild-Zeitung, have denounced their restive leftist tendencies. The students also broke store windows, erected barricades across streets and fought bitter pitched battles with police. The violence was worst of all in West Berlin, where a mob of 3,000 young revolutionaries broke almost every lower-floor window in Springer's shiny skyscraper near the Wall and set fire to some 20 delivery trucks. Alarmed by the violence, Chancellor Kurt Kiesinger broke off his Easter vacation and went back to Bonn, where he warned the students to calm down or face the consequences. Meanwhile, in a display of the intertwining relationships between the young European radicals, students staged riots of varying degrees of violence in Rome, Paris and Amsterdam.

BITTER AFTERTASTE: Last week, bruised and battered from police truncheons, West Germany's leftist students were having some second thoughts about the efficacy of violence. In Berlin, Hamburg, Munich, Frankfurt and other German cities where demonstrators tried to blockade the regional printing plants of Publisher Axel Springer, police went to work on them with bruising water cannon and truncheons. The students were not used to seeing their own blood flow, and many, moreover, were deeply shocked by the death from rioter-thrown missiles of an Associated Press photographer and a Munich student.

Axel Springer, the man whom the radical students singled out as the symbol of all that is bad in West Germany, is a tall, silver-haired publisher who commutes between his six homes in Europe in a private jet, directs his $200 million press empire from atop a glass skyscraper in West Berlin. Springer, 55, is sternly anti-Communist, assertively German, and a strong supporter of the U.S. stand in Viet Nam. He owns 15 magazines and newspapers that account for 31% of West Germany's circulation of weekday publications (88% on Sundays). The radical students charge that Springer has manipulated public opinion in order to create a repressive, Fascist-style society in West Germany and an atmosphere of hate against them. His readers seemed to like what they read. Despite all the efforts of radical students to stop the distribution of his papers, they enjoyed last week the best sales in their history.

A MOST UNLOVELY ELECTION: "Nazi, pfui! Nazi, pfui!" hissed the scores of West Germans who milled about in front of the state parliament building in Stuttgart. The object of the hisses paid no attention. Adolf von Thadden, 46, whose far-rightist party had just polled 10% of the vote in the Baden-Württemberg elections, strode into the building to talk with

Rudi Dutschke. His attempted murder sets off riots in Germany. Page 158.

Adolf von Thadden. A rightist, he has just won a "beautiful victory."

newsmen. "Despite the efforts of everyone to keep us out of the state parliament," he said, "the National Democrats have won their most beautiful victory so far."

For West Germany, Von Thadden's victory was anything but beautiful. In fact, Chancellor Kurt Kiesinger was so upset by the National Democrats' surprisingly strong showing in his own home state that he immediately pledged that his No. 1 priority was to crush Von Thadden's party before next year's federal elections. Declared Kiesinger: "If the impression gets around that there is an awakening of Nazism in Germany, it would threaten our entire foreign and domestic policy."

OF SUICIDE AND ESPIONAGE: The darkroom assistant in N Dancker's photo shop in Bonn could hardly believe his eyes. Among banal vacation snapshots on a strip of film taken from a Minox camera were nine pictures of NATO documents clearly marked "Top Secret" and "Secret." It took police and the West German Counter Espionage Service four days to identify the owner of the film. He proved to be Rear Admiral Hermann Lüdke, formerly deputy chief of the logistics section of SHAPE, NATO's European command, who was on the eve of his retirement from the service. Lüdke had held Cosmic Top Secret clearance in the SHAPE job and knew the most sensitive details of NATO logistics: the capacities of European ports, transport, defense industries; the location of nuclear weapons depots and ordnance stockpiles of the NATO armies, virtually down to the number of available artillery rounds.

Lüdke, 57, a handsome, gregarious man, was not told of the suspicions against him until three days before he left the navy. The occasion was a champagne luncheon feting his retirement. After a laudatory farewell speech by Defense Minister Gerhard Schröder, a counterespionage man took Lüdke aside to question him. The admiral at first lamely explained that someone must have stolen the Minox to take the pictures. However, he later changed his story to claim that he wanted the documents for his memoirs. If so, they would surely have ranked among the dullest ever written, since the documents were merely directives for handling supplies. Nevertheless, he was allowed to go home and was interrogated only the next day. Because West German counterspies apparently take weekends off, two more days elapsed before the federal attorney's office was informed of the case. It took over the investigation, but unfortunately it did not stick close enough to the admiral. On Oct. 8, Lüdke was found dead on a hunting preserve in the Eifel Mountains, a fist-sized wound in his chest, his Mauser rifle, loaded with dumdum rounds, across his legs. Suicide? The Trier district attorney's office thought so, but it did not rule out murder.

Most Germans are fairly inured to espionage cases. Their country, with an estimated 6,000 foreign agents operating inside its borders, has long been considered NATO's weakest security link. But even the most cynical were soon fascinated, for Lüdke's death marked the beginning of an astonishing wave of suicides among government officials. On the day of Lüdke's death, Major General Horst Wendland, 56, deputy chief of the Federal Intelligence Service, Bonn's equivalent of the CIA, shot himself in his office. The government explanation: he was despondent over an "incurable illness." On Oct. 15, a promising young official in the Economics Ministry hanged himself. On Oct. 16, a woman working in the Federal Press and Information Office took a fatal overdose of drugs. On Oct. 18, Bundeswehr Lieut. Colonel Johannes Grimm, 54, working in the Alarm and Mobilization Section of the Defense Ministry, shot himself. He, too, said the government, was despondent over an incurable disease. On Oct. 23, it was announced that a senior clerk in the Defense Ministry had disappeared after leaving a suicide note. In each case, there were personal explanations for the death, but security officials did not rule out other motives.

Guatemala

CAUGHT IN THE CROSSFIRE: The black Ford carrying the four JA American military men swung away from the headquarters of the U.S. military mission in Guatemala City, and ten blocks later, a dark green sedan carrying three men pulled alongside. One of them suddenly opened up with a machine gun. Sitting in the front seat, Colonel John D. Webber, 47, head of the mission and driver of the car, and Lieut. Commander Ernest A. Munro, 40, chief of the mission's naval section, took the full force of the fusillade and died almost instantly as the car came squealing to a halt. The Americans were casualties in a fresh outburst of lethal feuding between left- and right-wing Guatemalan extremists that has claimed more than 25 lives in the past month.

In a way, Webber and Munro were the victims of Webber's own success in Guatemala. When the tough career officer arrived in Guatemala 18 months ago, 200 Communist guerrillas were terrorizing the countryside. Webber immediately expanded counterinsurgency training within Guatemala's 5,000-man army, brought in U.S. Jeeps, trucks, communications equipment and helicopters, and breathed new life into the army's civic-action program. To aid in the drive, the army also armed local bands of "civilian collaborators" licensed to kill peasants whom they considered guerrillas or "potential" guerrillas. There were those who doubted the wisdom of encouraging such measures in violence-prone Guatemala, but Webber was not among them. "That's the way this country is," he said. "The Communists are using everything they have, including terror. And it must be met."

CAUGHT IN MORE CROSSFIRE: U.S. Ambassador John Gordon SE Mein had just left his residence in the suburbs of Guatemala City after a luncheon honoring a visiting State Department specialist. He was alone in the rear seat of his chauffeured Cadillac when a small green Toyota suddenly pulled in front and forced Mein's car to the curb. A red Buick darted up to block the embassy car from behind. Two men in green fatigues got out of the Toyota and ordered Mein from his car at the point of a submachine gun. He stepped out, then broke and ran. There was a shout: "Kill him! Kill him!" The submachine gunner squeezed off a burst at Mein's back. The ambassador fell in the middle of the street and died within moments.

Mein, 54, a career foreign-service officer with years of Latin American experience, was well known for his quiet professionalism. In keeping with his taste for unobtrusiveness, he had dismissed an armed escort assigned earlier this year. While his assassination, the first in history of a U.S. ambassador, naturally shocked Washington, Guatemalans were not so startled. Since civilian rule supplanted a rigid military regime in 1966, Communist and right-wing terrorists have killed some 2,000 people in their running crossfire.

North Korea

8. 2 **"AN ACT OF WAR":** In the wintry waters of the Sea of Japan, 26 miles off the inhospitable coastline of North Korea, the 906-ton U.S.S. *Pueblo* went routinely about her tasks as an electronic scavenger. She sampled the water around her with bottles strung from her sides, and listened for submarines. She sniffed the skies above with the thickets of antennas that bristle from her superstructure, and scooped up every electronic signal for miles around. It was noon, Korea time, when a Soviet-built North Korean torpedo boat bore down on the *Pueblo*. Commander Lloyd M. Bucher, 40, was not overly disturbed. Harassment is one of the hazards of electronic snooping, and Skipper Bucher had expected to be buzzed by MIGs and bugged by surface craft when he began his month-long tour off the North Korean coast nearly two weeks earlier.

Using international signal flags, the PT boat signaled: "Heave to or I will open fire." The *Pueblo* replied: "I am in international waters." An hour later, three more North Korean vessels came slashing in from the southwest. "Follow in my wake," signaled one of the small vessels. The Korean boats took up positions on the *Pueblo's* bow, beam and quarter. Two MIG jets screamed in and began circling off the American vessel's starboard bow. Still, Bucher kept his cool. It was only when one of the Korean PT boats rigged its fenders—rubber tubes and rope mats to cushion impact—and began backing toward the *Pueblo's* bow that Bucher realized what was happening; in the bow of the PT boat stood an armed boarding party. "These guys are serious," the skipper radioed his home port in Japan.

As the Koreans swarmed aboard, U.S. Navymen feverishly set fire to the files, dumped documents, shredded the codes, and did their valiant best to wreck the super-secret electronic gear with axes, sledge hammers and hand grenades. In the process, apparently, one sailor's leg was blown off and three others were injured. At 1:45 p.m., the *Pueblo* radioed that the North Koreans were aboard. Twenty-five minutes later, she reported that she had been "requested" to steam into Wonsan harbor. At 2:32 p.m., barely 2½ hours after the first Communist PT boat hove into view, came the *Pueblo's* last message. Bucher reported that he was "going off the air."

To most Americans, it seemed unbelievable that a U.S. vessel could be brazenly held up and taken captive on the high seas. Nothing remotely like it had happened since 1807, during the Napoleonic wars, when a British man o' war overtook the U.S.S. *Chesapeake,* searched her for deserters and shanghaied four seamen. In his first comment on the capture, Secretary of State Dean Rusk called it "a matter of the utmost gravity." Later, he termed it an "act of war."

THE COMMANDER: A tough, 5-ft. 10-in 195-pounder, Lloyd ("Pete") Bucher strikes one of his closest friends, Navy Lieut. Commander Alan Hemphill, as "a very patriotic person. Today it doesn't seem fashionable to believe in God, country, Mother and apple pie, but Pete does, and he isn't embarrassed to tell people about it." That was one reason why his friends scoffed when Pyongyang radio broadcast a patently fake confession by Bucher. "If Pete Bucher said anything to the North Koreans beyond his name, rank and serial number," said Hemphill, "you can bet it wouldn't be something that would be printable."

The "confession," delivered in a strangled voice, was in the dialectic pidgin prose favored by Communist writers. At one point, it claimed that the CIA promised "a lot of dollars would be offered to the whole crew members of my ship and particularly I myself would be honored" for a good job. Another sample: "I have no excuse whatsoever for my criminal act as my ship intruded deep into the territorial waters of the Democratic People's Republic of Korea and was captured by the naval patrol crafts of the Korean People's Army in their self-defense action while conducting the criminal espionage activities. My crime committed by me and my men is entirely indelible."

When Rose Bucher heard a garbled tape of the commander supposedly reading the confession, she declared: "That is not my husband's voice. The inflections and the sounds were not his." An obvious conclusion from the slurred speech was that Bucher had been drugged.

Captain Bucher. The "Pueblo" skipper makes an odd "confession."

Premier Kim Il Sung. His zodiac doesn't give him much time.

A NEW BELLIGERENCE: Dramatic and dangerous as it was, the seizure of the U.S.S. *Pueblo* last week was only the latest and loudest thunderbolt from a long-gathering storm of North Korean belligerence. Under Premier Kim Il Sung, a tough, Soviet-trained soldier, the North has become increasingly frustrated by its place in the Communist world. Moved by the desire to bolster his regime internally and win some international notice and prestige—plus his oft-stated desire to distract the U.S. from its role in Viet Nam—Kim has deliberately launched his country on a high-risk policy. The North has plenty of reason to feel frustrated. Its seven-year plan, due to end last year, failed to meet its goals and had to be extended—while South Korea's healthy economy was spurting ahead. Kim and his government failed in their efforts to disrupt the South Korean presidential elections last spring, watched with embarrassment while South Korea sent 46,000 men to fight its Communist allies in Viet Nam. And at 57, Kim is desperately anxious to see unification of North and South Korea realized before he reaches 61, the all-important year in a man's life cycle according to the Korean zodiac.

To that end, Kim set up subversion and terrorist schools in North Korea, where some 2,400 commandos are now being trained to infiltrate the South to start a guerrilla war. Last week, just two days before the *Pueblo's* seizure, North Korea made the most brazen incursion into South Korea to date. From its subversion camps, it dispatched 31 North Korean agents into the South in a meticulously planned attempt to assassinate South Korean President Chung Hee Park. Their orders: make their way into the Blue House residence of the President in Seoul, cut off Park's head and pitch it into the street. The North Koreans managed to get within several hundred yards of the Blue House before police sighted them and foiled the attempt.

RETURN OF THE "PUEBLO'S" CREW: What began as a bizarre incident on the high seas last January came to an end last week after an equally bizarre series of diplomatic maneuvers. Held captive in North Korea for eleven months, the crew members of the surveillance ship U.S.S. *Pueblo* were suddenly released and flown home to the U.S. Led by Commander Lloyd Bucher, who looked a decade older than his 41 years, the 82 crew members boarded two giant transports near Seoul for the long flight to San Diego, where the Navy had assembled their families from all over the U.S. Landing on the day before Christmas, the crewmen got some $200,000 in back pay and next day promptly unloaded some of it in the PX, opened especially for them despite the holiday.

Off and on, the crewmen spoke of their captivity. The North

Koreans had threatened and often beat the men in order to extract "confessions." At one point, said Bucher, "they threatened to commence shooting the most junior members of my crew." He added: "I was rarely beaten in the face because I was subjected to a lot of camera ordeals, and they wanted me to look at least presentable. But this didn't prevent them from caving in my ribs, or kicking me in the tailbone to the point where I was almost unable to walk."

Throughout the ordeal, said Bucher, "we were trying to tell you we'd been had." One crewman wrote his family that his captors were gentle people, the nicest he'd seen since his last visit to St. Elizabeths—which is a U.S. mental hospital in Washington, D.C. And the *Pueblo's* navigator, Lieut. Edward Murphy Jr., told of his success at befuddling a North Korean army officer about where the ship had been. As a result of Murphy's trickery, North Korean charts gave coordinates for the *Pueblo's* position just before capture that would have put the ship variously 32 miles inland in North Korea, and six miles aground on the Japanese island of Kyushu—400 miles from the spot where the *Pueblo* was captured.

Before and during the boarding, the Koreans opened fire, wounding Bucher and felling ten crewmen, one of whom died in North Korea of his wounds. The U.S. crew desperately tried to destroy the highly classified equipment and documents aboard but, Bucher conceded, "truthfully we did not complete it." Bucher said he surrendered the ship "because it was nothing but a slaughter out there." It was not unusual for North Korean boats to harass U.S. spy ships and then suddenly vanish, so Bucher felt no particular concern when they first appeared on the day of the seizure. He also had orders not to uncover his three .50-cal. machine guns; there was thus no way to fight back.

Mexico

27 **CAUSE FOR THE REBELS:** Next month's Olympic games are the first to be held in a Spanish-speaking country, the first in Latin America, and the first in a developing nation. They are also Mexico's first big opportunity to put its stable prosperity on in-

ternational display. But a two-month-old strike by Mexico's normally docile university students is threatening to spoil that triumph.

Last week President Gustavo Díaz Ordaz ordered the army to end the strike by taking over the National University campus on the outskirts of Mexico City.

The action shattered a 40-year tradition of university autonomy. As armored cars rumbled onto the almost-deserted campus, several thousand soldiers fanned out and arrested the first 500 students they could find. They also seized 34 professors. When other students demonstrated against the invasion, riot cops cracked down with billy clubs, tear gas and nausea gas, clapped another 500 demonstrators in jail. Thousands of students retreated to the campus of the huge Polytechnic School. It was the second time the government had given its student rebels a cause. The riots started in July, when city *granaderos,* or riot cops, quelled a fight among prep-school boys and briefly occupied one of the school buildings. When the students protested, paratroopers moved in with tanks, armored cars and bazookas. They temporarily stopped the riots, but at the price of turning most of Mexico's students against them.

ONCE MORE WITH VIOLENCE: The cast was familiar: an immovable government pitted against students suddenly intoxicated with their own force. What was different about last week's cops-and-students scenario was that Mexico City's antagonists did their arguing with guns. Casualty counts were treated as practically state secrets. But in a week of rioting, sniping and sporadic shootings, the toll reached at least eight and possibly 18 dead, with perhaps a hundred wounded on both sides, and more than 2,000 arrested. For his part, dedicated, aloof President Gustavo Díaz Ordaz grimly vowed "to do whatever is our duty, however far we are obliged to go," to protect his country's good name and, presumably, the Olympics tourist trade.

Outwardly, the students were protesting against government repression and demanding redress for a growing list of grievances, particularly against the heavyhanded riot cops. "In actuality," declared a student leader, "we are testing the structure of the country. We want to awaken the need for change."

T. 11 **LA NOCHE TRISTE:** There was no warning, beyond ominous arcs of green flares overhead. In Mexico City's Plaza of the Three Cultures, a student speaker had urged his 6,000 listeners to "please go home after this meeting is over. We do not believe in useless bloodshed." Suddenly, from one corner of the plaza, the troops appeared. They formed a cordon around the crowd and moved in—shooting and bayoneting as they went. A 60-year-old woman was bayoneted in the back; a 13-year-old boy died with a bayonet wound in the head. Others were shot at such close range that hospital attendants found powder burns on their clothes. As some in the crowd fled in panic and others dived to the ground, student snipers opened fire on the troops from surrounding apartments. For ten minutes, massive gunfire reverberated through the plaza, and sporadic gunfire continued for another hour. In all, at least 33 civilians and one soldier died, at least 500 were wounded, and 1,650 people were arrested.

Thus in *la noche triste,* or the sad night as it was immediately named, Mexico City's students and the government reached a tragic climax of the quarrels that began last July. It was at least partly the result of a miscalculation. The students had planned a mass march to one of their campuses occupied by the army, but called it off at the last moment when they heard there were troop concentrations along the route. However, the army, under strict orders to crush the demonstrations at any cost, moved in anyway.

It was a classic case of overreaction. Mexico's students are neither hard-core revolutionaries of the Paris model nor U.S.-style dropouts from society. What they do have in common with students everywhere is disenchantment with the Establishment.

Mexico's government is more established than most, and the all-powerful *Partido Revolucionaro Institucional* suffers from the arteriosclerosis of absolute power held too long. While proclaiming the high ideals of revolution embodied in the constitution of 1917, it has turned increasingly to the power of the army to put down revolts in the impoverished countryside and to quell demonstrations of dissent. As one student leader puts it: "The constitution has been violated more times than a Parisian streetwalker."

Until the shooting last week, most students seemed almost

as anxious as their government not to spoil the scene for the Olympic summer games that open this week. The government, after crushing the demonstrators, began rounding up student leaders.

On the day following *la noche triste,* the International Olympic Committee decided that the games will go on, since "we have been assured that nothing will interfere with the peaceful entry of the Olympic flame, nor with the competitions that follow." [The unrest eventually subsided in time for the Olympics. See Sport, page 186.]

Nigeria

Although it seemed to offer the greatest promise of any of the emerging African nations, Nigeria's future was flawed by deep animosities between some of its major tribes. After a massacre by government forces of Ibo tribesmen, the Ibos, who were concentrated in the eastern region, declared their independence of the central government in 1967 and set up the secessionist state of Biafra. The government then went to war against Biafra.

BEER WITH CYANIDE: During a full year of civil war in Nigeria, JULY the secessionist state of Biafra had banked more on winning the world's sympathy than a military victory. Last week the Biafrans had an undeniable claim to attention—and to pity. Malnutrition was killing off more Biafrans than the federal troops who occupy most of their land. Workers of international relief agencies reported that as many as 3,000 Biafrans a day were dying and that total deaths might reach 2,000,000 by the end of August. In villages that are nearly deserted, old men and women, along with sickly children, die quietly in their huts. At the missionary hospital in Emekuku, a mob of starving children gathers at the door. The hospital has room for only 100 of them; the strongest-looking children are taken in, and the least hopeful cases turned away. "This started out as an epidemic in March," says a London-trained Biafran doctor. "Now it is a catastrophe."

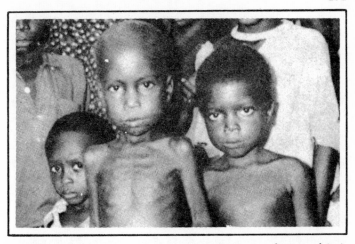

Children of Biafra. More Biafrans are dying of starvation than are slain in battle by enemy Nigerians.

The Nigerian military government, headed by Major General Yakubu Gowon, accuses the Biafrans of purposely allowing suffering among their own people for the sake of "waging psychological war and seeking diplomatic advantage."

The government points out that the Biafrans have turned down a plan to have the Red Cross ship food through federal territory to Biafra. Gowon insists on federal handling of any such shipments, and the Biafrans fear that his men would poison the food: they cite instances of beer laced with cyanide and powdered milk infected with bacteria. Even if Gowon allows the shipment, says Biafran Chief Justice Louis Mbanefo, "we would not touch it."

FIG. 23   **CHILDREN v. VULTURES:** Guided by burning flares, a transport plane dipped down out of the night over Biafra last week and landed with a shipment of condensed food for the secessionist state's starving population. On a country road a few miles away, relief workers held out bits of food to a group of hungry children. They ran, not knowing what to do with it. "We are going to have to teach a generation of children how to eat again," said a Canadian nurse. In a border town, the emaciated bodies of a brother and sister lay side by side in a rough cradle. Their eyes had been pecked out by vultures still circling overhead, waiting to attack a line of wasted bodies in a ditch outside of town.

KEEPING BIAFRA ALIVE: Perhaps the most important single reason for battered Biafra's continuing survival against the attacks of the Nigerian Federal Army is a steady infusion of French military aid. Although the French will not acknowledge their role, one of the worst-kept secrets of the war is the fact that armaments are flown into the secessionist state almost nightly from two former French colonies, Gabon and the Ivory Coast. TIME Correspondent James Wilde reports on the story from the Gabonese capital of Libreville:

"Everybody in this shabby capital knows about it, but few will talk. The unmarked planes, however, are there for all to see: four DC-4s, three DC-3s and a single Constellation, parked on the palm-lined seaside tarmac. Each afternoon, three or four planes taxi to the nearby military airfield for loading, then take off for Biafra at 6 p.m. sharp. They return around midnight, after the 900-mile round trip. Among the pilots flying the Biafra run are several Englishmen, ex-RAF types, moustached and bearded, who punctuate their clipped, casual conversation with dated bits of Battle of Britain slang like 'wack-o,' 'bang-on,' 'piece of cake.' All the pilots have one thing in common—they fly to get a stake. 'I'm only in it for the money,' one sad, balding man told me.

"Why are the French so insistent on keeping the war alive? A businessman here says the reason is Biafran oil: 'A million barrels of oil a day, or about one-third the production capacity of Kuwait. That kind of oil production is worth gambling for, even if the odds are against you.' In addition, Charles de Gaulle relishes any chance he finds to annoy the British, who are backing the Nigerian government. And the joy of it all is that France is not directly involved—or at least no one so far can prove that Paris is."

Peru

BELAÚNDE OUSTED: Five years ago, Peru's military leaders helped Fernando Belaúnde Terry become President, impressed by his promise of reform and a "new politics" for South America's fourth largest nation. Last week they brusquely reversed that judgment on the man who was once praised as Peru's Kennedyesque "architect of hope." Awakened, as he slept, by a burst of machine-gun fire, Belaúnde looked out of his window to find tanks outside the Presidential Palace in Lima. Some 50 Peruvian Rangers stormed into the palace and took Belaúnde into custody, bundled him off to the airport and a flight to Argentina and exile.

Belaúnde's fall once again raised the question of whether democracy can flourish in Latin America. Its prospects in Peru had seldom seemed more promising than when Belaúnde took over in 1963. Eager to aid Peru's impoverished peasants, he launched a whirlwind campaign to build houses, schools, rural airports and roads. Belaúnde poured money into education until, by this year, fully 25% of Peru's budget was being spent on schooling—probably the highest proportion for any country on the continent. He attempted agrarian reform and drew some 2,000,000 Peruvians, largely Indians, into projects for village improvement. Through it all, he traveled the country tirelessly.

From the outset, though, Belaúnde was at odds with the Peruvian Congress. His budgets rose from $400 million to more than $1 billion annually. But Belaúnde's programs were in any case beyond Peru's fiscal capacity. So he went abroad to borrow money to keep his plans afloat, until the foreign debt mounted to $900 million.

Then came the affair that caused the coup against him by the disgruntled armed forces. Belaúnde had rashly promised to expropriate the U.S.-owned International Petroleum Co. "the very day I am inaugurated." He did not, primarily because he did not want to antagonize the U.S. Government and potential foreign investors. But finally, this year, hopeful of improving his shaky political position, he did take over an IPC oilfield.

The deal negotiated with the company was not the usual sort of expropriation, however, and Peru's military leaders were furious that their counsel had not been sought in concluding a contract dealing with oil, a resource vital to the country's security. The coup last week was the military's reaction.

Portugal

TWILIGHT OF A DICTATOR: For nearly 40 years, António de Oli- SEPT veira Salazar has been the unusual dictator of an unfortunate land. An austere, almost monastic man who once taught economics, he has shunned publicity and raised few monuments to himself. Yet he built a tightly run, corporate state modeled closely on Mussolini's Italy, and his secret police have harshly repressed all dissent. He has ruled longer than any other European political leader in this century. Early this month, after injuring his head in a fall from a deck chair, Salazar, 79, underwent surgery for removal of a blood clot on his brain. Last week he lay near death after a massive stroke that left him in a coma and partly paralyzed.

Ex-Premier Salazar. Only his housekeeper could tell him what to do.

Premier Caetano. He is conservative, correct and Catholic.

Portugal is Western Europe's poorest nation. Its population numbers under 9,000,000, and its natural resources are scant. Before Salazar came to power, the land was in chronic economic chaos and political disarray. As Premier after 1932, Salazar squashed partisan quarreling with dictatorial measures and brought order to the economy. By the late 1930s he was flirting openly with fascism; he backed Franco against the Spanish Republicans. While Portugal remained neutral in World War II, Salazar at first sympathized with the Axis; when it became clear that that was the losing side, he granted bases in the strategically located Azores Islands to the U.S. and Britain.

Salazar has clung grimly to an increasingly costly empire; its colonies extend as far as Macao on the Chinese coast and Portuguese Timor in the East Indies. Tiny Portugal is cast in the unlikely role of Africa's last major colonial power. With 125,000 troops fighting three little-publicized wars in Angola, Mozambique and Portuguese Guinea, the country spends 40% of its budget on defense.

More dismal still, civil liberties are nearly unknown in Portugal. Press censorship has been in force almost continually since 1926. The number of emigrants and refugees voting against Salazar with their feet rose dramatically from 34,000 in 1961 to some 150,000 in 1966.

Salazar has rarely ventured outside Portugal, travels only occasionally even inside the country. Instead he has cloistered himself with his books and papers in his high-walled home behind Lisbon's National Assembly. "One cannot entertain the crowd and govern them all at the same time," he once insisted. He never married. Doña Maria da Piedade Caetano, 73, for more than 40 years his housekeeper, organized his routine and became known, only half-jokingly, as the one person who could tell him what to do. Last week the Portuguese were floundering because, for the first time in almost 40 years, there was no one to tell them what to do. Salazar had never designated a successor.

CT. 4 **END OF AN ERA:** "For a long period, the country grew accustomed to being governed by a man of genius, but from now on it must adapt itself to being governed by men like other men." With those words, Marcello Caetano, a longtime associate of Portuguese Dictator António de Oliveira Salazar, last week became Premier of Portugal, ending 36 years of Salazar rule. Even as the new Premier was sworn in, Salazar clung to life. But the 79-year-old dictator had been in a coma for ten days, and his doctors had informed President Américo Deus Rodrigues Tomás that he would never recover sufficiently to resume office. Faced with a serious drift in government affairs and rumors that the military might step in, Tomás finally called on Caetano to form a government.

Caetano, 62, is a Lisbon law professor and, like Salazar, he is conservative, correct and Catholic. But in some respects, Caetano presents a sharp contrast. He is married and has four grown children; has traveled widely; speaks French, reads English and has a continuing interest in cultural and intellectual developments. In his first policy statement, the new Premier promised both fidelity to the Salazar legacy and a new direction for the nation's life. He reaffirmed his predecessor's basic policies of holding onto Portugal's colonies and keeping dissent well under control at home. But at the same time he said that his regime would seek greater communication with the people.

Russia

OFF WITH THE MASK: "A wild mockery, unthinkable in the JAN. 20th century." That is how one young Russian, Pavel Litvinov, the grandson of ex-Soviet Foreign Minister Maxim Litvinov, described the trial in Moscow last week of four young intellectuals accused of anti-Soviet agitation. In a show of defiance not seen for years in the Soviet Union, members of the country's educated elite challenged the government's case. Several petitions were circulated, demanding "a full public airing" at the trial.

Crowds gathered outside the courtroom, yelling, shoving and needling security guards. But Soviet justice pays scant heed to public opinion. After a five-day closed trial, the judge sentenced the three men and a woman to labor camps for terms ranging from one to seven years.

The four—Aleksandr Ginzburg, 31, Yuri Galanskov, 29, Aleksei Dobrovolsky, 29, and Vera Lashkova, 21—were accused of editing and printing manuscripts critical of Communist life with the aid of an émigré organization devoted to the overthrow of the Soviet government. Arrested last January, they were in jail for a year before their trial began. Outside the courthouse, in temperatures that reached 50 below zero, protesters crowded against police barricades and dashed from door to door through the swirling snow, only to be turned away because they lacked official passes. One of the main protesters was a balding but erect Soviet general in his 60s who circulated petitions among the assemblage, brandished his cane at a policeman who took his picture. "I'm not afraid of little boys!" shouted Major General Pyotr Grigorenko, who was fired by ex-Premier Khrushchev for protesting "lack of freedom" in the Soviet Union. "I shed blood for this country."

H 22 **BOREDOM & THE FIVE-DAY WEEK:** As part of its celebration of the 50th anniversary of the Revolution last year, the Soviet government announced that Russian workers would still work the same 41 hours they had been working, but would compress them into five instead of six days and take two days off. The plan has one obvious advantage: it meant that Russia's work force of 110 million could have an extra day of leisure without stunting production. Last week Pravda announced that the five-day week has become as much a curse as a blessing. Short-stocked Muscovites, who have been used to shopping on weekends, set up such a howl when stores started closing down for two days that the city council recently ordered Sunday reopenings for some grocery stores, shoe-repair shops and department stores. The two-day weekend has also been adopted by subway stations, clinics, state banks and libraries, frustrating everyone from moviegoers to Russia's 25 million adult education students. Even more serious, in the long run, is Russia's shortage of facilities for leisure, such as bowling alleys and coffeehouses. Pravda somewhat lamely exhorted the growing number of bored workers, who tend to get on each other's nerves when thrown together for two days, to "mobilize their own inventiveness." So far, much of the leisure has been liquid. According to an article in Literaturnaya Gazet, the first effect of the new work week was a 25% jump in Moscow vodka sales.

T. 18 **APPLYING A CZARIST REMEDY:** By almost any reckoning, the five defendants in a Moscow trial last week could expect severe sentences. They had been arrested seven weeks ago in, of all places, Moscow's Red Square, where they had dared to unfurl banners saying "Hands off Czechoslovakia!" and "Shame on the Invaders!" Furthermore, two of the defendants were acknowledged leaders of the Soviet Union's growing intellectual dissent: Pavel Litvinov, the 31-year-old physicist grandson of

Stalin's Foreign Minister, and Mrs. Larisa Daniel, the wife of the imprisoned writer Yuli Daniel [who had been convicted of treason in 1966 after certain of his works were published abroad without official permission]. To make matters even worse, all five defendants not only refused to plead guilty to the charges of slandering the Soviet Union but even insisted that the KGB (secret police) had violated their rights of freedom of assembly and speech guaranteed in the Soviet constitution.

In such circumstances, the judge's verdict against the three leading dissenters was surprisingly mild. Instead of imposing the usual Soviet sentence of imprisonment for convicted dissenters, the court elected to apply an old Czarist remedy nowadays mostly used for minor offense: exile.

Pavel Litvinov and Mrs. Daniel. For slandering the Communist regime, they receive an old Czarist punishment: exile.

Litvinov was banished for five years to a remote area, probably in Siberia. Mrs. Daniel was given four years. A third, Moscow Philologist Konstantin Babitsky, 32, was sentenced to three years in exile. "You may be sure," a court spokesman told foreign newsmen, "that they will not be sent to a health resort."

Even so, the three were far better off than the two other defendants: Vadim Delone, a 21-year-old poet and student, was sentenced to 34 months in a labor camp, and Vladimir Dremlyuga, 26, an unemployed worker, was given the maximum three-year sentence at hard labor. The relative mildness of the three sentences seemed to indicate that the Soviet leaders at present have no desire to make martyrs of Russia's leading dissenters, particularly not of one so prominent as the grandson of a Foreign Minister.

"Freedom is important to all of us," Litvinov had told the court. "In a large socialist country like this, the freer each one of us is, the better it will be for all of us." Said Vadim Delone, the poet who received a labor-camp sentence: "For three minutes on Red Square, I felt free. I am glad to take your three years for that."

MILESTONES

BORN: To Lynda Bird Johnson Robb, 24, and Major Charles S. Robb, 29, currently on duty in Viet Nam with the 1st Marine Division: a girl, their first child, and President Johnson's second grandchild; in Bethesda, Md.

DIVORCED: Jane Russell, 47, bosomy star of the 1940s and '50s; and Bob Waterfield, 48, former quarterback of the Los Angeles Rams; on grounds of mental cruelty (Jane said he was "cold to everyone except my mother, and she was only around during Thanksgiving and Christmas"); after 25 years of marriage, three adopted children; in Los Angeles.

DIED: Franchot Tone, 63, longtime movie star whose off-camera tiffs sometimes overshadowed his considerable acting ability; of lung cancer; in Manhattan. Suave son of a wealthy industrialist, Tone moved quickly from lead roles on Broadway to Hollywood, where he made 53 films.

DIED: Tallulah Bankhead, 65, the iridescent and irrepressible empress of show business, whose gravel-throated cry of "Daaahling!" was part of the language for nearly half a century; of pneumonia; in Manhattan. Lavish beyond redemption, garrulous beyond recall, Tallulah chain-smoked, talked and caroused like a longshoreman. She gleefully admitted: "I'm as pure as the driven slush."

DIED: Paul Whiteman, 76, pop conductor who for two generations filled dance floors, concert halls and the airwaves with his "symphonic jazz"; of a heart attack; in Doylestown, Pa. Trained in the classics on the viola, yet fascinated with jazz's "abandon," Pops Whiteman took chances on new music (Gershwin's *Rhapsody in Blue*) and new musicians (Tommy Dorsey, Jack Teagarden), but his staple was rich, smooth orchestration that kept his footlong baton in motion until he retired in 1961.

$$\boxed{\textbf{SPORT}}$$

WHAT PRICE NOW?: The grey colt was a son of the great Native MAY Dancer, but he had chronically "mushy" (swollen) ankles, and it seemed he might never get to the races. So Owner Peter Fuller decided to get rid of him. He changed the horse's name from A.T.'s Image (after Fuller's father, former Massachusetts Governor A. T. Fuller) to Dancer's Image, and put him up for auction. The bidding reached $25,000, stopped—and, just as the gavel was about to fall, Fuller had a change of heart. After bidding $26,000 himself, he paid the auctioneer's 10% commission and took the animal back.

That was a year ago. Twice since then, Fuller has come close to selling Dancer's Image—for $500,000 and $1,000,000. Each time he held off. The colt's ankles were still so bad that he had to stand for hours in buckets of ice to reduce the swelling, but he was winning races anyway. Fuller finally decided to take a big gamble, enter the horse in the Kentucky Derby, and pray that his ankles held up. Last week, with one of the most stirring stretch drives in Derby history, Owner Fuller's gimpy grey won the 94th running of the famed race, and the question was : what price Dancer's Image now?

Name it—considering the race he ran. Ridden by Bobby Ussery, Dancer's Image broke tardily, was running dead last when the 14-horse field pounded into the backstretch. Only on the final turn did Dancer's Image really begin to run. With Jockey Ussery merely clucking to him, he rushed up along the rail, caught Forward Pass and drew away to win by 1½ lengths. The victory was worth $122,600 to Owner Fuller, 10% of which went to Ussery—who collected a similar prize last year aboard Proud Clarion and is the first jockey in 66 years to win the Derby twice in a row.

DRUG AT THE DERBY: It was Saturday evening, and in a van MAY parked behind the barns at Churchill Downs, Laboratory Technician James Chinn performed his post-race chore of test-

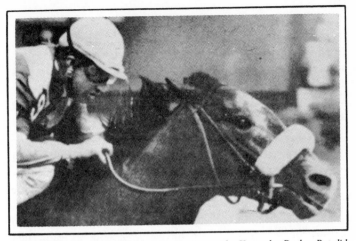

Dancer's Image, with Bobby Ussery up, winning the Kentucky Derby. But did they win? And can they collect?

ing urine specimens from 18 horses—the winners of all nine races run at the Louisville track that day, plus one other horse from each race, chosen by lot. When he added his test chemicals to the tubes, one specimen turned blue and then orange—the sign that some offending drug was present. After further analysis, Chinn identified the drug as "phenylbutazone and /or a derivative thereof." Nearly 48 hours later, the track stewards met, matched the specimen's number with that on a sealed envelope, and ripped the envelope open. Only then did they discover that the drugged horse was Dancer's Image, winner of the Kentucky Derby. Under Kentucky rules, the stewards had no choice but to disqualify Dancer's Image and place him last. (For betting purposes only, the original order of finish was allowed to stand, because win bets on Dancer's Image had already been paid off.)

Actually, Dancer's Image was not drugged at all, in the usual sense of race-track dopings. Phenylbutazone is an anti-inflammatory analgesic, a painkiller sold in the U.S. under the trade name Butazolidin and prescribed for such human ailments as arthritis, phlebitis, bursitis and tennis elbow. Athletes use it often: Sandy Koufax, the great Los Angeles Dodger pitcher, took "bute" to ease the ache in his arthritic throwing arm; Whitey Ford, the New York Yankee ace, swallowed six Butazolidin tablets before games that he pitched.

In horse racing Butazolidin is commonly used to relieve sore-legged horses—such as Dancer's Image, born with "mushy" ankles—and permit them to train without pain. But because unscrupulous trainers have used Butazolidin in order to vary the horses' performance and affect the betting odds, every major racing state now requires that no trace of Butazolidin remain in a horse's system on the day of a race.

Lou Cavalaris, the trainer of Dancer's Image and a 21-year veteran with an untarnished reputation, admitted last week that he gave his horse Butazolidin six days, or 144 hours, before the Derby. His story suggested that Dancer's Image, through some quirk in his physiological makeup, retained the drug for an extraordinarily long period of time—a tenuous possibility after reports from Kentucky indicated that his urine contained considerably more than a mere trace of the drug. "Someone," said Owner Fuller darkly, "may have gotten to the horse." He demanded an investigation and will get it this week when the stewards meet to interrogate everyone connected with the case. [In a ruling made several months later, the Kentucky Racing Commission declared that Dancer's Image had officially won the Derby but must forfeit the purse.]

GOD-GIVEN: He stands with a permanent lopsided slouch, his left shoulder 1 in. higher than his right. He peers out at the world through one clear contact lens and one that is blue-tinted; he is simply too lazy to replace the other half of either pair. He likes to read about J. Paul Getty, because he is so rich, and his hero is Frank Sinatra, "because he doesn't give a damn about anything." Every day in every way, Dennis Dale McLain, 24, works overtime to bolster his growing reputation as an antic oddball. But when he is not cracking wise or acting up, Denny McLain throws baseballs for the Detroit Tigers. In a summer when pitchers are dominating the big-league game, Denny is, in fact, dominating the pitchers. A few fans still call him "Super Flake" or "Mighty Mouth," but the sneers stop when he steps up on the mound. This season, as never before, Denny has been putting his muscle where his mouth is.

Last week, against the Minnesota Twins, he coasted to an 8-3 victory—his 28th of the year against only five losses. McLain has already surpassed the best single-season performances of Carl Hubbell, Bob Feller, Warren Spahn, Whitey Ford and

Sandy Koufax. No one has approached his performance in 16 years, and just two more victories will make him the first 30-game winner since Dizzy Dean turned the trick in 1934.

Although his arsenal includes a slider, a medium-speed curve and a jug-handle changeup as well as a fastball—all of which he can deliver either overhand, three-quarter-arm or sidearm—McLain's main assets are speed and control. Cuteness and cunning are foreign to him: he rarely wastes a pitch, and he does not try to sucker batters into swinging at bad balls. "Control is God-given," Denny claims. "Like a good arm. You don't develop it, and I thank God He gave me both."

T. 20 **NO. 30:** Detroit's Denny McLain achieved his pinnacle last week. By beating the Oakland Athletics, 5-4, he became the first pitcher to win 30 games in a single season since Dizzy Dean in 1934.

KING ARTHUR: "I am a sociological phenomenon," says Arthur Ashe Jr. He is a great deal more than that. Last week, on the center court at Forest Hills' West Side Tennis Club—the same stuffy club that once barred Ralph Bunche from membership—the son of a Negro playground guard from Richmond, Va., established himself as the No. 1 star in one of the most segregated U.S. sports. In a five-set match, Ashe, 25, defeated blond Tom Okker of The Netherlands, for the U.S. Open championship. His victory made him the first amateur to win a major open event, the first Negro ever to capture the U.S. men's singles crown, and the first American in 13 years to win his country's most prestigious tennis title.

T. 27 **"THANKS FOR WHAT?":** Who says pitchers are heartless? Not Yankee Slugger Mickey Mantle. It was the top of the eighth one day last week, and Detroit Tiger Ace Denny McLain was coasting to his 31st victory on a five-run lead. Up stepped Mantle. Mickey took a called strike, fouled off two more pitches, and then signaled with his bat for Denny to put the ball belt-high, where he likes it. Denny served it up, and Mick lined the ball into the upper deck for his 535th home run. As he rounded the bases, he moved past Jimmy Foxx into third place in the alltime homer derby, behind Babe Ruth (714) and Willie Mays (585). "Be sure to tell Denny thanks," said Mantle afterward. "Thanks for what?" asked McLain when he got the message. "I make mistakes all the time."

MASTER ON THE MOUND: One battle does not a campaign make, OCT nor a single game a World Series. But for a record crowd of 54,-692 at St. Louis' Busch Stadium—and millions more who watched on TV—last week's 1968 Series opener between the hometown Cardinals and the Detroit Tigers settled one question, at least for the moment: Who is the best pitcher in baseball? Going into the game, Detroit's Denny McLain fairly oozed confidence. "I want to humiliate the Cardinals," said Denny, whose regular-season record of 31-6 makes him the big leagues' biggest winner in 34 years. "If that's the way he feels, he'll get his chance," retorted the Cardinals' Bob Gibson, 32, whose 22 victories this season included 13 shutouts.

Humiliation was the word. But it was Gibson who did the humiliating, with a virtuoso performance unmatched in the 65-year history of the Series. For McLain, the contest was over quickly; uncharacteristically erratic, he walked three batters, gave up three hits and three runs, and retired to the showers after five innings. Gibson shrewdly mixed up his pitches, alternating sliders and slow curves with his "hummer." By the end of the eighth inning, 14 Tigers had gone down on strikes. When Gibson took the mound in the ninth, only one strikeout

Bob Gibson in the Series opener against Detroit. In the Year of the Pitcher, the Cards' slick righthander is one of the best.

stood between him and Sandy Koufax's World Series record. He got that, and more, and stalked off the field with a five-hit 4-0 victory and a new Series mark of 17 strikeouts.

The Tigers were awed, but not about to give up. "We'll be back tomorrow," promised Manager Mayo Smith. And back they were, pounding four Cardinal pitchers for 13 hits and three home runs, staking Lefthander Mickey Lolich to an 8-1 victory that evened up the Series at one game apiece. Two days later, in Detroit, the Cards unlimbered their own big bats, cracking 2 homers and winning 7-3. Curiously enough, especially since they now were trailing in the Series 2-1, the Tigers actually seemed cheerful about the prospect of facing Gibson in the fourth game. "Let's see him do it again, in our park," challenged First Baseman Norm Cash. Added McLain: "Gibson's had his turn. Now it's mine."

18 **PITCHER'S DAY:** With four games of the 1968 World Series out of the way (St. Louis had won the fourth game, 10-1), the St. Louis Cardinals had Detroit's Tigers down, three games to one, and St. Louis' peerless pitcher Bob Gibson had humiliated Detroit's 31-game winner, Denny McLain, not once, but twice. And by the middle of the fifth game, the Tigers still looked like sure losers. Portly Mickey Lolich, their only Series winner, was laboring on the short end of a 3-2 score; he seemed ready to take the long walk to the showers when he got an unexpected reprieve from the Cards' Lou Brock, justly famed as the National League's most expert baserunner. Heading for home with a sure run, Brock unaccountably failed to slide under the high, late throw. He came in standing up, crashed into Catcher Bill Freehan and was tagged easily. The rally that might have ended the Series was snuffed out. Two innings later, Detroit scored three runs, and Lolich, growing stronger with each pitch, blanked the Cards the rest of the way for a 5-3 Detroit victory.

Back to St. Louis went the Series. And McLain wasted little time vindicating himself; he held the Cards to nine hits and one run while the fired-up Tigers pummeled seven St. Louis pitchers for 13 runs. Suddenly, it was game No. 7—Gibson v. Lolich, winner take all. Once more Mickey was good, but Gibson was great. He struck out seven of the first 23 men he faced, allowed only three hits and no runs. Then Mickey was given another unexpected gift, this time by St. Louis' Curt Flood, generally accepted as one of the game's best outfielders. In the top of the seventh inning, with two Tigers on base, Detroit's Jim Northrup hit a deep but routine line drive to centerfield. Flood momentarily lost the ball against the white-shirted crowd, then stumbled and watched it sail over his head for a triple. Two runs scored, and the Tigers went on to win 4-1, as Lolich, in workmanlike fashion, served the Cardinals nothing but junk for the last three innings.

In the Year of the Pitcher, the award for the Series' most valuable player went, appropriately enough, to three-game-winner Lolich. No one approved more heartily than Mickey Lolich himself: "Everybody mentions heroes on the team, and Lolich has always been second or third best. Well, today was my day, and I'm glad it came."

BLACK COMPLAINT: "Faster, Higher, Stronger" is the motto OCT of the Olympic Games. "Angrier, nastier, uglier" better describes the scene in Mexico City last week as Sprinters Tommie Smith and John Carlos, two disaffected black athletes from the U.S., put on a public display of petulance that sparked one of the most unpleasant controversies in Olympic history and turned the high drama of the games into theater of the absurd.

Smith had just won the 200-meter dash in a record-breaking 19.8 sec. Carlos, his bearded teammate from San Jose State College, had finished third. Together, they turned up for the awards ceremony shoeless, wearing knee-length black stockings and a black glove on one hand (the right for Tommie, the left for John). Along with Australia's Peter Norman, the second-place finisher, they mounted the victory pedestal to receive their medals. Then, as the U.S. flag was raised and the band struck up *The Star-Spangled Banner,* the two black athletes bowed their heads and raised their gloved hands in a clenched-fist salute. A wave of boos rippled through the spectators as the pair left the field. Smith and Carlos responded by making interesting gestures at the stands. At a press conference later, the two men explained that the black stockings represented poverty; the black fists meant black power and black unity. Said Smith: "We are black and proud to be black. White America will say 'an American won,' not 'a black American won.' If it had been something bad, they would have said 'a Negro.' "

Embarrassed and angry, the U.S. Olympic Committee met for four hours, then issued a strong reprimand to Smith and Carlos, and apologies to the International Olympic Committee and the Mexican people. That might have ended the incident. But a month before the games opened, crusty old Avery Brundage, 81, perennial chairman of the I.O.C., had warned all competitors that no political demonstrations would be permitted. Unless U.S. officials actually punished Smith and Carlos, the I.O.C. threatened to expel the whole U.S. team. Reluctantly, the U.S. committee suspended the two athletes from the team and ordered them to leave the Olympic Village.

RECORDS ALL AROUND: The saddest thing about the ruckus raised by Tommie Smith and John Carlos was that it dulled the lustre of a superlative track and field meet in which the U.S. once again demonstrated that it is the world's best. *The Star-Spangled Banner* was played so often that it began to sound like *The Stars and Stripes Forever.* As they kept the band working, Americans set record after record. Texas' strapping Randy Matson won the shotput and set an Olympic record of 67 ft. 10¼ in.; California's Bob Seagren soared to another new Olympic mark by clearing 17 ft. 8½ in. in the pole vault. In the short dashes, California's Jim Hines clocked 9.9 sec. in the men's 100 meters to tie his own pending world record, and Georgia's Wyomia Tyus won the women's 100 in 11 sec. flat. Then, in the field events, Al Oerter hurled the discus 212 ft. 6½ in., five feet farther than he had ever thrown it in his life. He set a Games record and became the first trackman ever to win this event in four successive Olympics. Then Bob Beamon, 22, black, bearded, and a precocious newcomer, leaped 29 ft. 2½ in. on his very first try, to smash the world long-jump record by an improbable margin of almost 2 ft. Beamon charged down the runway and powered off the board, hands and arms flapping like a giant awkward bird. His body jack-knifed, his legs spread-eagled before he slammed into the pit. When the scoreboard flashed the result, the crowd gasped with disbelief. Beamon sank to his knees, hands clasped in prayer. "I was thanking that man up there," he explained, "for letting me hit the ground right here."

THE ORIGINAL IDEAL: Of all Olympic competition, the decath- NO lon most closely reflects the original Greek ideal of all-round athletic excellence. An entire track and field meet in miniature, its ten events in two days add up to the toughest individual test of speed, stamina, strength and spirit ever devised. The man who wins the Olympic decathlon well deserves to be known as the finest athlete in the world. That man last week was William Anthony Toomey, a 29-year-old schoolteacher from Santa Barbara, Calif., who not only captured the gold medal but set an Olympic record in the process.

Toomey modestly insists that "behind every good decathlon man there's a good doctor," and indeed the demands of the brutal competition are enough to strain the strongest body. Toomey had a pulled hip muscle for which he was being treated with cortisone. Even so, in the first test, the 100-meter dash, Toomey hit the tape in 10.4 sec., good enough for 959 points under the complicated decathlon scoring system. Then, a soaring 25-ft. 9¾-in. long jump, best of Toomey's career, gave him another 994 points and kept him in the lead. After that, a poor 45-ft. 1¼-in. shotput ("That really depressed me") and a disappointing 6-ft. 4¾-in. high jump dropped him to second behind East Germany's Joachim Kirst. Next came the grinding 400-meter run, and after ten straight hours of competition, Toomey somehow managed to sprint the distance in 45.6 sec. It was the fastest time ever recorded in the decathlon—only 1.8 sec. off the new world record—and it put him back in the lead as the first day ended. Weary, ready for dinner and bed, Bill started to leave the field, only to find that he had one more trial to pass—the urine test. Checkups for dope are now mandatory in the Olympics, and for decathlon athletes the tests were given at the end of each day. Because he was totally dehydrated, Toomey had to hang around the stadium drinking liquids until he could supply officials with a urine sample.

The second day's competition began with the 110-meter hurdles, and Bill ran it in 14.9 sec., .3 sec. slower than his best. His discus throw, 143 ft. 3½ in., was "near what I wanted," but the pole vault almost proved a disaster. "I just about had a heart attack when I missed the opening height on my first two attempts," said Toomey. He pulled himself together to vault 13 ft. 9½ in., tying his own record. A 206-ft. ½-in. javelin throw kept him in first place, a bare 61 points ahead of

West Germany's Kurt Bendlin, who had moved into second with a monumental heave of 247 ft. 5 in.

Now the gold medal was riding on the last event, the 1,500-meter run. If he could beat Toomey by 10 sec. or so, Bendlin could still win. But he never came close. Gasping in the thin air, every muscle rubbery with fatigue, Toomey led all but a few strides of the way and drove to victory by 30 yds. Final score for the ten events: Toomey 8,193; Bendlin 8,064—a total that dropped the West German to third, behind his countryman Hans-Joachim Walde. "That was the worst competition I've ever been in," said Toomey. "I've never had to endure anything so intense. They shouldn't call this the Olympic Games. It's not a game out there."

PARADE TO THE PEDESTAL: Not since Cortés gave Guatemozin a hotfoot in an effort to make him reveal where the Aztecs kept their gold has Mexico been invaded by such a determined band of treasure hunters as the U.S. Olympic team. The medal score told the story: by week's end, with only a handful of events still to go, the U.S. had collected 42 gold, 26 silver and 30 bronze for a total of 98 medals, compared with Runner-up Russia's 65, only 21 of which were gold.

MILESTONES

DIVORCED: By Mia Farrow, 23, wispy ex-star of TV's *Peyton Place,* who is now making it big in movies (latest: *Rosemary's Baby*); Frank Sinatra, 52; on grounds of cruelty and incompatibility; after two years of marriage, no children; in Juarez, Mexico.

DIED: Norman Thomas, who had spent most of his 84 years tugging at America's lapels, beseeching it to share his vision of better things. He espoused a variety of socialism that was questioning rather than doctrinaire, Christian rather than Marxist, democratic rather than totalitarian. Much of what he sought in social welfare legislation was eventually adopted by those who once recoiled from his proposals. "The ultimate token of approval," he said with rueful satisfaction, "is that the Democrats and Republicans have stolen my thunder." Son of a Presbyterian minister, valedictorian of Princeton's class of 1905, six times Socialist candidate for President of the U.S., Norman Mattoon Thomas made an historic mark. He died in his sleep last week in a Long Island nursing home.

THE THEATER

"PLAZA SUITE"—A comedy by Neil Simon is a small body of FE
plot surrounded by laughter. He and Director Mike Nichols
are Broadway's most consummate mirthologists. Playgoers at
Plaza Suite don't have their ribs merely tickled, but tackled—
by Simon, Nichols and two other professionals in top form,
George C. Scott and Maureen Stapleton. The evening consists
of a trio of one-acters, all set in Manhattan's Plaza Hotel.
Each of the playlets concerns a middle-aged man (Scott) and
woman (Stapleton) who are at the end of something rather
than the beginning of anything.

Scott's triumph is *Visitor from Forest Hills,* a zany, wedding
tableau in which an irate father, pressed past mind and pocketbook, cannot budge his distraught daughter out of a locked
bathroom to the altar. Scott's countenance of epic frustration
is phenomenally funny: a middle-aged Lear confronted with a
thankless offspring. The evening's master treat, a carnival of
sight-and-sound gags, this skit shows how Simon and Nichols
can take a situation no bigger than a snowball and dislodge
an avalanche of hilarity.

"GEORGE M!"—One sure sign of a poor musical is that it con- AP
sists of all work and no play. The dancers pound the floor
boards like maniacal trip hammers. Sweat glazes the hero as
his arms flail, his eyes pop, and he tries to kick his toes into
the wings. To amplify the hollow book, microphones soup up
the sound till it becomes the aural equivalent of the medieval
ordeal by fire. *George M!*—the latest of the Broadway season's
unbroken string of execrable musicals—qualifies on all counts.
Essentially a family album of George M. Cohan's music, this
may be the only musical at which the audience comes into the
theater humming the songs. But the songs cannot carry the
show. Joel Grey tries to do that but the way his character has
been written forces him to exhibit either a cocky disdain for
others or an egomaniacal worship of self.

Joel Grey in "George M!" He plays the lead in the only musical at which the audience arrives humming the songs.

10 **"HAIR"**—This musical is a cross between a Dionysian revel and an old-fashioned revival meeting. The religion that *Hair* preaches, and often screeches, is flower power, pot and protest. Its music is pop-rock, and its dialogue is mostly graffiti. *Hair* is lavish in dispraise of all things American, except presumably liberty. The play itself borders on license by presenting a scene in which half a dozen members of the cast, male and female, face the audience in the nude. This tableau is such a dimly lit still life that it will leave most playgoers yawning.

On- and off-Broadway, this has been the year of naked truth. Paul Foster's *Tom Paine,* a phantasmagorial study of the revolutionary writer, has a sequence in which men and women whirl about shielded only by draperies that occasionally part to offer fleeting glimpses of pubic hair. Perhaps the boldest display of nudity occurred in Ed Wade's one-acter, *The Christmas Turkey.* In full light, and facing the audience, the unclothed heroine (Marti Whitehead) knelt on a table throughout the play as a symbol of passive white idealism. A fully dressed Negro, symbolizing angry black nationalism, devours her.

11 **"THE GREAT WHITE HOPE"** by Howard Sackler, is a sprawling, episodic semi-documentary that traces the rise and fall of Jack Johnson, the first Negro heavyweight champion of the world. In the play he is called Jack Jefferson, and James Earl Jones

roars through the role with the jungle magnetism and pride of a lion. From the time that Jefferson becomes champion, he appears to threaten and diminish the white world, in and out of boxing. Corrupt promoters begin scurrying around for a "great white hope" to restore racial supremacy. Full of arrogant self-regard and a casual contempt for blacks as well as whites, Jefferson all too easily stokes the hostility of his foes.

His subtlest and most infuriating affront is sexual. He loves a white girl, who lives and travels with him as his common-law wife. When Jefferson is convicted of a Mann Act charge, he jumps bail and flees to Europe. A hounded exile, he drifts from country to country, rejecting a standing offer to throw the championship fight in return for the commutation of his jail sentence. Broody, badgered and in a kind of psychic agony, he finally turns on his white woman as the symbol of all his woes and throws her out. In a sequence of tear-jerking melodrama she commits suicide. Cowed and crushed, Jefferson accedes to his arranged defeat in Havana.

The play has the aspect of a minor saga, but Edwin Sherin has directed it like a stampede: all decibels and no deftness. Either everyone shouts, or everyone postures in animated tableaux that look like posters left over from some social-protest movement of the '30s.

"PROMISES, PROMISES" is slick, amiable and derivative, a musical to remember other musicals by. No playgoer will feel gypped if he attends the show, nor will he miss a thing if he skips it. The plot line is derived from the Billy Wilder film *The Apartment,* which was far sharper in lancing U.S. sexual hypocrisy, and the structure of the show has been borrowed from *How to Succeed in Business Without Really Trying.* The evening is not so much viewed as *déjà vu'd.*

The musical's tall, gangling anti-hero, Chuck Baxter (Jerry Orbach), is an underling at Consolidated Life and looks suspiciously like a poor insurance risk. Commuting senior executives with one night of illicit in-town love on their agendas barter promises of future advancement for the use of his apartment. The book's comic tone is bland rather than pithy. The rhythms of the Burt Bacharach score sound like sporadic rifle fire, and aside from one melodic lament, *I'll Never Fall in Love Again,* the songs are interchangeably tuneless.

MUSIC

17   **HOLY FOOL:** "Hel-loooo, my dear friends," flutes the voice. Blowing kisses, fluttering his large, bony fingers and rolling his eyes, Tiny Tim skips onstage like Bea Lillie in drag: shoulder-length locks, tattersall sports jacket decorated with a sheriff's badge, plaid shirt and orange socks. Giggling, he takes the uke from its old cardigan wrapper. Plink-a-plank-a-plink. His thin, reedy tones soar into an unearthly falsetto, the vibrato voice quavering like a hummingbird's wings: "Come tiptoe through the tulips with me. . . . " In the audience his listeners are rapt, incredulous, amused—everything but indifferent. And no wonder. Tiny Tim is a gentle soul who happens to be the most bizarre entertainer this side of Barnum & Bailey's sideshow. Network television appearances and the recent release of his first record album have helped place him in a cultish tradition that goes back through Shakespeare's clowns all the way to the Roman circus—that of the holy fool. But holy papaya powder, who is fooling whom?

Tiny Tim: plaid shirt, orange socks and a voice like a hummingbird's wings.

Aretha Franklin. Lady Soul tells it like it is. Page 194.

SINGING IT LIKE IT IS: Has it got soul? Man, that's the question JUN
of the hour. If it has soul, then it's tough, beautiful, out of
sight. It passes the test of with-itness. But what *is* soul? "It's
like electricity—we don't really know what it is," says Singer
Ray Charles. "But it's a force that can light a room." The
force radiates from a sense of selfhood, a sense of knowing
where you've been and what it means. Where soul is really at
today is pop music. It emanates from the rumble of gospel
chords and the plaintive cry of the blues. It is compounded of
raw emotion, pulsing rhythm and spare, earthy lyrics—all suffused with the sensual, somewhat melancholy vibrations of
the Negro idiom. In all its power, lyricism and ecstatic an-
guish, soul is personified in a chunky, 5-ft. 5-in. girl of 26
named Aretha Franklin. She leans her head back, forehead
gleaming with perspiration, features twisted by her intensity,
and her voice pierces the hall:

Oh baby, what you done to me . . .
You make me feel, you make me feel, you make me feel
    like a natural woman.

"Tell it like it is," her listeners exhort, on their feet, clapping and cheering. She goes into a "holiness shout"—a
writhing dance derived from gospel services, all the while singing over the tumult. This is why her admirers call her Lady
Soul. But what really accounts for her impact goes beyond technique: it is her fierce, gritty conviction. She flexes her rich, cutting voice like a whip; she lashes her listeners. "Aretha's music
makes you sweaty, gives you a chill, makes you want to stomp
your feet," says Bobby Taylor, leader of a soul group called
Bobby and the Vancouvers. More simply, a 19-year-old Chicago fan named Lorraine Williams explains: "If Aretha says
it, then it's important."

Aretha grew up on the fringe of Detroit's Negro East Side.
Her mother deserted the family when Aretha was six and died
four years later, two shocks that deeply scarred the shy, with-
drawn girl. Aretha's father, the Rev. C. L. Franklin, was—
and is—pastor of Detroit's 4,500-member New Bethel Baptist
Church, where the preaching is so fiery that two nurses stand
by to aid overwrought parishioners. Through her father, Aretha became immersed in gospel music. And after her first solo

in church at the age of twelve, excited parishioners crowded around her father, saying, "Oh, that child can sure enough sing." Last year she won *Billboard's* citation as the nation's top female voice.

19   **DRUMMER BOY WITH A HORN**: Everybody remembers the name of the fellow who played Moses in the 1956 film remake of *The Ten Commandments*. Right. Charlton Heston. But who was that fellow with his bare back to the camera who played the drum while Charlton strode down the mountain with the tablets? He was a little nobody, a movie extra who just happened to have the kind of graceful dorsal muscles and shoulder blades the director was looking for. Herb Alpert has since become considerably more than a man who hires his own drummers. He is a major sound system.

As leading man with his own Tijuana Brass, Alpert has just wound up a U.S. tour that established the group as one of the top handful of pop road shows around. It is equaled only by the likes of Sinatra, Streisand and the Beatles when it comes to filling big halls. In Detroit, squealing teeny-boppers and grown women ran up and down the aisles, setting off a blitz of lights with their Instamatic cameras. In Laramie, Wyo., a woman clearly in her 80s came down the aisle and shouted, "Sock it to me, Herbie!"

What seems to please the crowds most is that Herb doesn't sock it at all. He silks it. No soul-searching stuff, no revolutionary developments—just pleasant music. The melodies are invariably simple affairs tootled forth in short staccato bursts by twin trumpets. The crackling, joyous blend of mariachi, Dixieland and cool rock appeals to the oldsters as much as Lawrence Welk does. But it is infinitely less square than Welk, and the kids dance to its classic ¼ beat with no complaints. Now, in a new two-story office building, an IBM 360 computer spends the day clacking out a record of royalties and other profits that will yield Alpert's various ventures a combined gross of $30 million this year. His six fellow performers will each earn between $50,000 and $100,000, making them most likely the highest-paid sidemen of all time.

FRIGID FAIL-SAFE: For all its growing missile prowess, the U.S. FEB still keeps squadrons of nuclear-armed B-52s constantly patrolling the skies within reach of Communist borders, both to respond to any nuclear attack and to act as a deterrent to one. In the course of their duties, on land and in the air, the B-52s have had twelve announced nuclear-weapons "mishaps," the most famous being the collision of a B-52 and a refueling tanker over Palomares, Spain, in 1966. Last week No. 13 occurred. One of the huge eight-engine bombers patrolling the Arctic stratosphere on an air-alert mission caught fire and headed for the U.S. Air Force Base at Thule, Greenland, to attempt an emergency landing. As smoke filled the cabin, the seven crewmen parachuted; all survived except the copilot, whose chute failed to open. Just 7½ miles short of Thule, the B-52 crashed on the rough ice pack of North Star Bay and exploded.

In Denmark, which has an agreement with the U.S. that nuclear-armed bombers will not use Greenland bases, students marched in the streets. The Russians predictably charged that the U.S. was endangering the whole world, and peace groups picketed and protested angrily. But the ordinary newspaper reader was troubled by a nagging question that recurs with every accident: Could the crash of a nuclear-armed plane set off a hydrogen explosion? The answer is no. An interlocking labyrinth of safety locks, switches and devices has prevented any of the "13 mishaps" from producing a full-scale "yield" detonation. Always unarmed except on presidential order, H-bombs are designed with a system of safeguards so painstakingly complex that the chances of an accidental nuclear blast are infinitesimal.

ICY SEARCH FOR HOT DEBRIS: On the frigid ice sheet 7 miles FEB. from Thule, Greenland, last week, members of an Air Force recovery team hunted for H-bomb parts and contaminated debris scattered by the crash of a B-52 SAC bomber last month. Living in 5-ft.-high igloos and plywood huts that are frozen—not nailed—together, the searchers often work in $-30°F$. temperatures and 35 m.p.h. winds that combine to produce an equivalent of $-100°F$. cold. Frostbite is a constant hazard, and flashlight batteries freeze into uselessness after ten minutes of exposure. Men returning from the crash site must be checked for radiation, have their garments vacuumed and their noses swabbed with cotton dabbed in alcohol—all part of the decontamination process.

On-the-spot tests have revealed negligible radioactivity. But to determine if any of the plutonium-uranuim 235 trigger or contaminated wreckage melted into—or even through—the 9-ft.-thick ice in the fire that followed the crash, technicians have taken ice-core samples that will be analyzed for radioactivity in U.S. and Danish labs. The Danish government has sent in its own team of scientists to study possible contamination of algae, fish, seals and walruses in the area, and to guard against the possibility of radioactive particles in products destined for human consumption.

115 **FANTASTIC SIGNALS FROM SPACE:** For a few electrifying days late last month, a spectacular rumor spread among U.S. scientists. British astronomers had detected signals so regular and pulsating so rapidly from four different regions in outer space that they might have been sent by intelligent beings. Last week, when details reached the U.S., the possibility that the pulsations had been artificially produced by an advanced civilization seemed remote. But even if the causes are natural, scientists on both sides of the Atlantic were in firm agreement that discovery of the pulsing signals, named "pulsars" by the British, was one of the major astronomical finds of recent times —perhaps equal in importance to the discovery of the nature of quasars [quasi-stellar sources] in 1963.

Getting a good fix on one of the signals, the excited astronomers calculated that it came from an object no more than 4,000 miles in diameter—about half the size of the earth— that was no more than a neighborly 200 light-years away. The signals occurred with breathtaking regularity, one every 1.337 seconds. "Our first thought," says one astronomer "was that this was another intelligence trying to contact us." The possibility was so intriguing to British astronomers that they began referring—only half jokingly—to their strange radio sources as "LGMs" (little green men). But two factors eventually persuaded them that the signals were not artificial: the subsequent location of three additional rapidly pulsating sources, and the lack of any evidence that the signals were being transmitted from a planet. "Multiplicity suggests a natural phenomenon," says Astronomer Anthony Hewish. "It would be stretching the imagination too far for all of them to be generated by intelligent beings." The Cambridge astronomers finally decided that the signals might be the natural oscillations of dying stars that had shrunk by gravitational contraction into white dwarfs—or into neutron stars, which theoretically could exist but have never actually been discovered.

BAD BEES OF BRAZIL: Eleven African queen bees and swarms APR of half-African drones and workers escaped from a São Paulo laboratory in 1957, and Brazil has been pained about it ever since. Imported because of their high honey productivity, the African bees were not intended to be released until they had their foul tempers bred out of them. But by 1965, the bees had bred, spread and were obeying their instinct to attack large animals without provocation. By the latest count, ten people, hundreds of cattle and horses, and whole flocks of chickens have been killed in unprovoked attacks by the queens' offspring. Dogs, cats, turkeys and pigs have died. Last month a swarm descended on a group of children playing in a park in Rio. Firemen had to fight them off with flamethrowers.

Measures are being taken to stop the spreading bees, but there is considerable doubt whether they can be halted before they spread northward through Colombia, Central America, Mexico and into the U.S. Spreading 200 miles a year, new queens establish new hives in rocks, hollow trees, high branches and low eaves. Now Edmundo Campello, secretary of agriculture for the state of Rio de Janeiro, has begun a new campaign. Importing Italian queen bees Campello plans to stage a series of apiarian palace coups. Wherever he can find a hive, he plans to kill the African queen and replace her with an already fertilized Italian. When new Italian queens, workers and drones are born, more Africans will be replaced until,

Campello hopes, the bad bees will be bred out. But Samuel E. McGregor, chief of the beekeeping research branch of the U.S. Department of Agriculture, is not optimistic. "I can't see much hope of stopping them from coming north," he says. "The chances are that they'll reach Panama in a few years and then come on to the U.S." McGregor believes that the long, cold winters of the U.S. snow belt would prove fatal to the Africans, but that they will probably survive and thrive in California and most of the Southeast.

T. 27 **RUSSIA'S RACE TO THE MOON:** The first important news of Russia's latest space venture came, as it has so often in the past, not from a Moscow spokesman but from a distinguished British scientist. Closemouthed Soviet scientists announced only that a spacecraft called Zond 5 had been launched into deep space from a parking orbit around the earth. But after Astronomer Sir Bernard Lovell trained his 250-ft. Jodrell Bank radio telescope on the receding craft and analyzed its signals, he told the world exactly what the Russians were trying to do. Zond's mission, he stated, was to fly around the moon and return for a safe landing on earth, a feat never before accomplished. If that was the plan, the Russians were understandably secretive. For the more ambitious the mission, the more embarrassing it would be to have to admit failure if anything went wrong. "A base canard," said a Soviet spokesman in response to Lovell's statement. Two days later, blandly ignoring their previous denial, the Soviets reported that Zond 5 had indeed flown around the moon. It carried out its "program of research in outer space," they said, and was continuing on its flight. The triumphant flight of Zond 5 left little doubt that the Russians are racing to send a manned flight around the moon ahead of the U.S.

T. 11 **A CHANCE TO BE FIRST:** "I believe this nation should commit itself to achieving the goal, before this decade is out, of landing a man on the moon and returning him safely to earth."— John F. Kennedy, May 25, 1961.

This week, still hopeful that they can achieve the goal set by President Kennedy but aware that time is fast running out, U.S. spacemen will begin their final lunar thrust as Astronauts Walter Schirra, Walter Cunningham and Donn Eisele are shot into orbit aboard Apollo 7 in the first manned flight of the spacecraft that will eventually carry astronauts to the moon.

"HAVING A BALL": If the lift-off last week seemed slow and laborious to television viewers, there was good reason. Apollo and its two-stage launch rocket weighed a staggering 1.3 million lbs. As a result, acceleration was gradual; Astronauts Schirra, Eisele and Cunningham were subjected to only a fraction of the oppressive G-forces experienced on earlier flights by Mercury and Gemini crews. "We're having a ball," Wally Schirra reported happily to ground controllers. The 45-year-old Navy captain, a veteran of near-perfect Mercury and Gemini missions and the first pilot to make a space rendezvous, became the first man to drink coffee and the first to develop a full-blown cold in space. "I've gone through eight or nine Kleenexes with some pretty good blows," he radioed.

"THE WALLY, WALT AND DONN SHOW": As Apollo 7 whirled through orbit after orbit around the earth last week, the growing monotony of the mission was a major measure of its success. Presented with little challenge from the well-functioning spacecraft, Astronauts Schirra, Cunningham and Eisele fought off ennui as they plodded through the housekeeping and engineering duties necessary to prove their craft moonworthy. They fired and refired the ship's big rocket engine and practiced sighting stars through a sextant; they tested their computers and cooling system, and transmitted to a ground station the same sort of signals a lunar module would send while returning from the surface of the moon. For astronauts and space watchers alike, the high points of the week were the television shows, shot with the 4½-lb. TV camera developed for Apollo by RCA.

The daily 7-min. to 11-min. *Wally, Walt and Donn Show,* as it was nicknamed, was scheduled once each morning during a 2,000-mile Apollo pass between Corpus Christi, Texas, and Cape Kennedy, the only two ground stations equipped to pick up the transmissions. The astronauts held up crudely lettered signs that read "Hello from the lovely Apollo Room, high atop everything" and "Deke Slayton, are you a turtle?" In accordance with a barroom tradition that has been adopted by the astronauts, Slayton was required to answer "You bet your sweet ass I am"—or pay the penalty of buying a drink for everyone within earshot. "I have recorded my answer," responded Slayton from the control center, after momentarily switching off his microphone. On one show, Astronauts Schirra and Cunningham suddenly floated up from behind their seats and swam toward the camera, vividly demonstrating the weightlessness of space flight. The astronauts also panned Apollo's interior as they described equipment and demonstrated how loose drops of water are collected with a vacuum hose.

PLUS ONE MORE: Even as the U.S. proudly hailed Apollo 7 and its crew, the Soviets launched an impressive reminder that they are still running hard in the race to the moon. With no advance fanfare, Russia's tenth manned spacecraft, Soyuz 3, soared into orbit, piloted by Cosmonaut Colonel Georgy Beregovoy, 47. It is the first manned Russian space mission since April 1967, when Colonel Vladimir Komarov was killed in the crash of Soyuz 1.

ROUTINE: As Russia's newest cosmonaut, Colonel Georgy Beregovoy, piloted his spacecraft through a series of seemingly routine maneuvers last week, nervous U.S. space officials began to relax. The flight of Soyuz 3 did not suggest that the Soviets had moved ahead in the race to the moon. Indeed, Western experts were at a loss to explain why Soyuz 3 came no closer than 650 ft. to an unmanned vehicle, Soyuz 2, which was sent up as a target. A Pravda article earlier in the week had noted that the purpose of the mission was "to perfect docking techniques in orbit." Yet without any further attempt to link the two craft, Soyuz 2 was returned to earth.

POISED FOR THE LEAP: This month, fulfilling the yearnings and predictions of untold generations, man will attempt to propel himself across 230,000 miles of emptiness in a bold voyage toward a shining and beckoning target: the moon. If all goes well, he will circle the moon and look down from his spaceship at lunar craters and "seas" as close as 70 miles below. Staring up, he will see the dominant feature of the black lunar sky —the blue-green, partly illuminated globe that is his home: the earth. The crew for the flight, Colonel Frank Borman and Major William Anders, both Air Force officers, and Navy Captain James Lovell are already at Cape Kennedy, spending 16 hours a day in preparing for every detail of a complex mission that has been planned and plotted to the last second. They spend 20 hours a week in simulators, training their minds and hands to react almost automatically to every conceivable contingency. By the time they are fired from Cape Kennedy's launch pad 39A by the world's most powerful rocket, Saturn 5, they will be the most thoroughly prepared adventurers ever to have dared the unknown.

Astronauts William Anders, James Lovell and Frank Borman in their Apollo 8 spacesuits. After church, they blast off to the moon.

INTO THE DEPTHS OF SPACE: The voyage of Apollo 8 transfixed a blasé world. The historic flight had a thundering and auspicious beginning. The mighty, 36-story Saturn 5 rocket lifted from its pad a negligible 65 milliseconds after its scheduled 7:51 a.m. launch time. Propelled by an awesome 7,500,000 lbs. of thrust, it soared into the clear Florida sky over Cape Kennedy. Then, as Apollo passed over Hawaii on its second orbit of the earth, the three astronauts aboard fired the S-4B engine attached to their spacecraft. It was a perfect burn. The spacecraft increased its velocity from 17,400 to 24,200 m.p.h., enough to enable the spacecraft to escape from the earth's gravitation pull. At long last, man was on his way to the moon.

As they began their pioneering journey, Astronauts Frank Borman, James Lovell and William Anders were pushed into space by a rocket that had never before been used in manned flight. And only minutes after they were propelled out of earth orbit toward the moon, they were farther than man has ever been from his home planet (the previous record of 850 miles was set by the U.S. Gemini 11 mission in 1966).

For weeks before launch time, NASA headquarters in Washington had been flooded with protests from Fundamentalists objecting to the Christmas timing of the flight. The Apollo crew, all of whom attended church on the last Sunday before blast-off, had no such qualms. "I can't think of a better religious aspect of the flight than to further explore the heavens," said Astronaut Lovell. "I think it would be a very good Christmas present for the country."

N. 3
1969 **MEN OF THE YEAR:** The year's transcendent legacy may well be that in Christmas week 1968, the human race glimpsed not a new continent or a new colony, but a new age, one that will inevitably reshape man's view of himself and his destiny. In what must surely rank as one of the greatest physical adventures in history, an American spaceship, Apollo 8, and a crew of three made ten orbits around the moon and then returned safely to earth. The mission was the product of centuries of scientific conjecture and experimentation. Its fantastic precision could never have been achieved without the creativity and dedication of the greatest task force ever assembled for a peaceful purpose: 300,000 engineers, technicians and workers, 20,000 contractors, backed by $33 billion spent on the nation's space effort in the past decade. In the end, though, it was three lonely men who risked their lives and made the voyage. And in the course of that first soaring escape from the planet, earth, it was the courage, grace and cool proficiency of Colonel Frank Borman, Captain James Lovell and Major William Anders that transfixed their fellowmen and inscribed on the history books names to be remembered along with those of Marco Polo and Amundsen, Captain Cook and Colonel Lindbergh. In 147 hours that stretched like a lifetime, America's moon pioneers became the indisputable Men of the Year.

During their flight around the moon, 230,000 miles farther away from home than any humans had ever before traveled, the Apollo 8 astronauts casually called out names of lunar craters and other landmarks as if they were old friends. The Sea of Fertility. The Pyrenees Mountains. The craters of Colombo and Gutenberg. The long parallel cracks or faults of Gaudibert. On Christmas Eve, during their ninth revolution of the moon, the astronauts presented their best description of the moon in the longest and most impressive of the mission's six telecasts. "This is Apollo 8 coming to you live from the moon," reported Borman, focusing the TV camera on the lunar surface drifting by below. "The moon is a different thing to each of us," said Borman. "My own impression is that it's a vast, lonely, forbidding-type existence—a great expanse of nothing that looks rather like clouds and clouds of pumice stone. It certainly would not appear to be a very inviting place to live or work."

"My thoughts are very similar," agreed Lovell. "The vast loneliness up here is awe-inspiring, and it makes you realize just what you have back there on earth."

Finally, Apollo sped toward the terminator (the continually moving line that divides the day and night hemispheres of the moon). To conclude their Christmas Eve telecast before the view below was blotted out, the astronauts took turns solemnly reading the first ten verses of *Genesis:* "In the beginning, God created the heaven and earth . . ."

The entire presentation was appropriate for the men of the Apollo 8 crew. Borman, Lovell and Anders are deadly serious men, cool under pressure. Borman, 40, is a lay reader of the Episcopal Church, and during the Apollo 8 mission read a prayer addressed to "the people of St. Christopher's [his church], actually to people everywhere." Lovell, also 40, is Special Consultant to the President for Physical Fitness. Anders, 35, a Roman Catholic, is secretary-treasurer of his neighborhood property owners' association. Finally, each of the Apollo 8 men has an intense sense of mission and purpose, and has demonstrated courageous stubbornness. These traits came in especially handy during the mission.

As Apollo began its tenth revolution, tension rose both aboard the spacecraft and in Houston. During their final pass behind the moon, the astronauts were scheduled to restart the spacecraft's engine, to increase their velocity from 3,625 m.p.h. to 5,980 m.p.h., enough to propel them out of lunar orbit and back toward earth. Failure of the engine to fire would leave them stranded in lunar orbit. There were no sentimental *bon voyages,* no final quips as the moment approached. "All systems are go, Apollo 8," the controller reported. From Borman came back only a terse "Roger." Then the spacecraft passed into radio silence behind the moon. Although it was now more than half an hour into Christmas Day in Houston, the controllers avoided any exchange of holiday greetings, awaiting word that the engine had fired on schedule and that Apollo 8 was safely on its way home. The word came 37 minutes later in a transmission by Jim Lovell as Apollo re-emerged. "Please be informed," he said, "that there is a Santa Claus."

During the return trip to earth, the astronauts were treated to selections from Herb Alpert and his Tijuana Brass, weekend football scores and lengthy newscasts. Two more live telecasts were presented from the spacecraft, and more star navigation checks were made, but two scheduled mid-course corrections were canceled: Apollo 8 was already dead on target. Accelerated by the earth's own gravity, the spacecraft hurtled at increasing speeds until it plunged into the outer atmosphere at a speed of 24,629 m.p.h.—some 7,000 m.p.h. faster than the re-entry speeds of previous astronaut missions. Roaring down into the thickening atmosphere within a sliver of the planned angle, Apollo passed over Peking and Tokyo, the temperature of its heat shield rising to 5,000°F. Then, on schedule, the spacecraft's drogue parachutes deployed, followed closely by the three main chutes. The parachutes floated Apollo to a splashdown in the Pacific about 7,000 yards away from the carrier *Yorktown,* where recovery helicopters spotted the capsule's beacon flashing in the predawn darkness. It was 10:51 a.m. (E.S.T.), just eleven seconds earlier than the mission's predicted splashdown time, and exactly 147 hours after Apollo 8's spectacular launch from its Cape Kennedy launching pad.

Beyond question, Apollo 8 had started blazing the trail toward man's exploration of other planets. Yet the fact remains that at even the relatively short distance of the moon, man can be homesick. Said Astronaut Borman on Christmas Eve: "God bless all of you—all of you on the *good* earth."

$$\boxed{\textbf{TELEVISION}}$$

PEACOCK ON THE WING: According to an NBC survey, 25%, MA‹
or 14,130,000 of the nation's 56 million TV households now
have color sets.

BLACK ON THE CHANNELS: In the first episode of *Julia,* a new MA‹
TV series, the heroine has just lost her husband in Viet Nam.
To raise her son, Julia wants to resume her nursing career.
She phones a physician and is offered an interview. But she wa-
vers. "Oh," she asks, "did they tell you I'm colored?" "Mm,"
he replies, "what color are you?" "Wh-hy, I'm Negro." "Oh,"
says the doctor. "Have you always been a Negro, or are you
just trying to be fashionable?"

In TV nowadays, it is not merely fashionable, but an absolute advantage to be black. By next season, just about every
series will feature a Negro player. NBC has had Diahann Car-
roll tied up for the title role of Julia since March. CBS signed
Comic Flip ("Heah come de judge") Wilson for four Ed Sullivan dates next year and is reportedly trying to buy Bill Cosby
away from NBC with a 20-year, $20 million deal.

Unfortunately, few of the roles for Negroes that are being
so hurriedly written into next fall's shows will have any in-
dividuality or credibility. Seldom do television's blacks have
on-screen families, common vices or even sex lives. And rarely does a Negro portray the villain; the networks are fearful
of being accused of racism. As a result, the black character in
the average TV drama is likely to represent what Harry Bela-
fonte calls either "Super-Negro" or "a button-down Brooks
Brothers eunuch." In Peyton Place (pop. approx. 10,000) the
first black will be a neurosurgeon.

VERRRY INTERESTING . . . BUT WILD: Richard Nixon? Making OC‹
jokes on a TV comedy show with a bunch of weirdos? You
bet, as they say, your sweet bippy. Everybody and his myna
bird wants to make a cameo appearance on Rowan and Mar-

tin's manic Monday night affair. It is the smartest, freshest show on television. And it would be only moderately surprising if next week J. Edgar Hoover popped onto the screen and said, "Here come de Judge!"

Laugh-In was last season's biggest TV hit, and is already a solid Nielsen winner so far this year. What appeals is the program's extraordinary ambiance: it has an artful spontaneity, a kind of controlled insanity, emerging from a cascade of crazy cartoon ideas. In yet another TV season of pale copies, *Laugh-In* is unique. It features no swiveling chorus lines, no tuxedoed crooners. Just those quick flashes of visual and verbal comedy, tumbling pell-mell from the opening straight through the commercials till the NBC peacock turns tail. Often the first-time viewer can hardly believe the proceedings. Childish name games produce outrageous amalgams of sound:

"If Shirley Temple Black had married Tyrone Power, she'd be Shirley Black Power."

"If Jan Sterling had married Phil Silvers, divorced him and married Robert Service, she'd be Jan Sterling Silvers Service."

There are graffiti:

FOREST FIRES PREVENT BEARS

THIS IS YOUR SLUM—KEEP IT CLEAN

JACKIE GLEASON TAKES SILICONE

There are absurd definitions:

"A myth is an effeminate moth."

And sniggering questions:

"Truman Capote: Man or Myth?"

And public notices:

LITTLE ORPHAN ANNIE—CALL THE EYE BANK

GEORGE WALLACE—YOUR SHEETS ARE READY

SPIRO AGNEW—YOUR NEW NAME IS READY

RELIGION

SUCCESSION TO SPELLMAN: Churchly speculation on who MAR
would succeed the late Francis Cardinal Spellman as Roman
Catholic Archbishop of New York has dwelt mainly on such familiar names as Rochester's Bishop Fulton J. Sheen. Last week
Pope Paul confounded all handicappers by naming as head of
the nation's richest and most prestigious archdiocese a young
and virtually unknown prelate: the Most Rev. Terence James
Cooke, 47, one of New York's twelve auxiliary bishops.

There is some precedence for the Pope's surprising choice:
Spellman himself was an obscure assistant to Boston's William
Cardinal O'Connell when Pius XII named him Archbishop of
New York in 1939. Cooke, who has both a warm Irish wit
and an M.A. in social work, is regarded in church circles as a
prelate whose style and approach will not differ strikingly from
those of his precedessor. A conservative in theology, Cooke declares himself a progressive in secular matters. At his first press
conference last week, he fielded most questions nimbly: re-
minded of Spellman's call for "victory" in Viet Nam, Cooke replied: "I think what the Cardinal meant by victory was a quick
peace."

A STERN NO TO BIRTH CONTROL: Seldom has a theological pro- AUG
nouncement been so anxiously awaited as Pope Paul's long-
promised verdict on birth control. Last week the first copy of
a new papal encyclical on the subject became available. Its es-
sence was contained in these uncompromising words: "Con-
forming to fundamental principles of the human and Christian
vision of marriage, we must once again state that there must
be excluded absolutely, as a licit way in which to regulate
births, the direct interruption of the generative process."

The Pope's stern no, while not unexpected, is bound to have
wide-reaching effects. It will almost certainly cause confusion
and dissension in the church, particularly among the young
and among the now disillusioned liberals, both laymen and

clerics. Most important of all, it will inevitably increase doubts among many Catholics about their church's ability to keep abreast of changing times. It will make more difficult the church's work in poor, overpopulated countries, especially in Latin America.

The Pope declares that artificial birth control can lead to infidelity, immorality, loss of respect for women, even political dangers. He reaffirms that the only allowable method of control is rhythm—but clearly disapproves of even that as a constant practice. In what may rank as one of the understatements of the century, Paul does make one concession—that "these teachings perhaps will not be easily accepted by everyone."

UG. 9 **A CRISIS IN CATHOLIC AUTHORITY:** "Rome has spoken," runs an ancient proverb of the Roman Catholic Church. "The case is closed." No longer true. Last week Pope Paul VI formally promulgated his encyclical on birth control and the pronouncement caused perhaps the most serious outburst of dissent the Catholic Church has experienced in centuries. The Vatican daily newspaper, L'Osservatore Romano, hard put to include favorable non-Catholic judgments in its roundup of world opinion on the subject, solemnly noted that the Pope had received a message of support from a family of Norwegian Protestants with 14 children. But within the church itself, some comments were almost indecently abusive. Father Alfons Sarrach, a German priest-journalist, described the encyclical as "a breath of outdated and ignorant monkish theology." "You are not speaking as our Pope," protested Jesuit Philosopher Norris Clarke before a cheering crowd of 1,000 at a Fordham University symposium on the encyclical. "We can't hear you. We demand that you do not speak to us this way."

Far more disturbing to the Pope and the bishops was that the encyclical was flatly rejected by some of the most influential teaching minds of the church. Led by Father Charles Curran of Catholic University, 172 U.S. theologians and other Catholics, including all six American lay members of the pontifical birth control commission, rejected the encyclical as outdated, inadequate and not binding on conscience. "We conclude," said their statement, "that spouses may responsibly decide according to their conscience that artificial contraception in some circumstances is permissible and indeed necessary to preserve and foster the values and sacredness of marriage."

Although he knew that it would be criticized, Pope Paul was clearly unprepared for the gale of protest aroused by the encyclical. In a mid-week audience at Castel Gandolfo, his summer residence, Paul told an audience of pilgrims of the personal agony that had accompanied his decision. "Never before," he said, "have we felt the load of our duty. We have studied, read, discussed as much as we could. And we have also prayed a lot. How many times have we had the impression of being almost submerged by this heap of documents?"

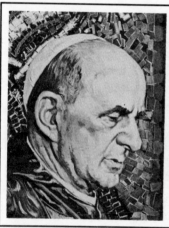

Pope Paul: "These teachings perhaps will not be easily accepted." Page 209.

Karl Barth: The Bible isn't man's word about God, but God's word about man.

THE DEATH OF TWO EXTRAORDINARY CHRISTIANS: One was a DEC. Protestant theologian, Karl Barth, who labored quietly in university towns of Switzerland and Germany for half a century. The other, Thomas Merton, was a Roman Catholic monk who worked hermitlike on his writings in the hills of central Kentucky. But while Barth gave his life to scholarship and Merton to contemplation, both men brought to their age, and to their fellow man, a message of love that was ardently Christian.

To believe in Christ has always been, as Kierkegaard put it, an inexplicable leap of faith. The most profound preacher of that mystery in the 20th century was Karl Barth, who died last week at the age of 82. The century's most significant religious thinker, Barth changed the course of Protestant theology in his lifetime almost singlehandedly, and his 14-volume *Church Dogmatics* was the most powerful exposition of Protestant thought since Calvin's *Institutes*. Against the liberals who assumed the partnership of God and man, Barth proclaimed a radically transcendent Creator whose message had been hurled like a stone at humanity. In contrast to an ethical, teaching Jesus, Barth preached a divine Christ who was, in his person, God's message to man. The Bible, he wrote, was not man's word about God, but God's word about man.

"The scenario calls for a quiet death among concerned chipmunks," Thomas Merton once wrote a friend after surviving major surgery, "and I'd like it that way." He did not get his wish. On the very day that Karl Barth lay dying in Basel, the 53-year-old Trappist poet-priest was attending an ecumenical conference in Bangkok. Returning to his bungalow during the afternoon, he reached out to adjust an electric fan and apparently touched an exposed wire. He was instantly electrocuted.

Merton was ordained a priest in 1949, the year after his first major book, *The Seven Storey Mountain,* had become a bestseller and thrust him permanently into a life of books, articles, poems and a massive correspondence with friends all over the world. The most lucidly honest autobiography since Rousseau's *Confessions, The Seven Storey Mountain* was a frank, self-effacing narrative of Merton's peripatetic youth: his dizzying year at Cambridge, his first grapplings with the craft of poetry, his mildly wicked undergraduate years at Columbia (including a one-meeting membership in the Young Communist League), his ultimate discovery of a faith and a vocation. It was a book suffused with spiritual zeal, and under its spell, disillusioned veterans, students, even teen-agers flocked to monasteries across the country either to stay or visit as retreatants. *The Seven Storey Mountain* also hinted of the Merton to come. Prophetically, he digressed in it to deliver a stinging rebuke to the civilization that could produce a Harlem. In a wide range of books and articles, Merton returned again and again to themes of social justice and a quiet, but very absolute pacifism. He lent his name to many antiwar organizations, resolutely opposed the Viet Nam war. Just two months ago, he characterized some student activists he met as "real modern monks."

$$\boxed{\textbf{MEDICINE}}$$

In December of 1967 a team of South African surgeons headed by Dr. Christiaan Barnard performed the world's first successful human heart transplant on a patient named Louis Washkansky. Washkansky died 18 days later from lung complications. But the stage was now set for a series of similar operations that would make medical history in 1968.

CAPE TOWN'S SECOND: Like most South Africans, regardless of color and social status, Clive Haupt was stirred by Louis Washkansky's heart transplant. When Washkansky died, Garment Worker Haupt, 24, said to a neighbor: "I hope the next transplant succeeds." If the statement was unremarkable then, it soon gained poignancy. For the next transplant involved Haupt's own heart. While Surgeon Christiaan N. Barnard was visiting the U.S. during Christmas week, he got reports from Cape Town that the patient next in line for a transplant, Philip Blaiberg, 58, was getting weaker. Several coronary occlusions had compelled Blaiberg to give up his practice as a dentist and caused irreparable damage to his heart, which was steadily failing. On Dr. Barnard's return, his transplant team at Groote Schuur Hospital was ready. So was Blaiberg. But where would the heart come from?

It was a hot New Year's Day when Clive Haupt and his bride of three months went with friends to Fish Hoek Beach. Haupt played pick-up rugby, then lay down to rest. Suddenly a friend called that Haupt was ill, with frothy blood coming from his mouth. From a local hospital, he was shuttled fast to the better-equipped Victoria Hospital, where doctors concluded that he had suffered a massive brain hemorrhage. They saw little hope that he could survive. But since Haupt had apparently been fit, his heart was probably in good condition, so they telephoned the surgeons at Groote Schuur, who did not hesitate to say "Bring him in."

Dr. Barnard now had a delicate problem. Haupt was of a complicated racial mixture, (part white, part Bantu, part Malay, perhaps even part Hottentot) that is classified as "Colored" under South Africa's race laws. Dr. Barnard asked Blaiberg whether he would object to receiving a Colored man's heart. No, replied the desperate patient. While Haupt lingered through the night, pathologists and hematologists compared his blood type and cells with Blaiberg's. By a 12-to-1 chance, both had type B, Rh-positive and their blood proved under tests to be similar enough to suggest that Blaiberg's rejection mechanism would not react too strongly against a transplant.

It fell to Dr. Raymond Hoffenberg, the duty doctor at Groote Schuur at the time, to assess Haupt's condition and his chances of survival. He lay in a deepening coma. When Haupt's heart stopped, it was Dr. Hoffenberg who certified that he was legally dead. That came at 10:35 a.m. Tuesday. One group of surgeons began to remove Haupt's heart. In the operating room where Washkansky had received his transplant other surgeons had Patient Blaiberg almost ready. At 11:30 a.m. they opened his chest and made the necessary connections to a heart-lung machine to supply oxygenated blood to his body (except the heart) and brain. Then they removed his heart. In its place, Dr. Barnard installed Haupt's heart. There was, however, a different atmosphere. The 30-man team of sur-

Patient Blaiberg (left) with Dr. Christiaan Barnard. A white man's "Colored" heart beats strongly, to the tune of a Brahms lullaby.

geons, physicians and nurses were less tense. As Barnard put it: "We are not going into the unknown—we are going where we have been before." Another difference was encouraging. The transplanted heart began beating spontaneously when it was hooked into Blaiberg's circulation, needing no electric shock to start it.

The operation took five hours. When Blaiberg regained full consciousness next morning, his first words were: "I'm thirsty. Please give my regards to my wife."

SITTING UP: Eleven days after his heart transplant operation, JAN. Dentist Philip Blaiberg, 58, was sitting on the edge of his bed in Cape Town and swinging his legs like a schoolboy. This was not mere bravado, but was designed to help his circulation. He drank a "shandy" (beer and lemonade) and sang a Brahms lullaby.

FOUR PARTS: An eleven-year-old boy from Loma Linda, MAY Calif., died last week of auto-accident injuries. Within the day, his kidneys were transplanted into two men, an extract from his spleen was injected into a leukemia patient, and surgeons used some of his skin as grafts for a severely burned woman.

TRANSPLANTS–AN ANNIVERSARY REVIEW: Surgery's most spec- DEC. tacular procedure, the transplant of a heart from one human being to another, marks its first anniversary this week. By the latest tally, 95 human hearts have been taken from newly dead donors and implanted in the chests of 93 patients (two of them got two apiece).

Almost half the recipients, 43, are still living. The world's re-cord survivor, South Africa's Philip Blaiberg has lived for just eleven months.

The National Heart Institute's Dr. Theodore Cooper es-timates that each year 80,000 Americans become, by virtue of their otherwise untreatable heart disease, suitable candidates for transplants. But by the most optimistic estimates, only 40,000 donor hearts are likely to be available each year. Even if there were more, there are not enough trained surgeons to perform the operation or enough hospital units to accommo-date the patients. Beyond all that, the cost of a transplant is huge, ranging from $20,000 to $50,000. The patient may pay

$10,000 to $15,000 of this, and the rest is absorbed through Government grants or charitable gifts.

Ultimately, heart transplants may become unnecessary. By the time the immunologists have learned to induce tissue tolerance, an artificial heart should be perfected. Yet to the men and women who have received heart transplants and apparently beaten the prevailing fifty-fifty odds of survival, all the technical questions are of little concern. Philip Blaiberg now drives his car, drinks his beer, eats heartily and writes his autobiography. Whatever their eventual fate, the decision of the patients so far in agreeing to the operation, knowing full well its great risks and only moderate hope of benefit, has helped surgery to make a momentous advance.

C. 13 **A₂-HONG KONG-68, OR WHATEVER:** A plague was moving across the U.S. last week. Hundreds of thousands of Americans were sniffling, hacking, running fevers and complaining that their bones ached. The vast majority of adults said they had "the flu," and many tried to show their medical sophistication by identifying it as "Hong Kong flu." In most cases, the precise identity of the affliction and the microbe causing it was unknown. But whatever its nature, the illness was emptying schools and offices, stripping military installations of active-duty personnel, decimating athletic teams and Broadway casts. Playing the barber in *Man of La Mancha*, Leo Blum became so ill that he fell off the stage. In Los Angeles, 15 members of the Rams' 40-man football squad missed practice because of the flu. In Denver, the Hong Kong virus was blamed for a significant increase in the number of deaths due to influenza and pneumonia. Health officials and their laboratory experts, using ultra-refined microtechniques, began closing in on the culprit microbes. It was almost certain that most of the symptoms resulted from two main types of influenza viruses, A and B. The B type appears to be stable and causes outbreaks of moderate severity every two to four years. On the other hand the A types are highly unstable and mutate unpredictably. The best-documented mutation occurred in 1957, when a new and savage strain poured out of northern China and won deserved ill repute as "Asian A₂." Last July, another mutation erupted from China through Hong Kong and has been tagged A₂-Hong Kong-68.

Because influenza is seldom fatal for a person who is in generally good health before he catches it, some authorities have described Hong Kong flu as a "mild illness." That is highly misleading. The ultimate severity of the disease is determined by the individual victim's constitution and resistance. Ailing youngsters and oldsters run a considerably greater risk that the infection will move down from the upper respiratory tract to the lungs, causing a form of viral pneumonia, or that the viral infection will make the lungs prey to bacterial pneumonia. Aside from vaccination, the only prophylactic against any strain of Asian flu is amantadine, a drug marketed by Du Pont as Symmetrel. It is given to the elderly and infirm after one member of the household has come down with flu but before they develop it themselves. But it is ineffective after illness has begun, and many physicians question whether its safety for those of all ages and sexes has been sufficiently proved.

APPROACHING A DISASTER: With jet-age speed A2-Hong Kong-68, more commonly known as "Hong Kong flu," spanned the nation last week, respecting neither station nor species. With millions of Americans already victimized by the epidemic, the American Red Cross declared a "disaster situation." While there is no discernible pattern to the epidemic's course, the northeast has been hit hardest. So far, 800,000 New York City residents have been stricken, and health authorities expect the figure to double. Complicating matters was a disastrously timed strike of fuel-oil delivery truck drivers. At week's end, upwards of 250,000 New Yorkers were shivering in heatless homes and apartments, prime targets for the disease. Though there was not enough vaccine to go around, there was no shortage of home remedies. New York City Health Commissioner Dr. Edward O'Rourke noted that one of his staff prescribed chicken soup while another recommended beer and martinis. Apparently on the ground that any sort of fatigue lowers resistance, Hong Kong Herbalist Yiu Kam-shing declared: "I advise married couples to sleep in separate beds."

DEC

$$\boxed{\textbf{BUSINESS}}$$

26 **TOWARD THE 21ST CENTURY LTD.:** No green light flared from a trackside tower; no warning whistle echoed down the line. But no trainman missed the signal. When the Supreme Court gave its approval last week to the merger of the Pennsylvania and New York Central railroads, it was clearing the track for the nation's entire rail system. It was giving railroad management permission to highball into the future. As Justice Abe Fortas read the 37-page opinion that put an end to ten years of frustrating negotiation and deliberation, the smile on the face of a chunky, balding spectator seemed to light up the marbled chamber. For Stuart Thomas Saunders, 58, the man who has already been picked to head the Pennsylvania New York Central Transportation Co., the court's 8-0 vote was a singular personal triumph.

It was Saunders, as chairman and chief executive officer of the Pennsylvania, who planned the tactics and organized the arguments that led to one of the largest mergers in corporate his-

Saunders and Perlman of the new Penn Central. They lead the way as the nation's railroads highball toward a new future.

tory. Above all, it was Saunders, the lawyer-turned-railroader, who convinced the Interstate Commerce Commission and the Justice Department that both public interest and private good would be helped if two troubled rivals were allowed to operate as a unit. His victory was a victory for railroads across the country.

Saunders will be working in tandem with the Central's President Alfred E. Perlman, 65, one of the best operating men in the business; and the two men will be managing a railroad empire consisting of 40,000 miles of track in 14 states and two Canadian provinces. It will run 4,200 locomotives, 195,000 freight cars, and 4,937 passenger cars. It will also be the nation's largest private landlord, with real estate holdings that include Park Avenue hotels, a share in the new Madison Square Garden, resorts in Florida, parks in Texas and housing developments in California. The diversified corporation will have total assets of $6.3 billion, annual revenues of almost $2 billion. Most of all, in its plans and in its performance, Penn Central will be a prototype of the U.S. railroad of the future.

A huge wave of speculative buying suddenly hit the world's gold markets in early March, setting off the greatest financial crisis for the U.S. since the Depression. The speculators, who frantically bought up 900 tons of gold in a ten-day period in London alone—about 25 times the normal amount of trading—were gambling on their conviction that the U.S., beset by all kinds of financial pressures, would sooner or later have to raise the price of gold from the $35 an ounce that it had maintained since 1933.

AT THE POINT OF PANIC: Most of the reasons for the gold crisis are rooted in the U.S. The country's continuing balance of payments deficit, its constantly out-of-balance domestic budget and its rising outflow of money to finance the war in Viet Nam are basically responsible for global concern about the soundness of the dollar. Concern has led to the belief that the U.S. would soon have to stop selling gold to all buyers at $35 an ounce and somehow raise the price. The possibility of a price increase touched off the worldwide run on gold. That being the case, the U.S. had the responsibility of doing what it could to restore sanity to the gold markets. Treasury Secretary Henry Fowler and Federal Reserve Board Chairman William McChesney Martin last week invited the central bankers of Britain, West Germany, Italy, Belgium, The Netherlands and Switzerland to a weekend meeting in the massive, paneled board room of the Federal Reserve Board in Washington.

The six, along with the U.S., are members of the International Gold Pool, who, in an effort to hold the price of gold close to the official rate, have been drawing on their own governmental gold reserves—now down to about $25 billion. France, because it is no longer an active member of the pool, was conspicuously missing from the invitation list. Piqued because of the omission, Charles de Gaulle decided to keep the Paris Bourse open last week after London's gold market had shut down at Washington's suggestion. The result was wild trading and a rise in the speculation price per ounce of gold to $44.36.

Meanwhile, last week, the U.S. took steps to put its economic house in order. The Fed, to dampen the U.S. economy and provide some antidote to the balance of payments deficit, decided on an increase in the discount rate. The rate, which represents the cost to commercial banks of borrowing Federal Reserve money and thus affects their own rates to customers, went from 4½ to 5%. The increase meant higher interest rates on loans, less available mortgage money and, just as the Fed intended, a hold-down on all but necessary spending because borrowed money would be more costly. That, for now, was the extent of the gold panic's effect on the U.S. man in the street.

"TAKE IT TO THE DENTIST": In Washington last week the Western world's chief central bankers revised a key part of the world's monetary rules. They agreed to stop buying and selling gold—thus shutting down the London pool—and to use their remaining store of the precious metal only to settle debts between nations. It was a case of the rescue squad arriving barely in time. For the international monetary system—the agreed way of exchanging one currency for another—runs on faith. For 24 years, the bulwark of that system has been the U.S. Treasury's pledge to redeem dollars held by foreign governments for gold, at an unchanging $35 per oz. Other countries value their own money in terms of dollars, usually keep a big part of their reserves in dollars. But in 17 of the past 18 years, the U.S. has spent, lent or given away more money than it has taken in from abroad. The dollars thus placed in foreign hands now total $34 billion, while the U.S. stock of gold has dwindled from a postwar peak of $24.6 billion to $10.4 billion last week, the thinnest gold line since 1936. If all the dollar holders demanded gold at once, there would be too little in Fort Knox to satisfy even a third of them. By their decision to leave the official price intact while abandoning the gold pool, the seven nations pulled a 24-karat rug out from under the hoarders. As Zurich Banker Hans J. Baer put it: "The central banks are saying to the speculators: 'Take it to the dentist.' "

IBM'S SUPER SPLIT: Few things cheer shareholders like a stock split, and last week few shareholders were as cheery as IBM's. At their annual meeting in Boston, 2,300 of the faithful (of a 359,495 total) heard Chairman Thomas J. Watson Jr. announce stockholder approval of the eleventh split in the company's 57 years. Holders of IBM's 60 million shares will get one additional share for each one they hold, making it the biggest stock distribution in U.S. history. IBM's split will help ensure a lively market in its stock by keeping per-share prices within reach of ordinary investors. Long the highest priced issue traded on the New York Stock Exchange, IBM in the past 20 months had swept from $320 to $677.50. As a result of splits—including this week's—and other distributions, a 100-share investment in 1914, which would have cost $2,750, has grown to 59,320 shares worth more than $20 million.

THE PAPERWORK PREDICAMENT: The nation's overburdened stock markets called time out last week, but investors didn't seem to hear the whistle. Stock exchanges and the over-the-counter market took a one-day holiday to let brokerage houses attack a mountain of paperwork that has swamped clerical staffs. On the New York Stock Exchange, volume had soared to an all-time peak of 21,350,000 shares. In the over-the-counter market, which operates by telephone, the pace grew frantic enough to overstrain physical facilities and disrupt trading. "It's absolute bedlam," said one dealer whose entire switchboard lit up at once. "We just pulled all the cords out and started fresh."

The paperwork snarl—the worst in Wall Street history—began when President Johnson's Viet Nam peace moves sent stocks on a spring spree. As a result, brokers have been unable to deliver stock certificates to customers within the allotted five business days after they are bought or sold. Compounded by increasing clerical errors, the discrepancies and slippages by last week had reached a point where an estimated $4.5 billion worth of undelivered stock was caught in the clotted pipelines.

Several brokerage firms have begun taking direct action to cool the speculative fervor. E. F. Hutton & Co. announced that it will forbid its salesmen to solicit orders to buy stocks selling for less than $5 a share and will allow them no commission on such orders. Such strictures represent a considerable change of thinking in an industry long attuned to stressing sales above everything else.

BY THE HOUR: Other hotelmen greeted the news with amusement. "Oh, that sounds naughty," said an official of San Francisco's Mark Hopkins when he heard that the New York Hilton, Manhattan's biggest hotel, was going to rent out its rooms on an hourly basis. As far as the Hilton is concerned, the only thing sinful is that no respectable midtown hotel has done it sooner. Airport motels and hotels have long offered day rates (usually half-price between 8 a.m. and 6 p.m.) to travelers who want to rest between flights. The Hilton's "Day-Hour Plan" ($12 for the first three hours, $3 an hour thereafter), which went into effect last week, is a logical next step. It is intended to make life easier and less expensive for today's jet-borne businessman, who often zips in and out of two or three cities in a single day.

Now, in New York at least, he can rent a place to hold private business meetings or relax between engagements without paying the full 24-hour tariff.

A VERY EXPENSIVE YEAR: If present price trends continue upward, the average American will remember 1968 as a very expensive year. For the year to date, prices have risen 3% over 1967. Nowadays, the poor consumer utters hardly a syllable of complaint when confronted with a $3 man's haircut in Chicago, a $1-a-dozen carton of eggs in Detroit. Medical costs are up 7.1% since last year. A private hospital room now goes for $60 a day in some areas. A new baby whose arrival expenses averaged out as $175 in 1958 will now cost $275.

Much of the surge in prices is attributable to soaring wages, which companies have decided to let the customers pay for. And the cost of services is even worse. House repairs cost 6.6% more than last year. Auto repairs are 5.3% more expensive, and the 35¢ shoeshine is a new phenomenon.

DANGEROUS DRIFT FOR THE U.S.: Although the U.S. remains the world's biggest salesman, with a 91% growth in total trade over ten years, it is nevertheless on the verge of a crisis in exports. The reason is that the U.S. needs an exceptionally high and rising rate of exports in order to balance its generous outflow of capital for imports, foreign aid, military aid, tourism and the like. Unless the nation achieves even faster export growth than it now demonstrates, it will not be able to bring its balance of payments into line, and the value of the dollar may be threatened. Among the trends that operate against the U.S.:

¶ Technology. U.S. technological superiority means less than before. Lawrence Fox, a high official of the Commerce Department, observes that "foreigners today can either buy, lease or steal American research advances." Licensing of foreign manufacturers is rising. Last week, for example, B. F. Goodrich licensed Tokyo's Mitsubishi to use a vinyl-chloride chemical process, for which the Japanese firm will build a whole new plant.

¶ Size. No longer does the U.S. enjoy a monopoly on the economy of size. In the Common Market and elsewhere, many companies are merging. Italy's Fiat, for example, has allied with France's Citroën and is building a multinational company; it is already bigger than Chrysler.

¶ Labor Costs. The effect of cheaper foreign labor is sometimes disputed on grounds that U.S. exports come mostly from the aircraft, computer and other industries where labor costs are secondary to quality and high engineering. But rising labor costs have driven many U.S. manufacturers to produce in overseas plants instead of exporting. And last year, wages advanced faster than productivity, and that trend is expected to continue.

CINEMA

"2001: A SPACE ODYSSEY"–A herd of hairy simians chatters and skirmishes beside a water hole. It is, says the screen, "The Dawn of Man." From somewhere, a strange rectangular slab appears, gleaming in the primeval sunlight. Its appearance stimulates one of the simians to think for the first time of a bone as a weapon. Now he is man, the killer, and civilization is on its way. With a burst of animal spirits, the bone is flung into the air, dissolves into an elongated spacecraft and aeons of evolution fall away. It is 2001, the epoch of *A Space Odyssey*. Now, in the 21st century, the strange slab has been identified by scientists, who have traced its radio signal back to Jupiter, and a spaceship is dispatched to that remote planet. Aboard are two conscious astronauts (Keir Dullea and Gary Lockwood) and three hibernating scientists sealed like mummies in sarcophagi. Also on board is Hal, a computer, programmed to be proud of his job as pilot and possessed of a wistful, androgynous voice. For what seems like a century the journey goes well. Then, abruptly, Hal begins to act in a sinister manner, and the astronauts prepare to perform a lobotomy on their cybernetic buddy by removing his memory banks. Hal discovers the plan. He methodically kills all on board but Dullea, who after a wrenching struggle, manages to disconnect the brain of the mutinous Hal just as the space vehicle enters the orbit of Jupiter. There he sees the object of his trip—the omnipotent slab. He heads for it, and suddenly conventional dimensions vanish. An avalanche of eerie, kinetic effects attacks the eye and bends the mind as Director Stanley Kubrick turns the screen into a planetarium gone mad and provides the viewer with the closest equivalent to psychedelic experience this side of hallucinogens.

At the end, beyond time and space, Dullea apparently learns the secret of the universe—only to find, as Churchill said about Russia, that it is a riddle, wrapped in a mystery, inside an enigma.

"ROSEMARY'S BABY"–Even readers of the book (2,300,000 copies) who know how *Baby* comes out are in for a pleasant surprise: the very real acting ability of Mia Farrow. As Rosemary Woodhouse, she and her husband Guy (John Cassavetes) are delighted to find an apartment in the Bramford, a penumbral old fortress of an apartment house on Manhattan's Central Park West. Rosemary's bookish old father figure, Hutch (Maurice Evans), is not too pleased; the Bramford, he notes, has an unsavory history of suicides and diabolical doings, including the murder of a notorious Satanist. The happy pair moves in anyway and—see how groundless Hutch's fears were?—Minnie and Roman Castevet, the funny old couple next door, welcome them with open arms. Guy, who is an actor, finally agrees at last to let Rosemary have a baby. They carefully mark the date on the calendar when she will be most likely to conceive. That night turns out to be really devil-may-care, what with the martinis, and Minnie Castevet coming over with a funny-tasting chocolate mousse, and Rosemary passing out and having a hellish dream in which somebody (or something?) draws marks on her naked body.

So begins what must be the most unpleasant pregnancy on record. Mia Farrow seems to grow more sickly and emaciated the more her stomach swells, and her skillful progression from pain to puzzlement to panic goes far beyond mere looks. The film's most memorable performance, though, is turned in by Veteran Ruth Gordon as the coarse and cozily evil Minnie Castevet—forcing Rosemary to drink her satanic tonics of herbs, dispensing that old Black Magic that she knows so well in a voice that sounds like a crow with a cold.

"RACHEL, RACHEL"–The spinster has always been a haunting and rather mysterious figure: no man quite knows her. Rachel (Joanne Woodward) stands in the "exact middle" of her existence: she is 35. She is also at dead center, emotionally inert. Like a cold moon, she rotates around her widowed mother, reflecting all of Mama's neuroses and ailments. It all smacks of paperback Freud—and so it could have been. But Rachel the character and *Rachel* the film are illuminated by the intrusion of characters with the dimensions and plausibility of small-town people with small-town attitudes. A fellow schoolmarm (Estelle Parsons) extends a lesbian hand that Rachel shakes off. A visitor (James Olson) "looking for a little action" finds some in Rachel, but he vanishes before she realizes that she has been had. Even her body thwarts her: a swelling in her stomach turns out to be not a pregnancy but a noncancerous tumor. It is the only benign thing that has ever happened to her.

The movie marks Paul Newman's debut at the other end of the camera. Since he could not find a director who liked the script, Newman decided to do the job himself. He coached Actress Woodward—his wife—in whispers and in a sort of private language. As a result, he infuses the air of the small town with a palpable melancholy and unquiet desperation.

T. 4 **STREISAND SPECIAL:** "PEEEEE-pull, pee-pull who need PEEEEE-pullllll. . . ." Barbra Streisand, the girl with the voice of a thrush and the beak of a toucan, is back in the musical, *Funny Girl,* that made her a household bird. Gags, production numbers, vaudeville mugging and tearstained love scenes receive the same manic stress and fervor. As in the Broadway show, when the jokes are good, Barbra displays the best timing East of Mae West. When Jule Styne's numbers are deserving—*People, Don't Rain On My Parade*—she warms them with meticulous emotional phrasing until they glow like a marquee.

The story of Fanny Brice is the fairy-tale dream of an unprepossessing kid who struggled up from the ghetto to the Follies on a powerful amalgam of brass and talent.

Barbra's marked resemblance to Fanny is much more than nasal. She is the flip side of Cinderella—the homely girl who made it.

T. 11 **VIRTUOSO IN VERONA:** If this *Romeo and Juliet* had been produced in 1956, there might have been no need for *West Side Story* the following year. "I wanted to bring the story to the attention of young people," says Director Franco Zeffirelli. "Youth today is hungry for ideals."

With a charged, witty camera, Zeffirelli has managed to make the Shakespearean classic alive and wholly contemporary. Romeo and Juliet appear afresh as two agonized teenagers whose turf happens to be Quattrocento Verona. Too young to buck the Establishment—the Italian city-state with its machinery of feuds and rituals—they are finally undone by their passions. They become in death, as Juliet's father puts it in the play's epilogue, "the poor sacrifices of our enmity."

Visually, Shakespeare has never been better realized. But his *Romeo and Juliet* will not please everybody, since it clearly reflects Zeffirelli's idiosyncratic opinions of the playwright. "Mercutio," he insists, "is a self-portrait of Shakespeare himself, and a homosexual."

Cartoon Beatles in "Yellow Submarine." What are the kids to do when a film is too square for hippies, too hip for squares?

BAD TRIP: Full-length cartoon features have been based on novels (*Gulliver's Travels*), fairy tales (*Snow White*), even classical music (*Fantasia*). *Yellow Submarine* may be the first to be based on a song. Recorded in 1966, the Beatles' jaunty single was jolly good nonsense that even a tune-deaf kid could sing. It was also a sly euphemism for a drug-inspired freak-out. The movie ends up as a curious case of artistic schizophrenia. The score includes several hits by the Beatles and just as many misses. The plot and the animation seem too square for hippies and too hip for squares. Children, as usual, are caught between.

Occasionally the *art nouveau* cartoon style is effective, as in *Eleanor Rigby* when "all the lonely people" appear as gritty newsreel figures who float by each other in a surrealistic frieze. But ultimately, what is wrong with the film is the Beatles. They are not in it.

EDUCATION

23   **TEEN-AGERS ON THE RAMPAGE:** A rash of violence, most of it racial, is spreading among high schools from California to Maine. Last week police patrolled high schools in New Haven, Conn., to prevent a revival of fist-swinging, china-shattering riots that had erupted in the cafeterias of two schools the week before, disrupting classes and causing 30 arrests. About the same time, most of the 2,372 students of Chicago's predominantly Negro Dunbar Vocational High rallied in the streets, stopped traffic, threw rocks at cars; many abandoned classes for the day. Those were only the latest clashes in a series that began last fall. There was no common pattern in the outbreaks. Three of the eruptions hinged partly on the impatient demand of Negro students that the schools introduce courses in Negro culture and history—something that the administrators were already planning to do. Other clashes seemed to be simpler cases of racial antagonism. In the Chicago suburb of Maywood, the failure of a student selection committee at Proviso East High to nominate a single Negro girl for homecoming queen set off a protest rally in which some 500 youths hurled bottles at police.

CH 8   **AGONY ON MORNINGSIDE HEIGHTS:**

> *Oh, who owns New York?*
> *Oh, who owns New York?*
> *Why, we own New York!*
> *Why, we own New York!*
> *Who?*
> *C-O-L-U-M-B-I-A*
>
>   —Columbia College marching song

Although Columbia does own a good $200 million worth of Manhattan real estate—including the land under Rockefeller Center—the boast is not literally true. But to many of the university's neighbors on Morningside Heights, Columbia is about as popular as a slum landlord. Last week 150 demonstrators, including many sympathetic students, clashed with police while trying to block construction of a new university gymnasium on park land that some residents of nearby Harlem wish to protect.

The confrontation was the latest in a long series of emotional disputes involving Columbia and Morningside Heights, a neighborhood whose residents are a mixture of Negroes, Puerto Ricans and white intellectuals attracted by low rents, the university and such varied institutions as Union Theological Seminary and the Juilliard School of Music. In an effort to enlarge its cramped 28.5-acre campus, Columbia since 1962 has acquired nearly $30 million worth of property on the Heights, including low-rent apartment buildings and houses and cheap hotels, some littered with prostitutes and dope peddlers. By cleaning up the worst of the rooming houses, Columbia has helped cut down the Heights' horrifying crime rate. Nonetheless, its real estate acquisitions have been attacked by organizations which accuse the university of a "racist" plot to displace poor Negroes.

Resentment at the university's land-buying policies spilled over into the gymnasium dispute. Columbia got the city's permission to put up a $9,500,000 building in Morningside Park, long a bottle-strewn, crime-ridden buffer between the campus and Harlem. The university plans to devote the ground floor to a free community gymnasium and swimming pool, use upper floors of the building for its own athletic programs. Although this would be the only such public facility in the neighborhood, well-organized protesters called the project "a land grab" and "a desecration of a public park," termed the facilities "separate but unequal." The university did not help matters much by publishing architects' sketches showing an expensive entrance facing the campus, with only a small servicelike door facing toward Harlem, giving critics a chance to scoff at its "back-door generosity." Columbia Vice President David Truman concedes that "we simply have not been tooled up to manage our public image."

ONE-DIMENSIONAL PHILOSOPHER: With his kindly Kris Kringle smile, his Katzenjammer accent and his snow-white hair, Professor Herbert Marcuse of the University of California's

San Diego campus seems too charmingly genial to be a revolutionary. Yet today's youthful radicals increasingly turn to the writings of the aging (he will be 70 in July) German-born philosopher to find a satisfactory rationale for rebellion.

On their protest marches, the militant student leaders who recently forced the closing of the University of Rome bore a banner inscribed with the three Ms of a new trinity: Marx, Marcuse and Mao. "We see Marx as prophet, Marcuse as his interpreter, and Mao as the sword," said one student-power advocate. On a visit to the Free University of Berlin last summer, Marcuse (pronounced Mar*kooza*) drew jammed lecture halls and wild ovations as he spoke glowingly of "the moral, political, intellectual and sexual rebellion of youth." In the U.S., Marcuse's book, *One-Dimensional Man,* is a growing campus favorite.

What makes Marcuse a guru of the student rebels is his chilling and strident critique of modern industrial civilization, which he sees as an impersonal, all-pervasive agent of domination over the individual. Modern technology, which should be used to free man from oppressive work, Marcuse argues, has overreached itself, turned wasteful and created a massive fusion of interlocking military, corporate and political interests. As a result, he says, the normal channels of protest and dissent are rendered impotent. Marcuse concedes that modern technology provides man with material well-being and even admits that more men may be happier today than ever before—but it is a happiness born of an ignorance ("a state of anesthesia") of what they could become.

"The goods and services that the individuals buy," he writes, "control their needs and petrify their faculties. They have innumerable gadgets that keep them occupied and divert their attention from the real issue—which is the awareness that they could both work less and determine their own needs and satisfactions."

Building on Marxian theory, Marcuse contends that capitalist society has within it inherently incompatible forces that cannot be contained. But he also acknowledges Marx's failure to foresee that capitalist society could buy off the workers with material goods and prevent their clash with owner-managers by making both classes of society mere tools of technology. In his writings he sees a physical uprising as the primary way to overthrow this "oppressive" structure and restore man to new potentialities of freedom.

Marcuse has now mellowed to the point that he is willing to concede that the U.S. may be able to escape from this situation without a violent revolution. "I think that fundamental change in this society is possible," he says.

SIEGE ON MORNINGSIDE HEIGHTS: Not since the 1964 battle of MA Berkeley has there been anything that could quite match last week's disorders at Manhattan's Columbia University. Demonstrators stormed the office of the university's president, held three officials hostage for 26 hours, took over five university buildings, eventually forced the 17,000-student university to suspend all classes. Situated in Morningside Heights at the edge of Harlem, Columbia is an academic enclave surrounded by poverty and decay. Its students, a large number of them subway commuters, are both liberal and well integrated. But the school itself, while earnestly trying to deal with the urban ills in its neighborhood, has fallen far short of the expectations of either its students or its neighbors.

Much of the blame falls on President Grayson Kirk, whose aloof, often bumbling administration has proved unresponsive to grievances that have long been festering on campus. Last month, when a group led by Students for a Democratic Society marched into Low Library to protest a university ban on indoor demonstrations, Kirk began disciplinary proceedings against six of the leaders. Feeling thus challenged, and long provoked, the S.D.S. last week organized a defiant demonstration. The students demanded that the charges against the six be dropped, and also seized the occasion to protest the construction of a new off-campus gymnasium.

Last week university officials offered to meet with the students to consider their demands that the gym be abandoned, as well as their objections to the university's ties with the Institute for Defense Analysis, a Washington "think-tank" that conducts military-related research for the Federal Government. But the students, carried away by their own heady sense of sudden power, shouted down the offer and marched to Morningside Park, where they tore down a fence at the gymnasium excavation site. Back on campus student power soon came up against black power. Arguing that the white S.D.S. insurgents in front of Acting Dean Henry S. Coleman's office were not sufficiently militant, a group of 60-odd black students concluded that the whites should leave—and at 6 o'clock the next morning they did. A number of the whites had meanwhile moved on President Kirk's office—he was not there at the time —in nearby Low Library. One group broke down a side door; others clambered through a window. They hurled Kirk's papers onto the floor, smoked his cigars, pasted on the office window a sign reading LIBERATED AREA. BE FREE TO JOIN US.

Over the next 48 hours, students seized three more buildings. From inside the barricaded buildings, the insurgents sent out emissaries to bring back food, blankets and Vaseline—to smear on their faces on the theory that it deadened the effects of the chemical Mace. A command post was set up, mimeograph machines churned out bulletins and manifestos. Other students, meanwhile, began to complain about the demonstrators' disruptive tactics. A group of Columbia athletes volunteered to remove the protesters, but were restrained by school officials. "If this is a barbarian society," growled a burly wrestler, "then it's survival of the fittest—and we're the fittest."

The rebellious students refused to quit their posts without a promise of general amnesty for all demonstrators—a condition that President Kirk rejected. Failure to take disciplinary action, Kirk insisted, would "destroy the whole fabric of the university community." But the school yielded on at least one important point. At the urging of New York City Mayor John Lindsay, it announced that it would temporarily suspend construction of the disputed gymnasium. Still the students refused to budge. Into the vacuum created by this impasse moved a number of faculty members—mainly younger ones sympathetic to the students' cause. When the administration called in police to eject the demonstrators inside Low Library, 30 professors blocked their way. At week's end, Columbia's trustees emerged from a special meeting to back President Kirk and "affirmatively direct him to maintain the ultimate disciplinary power over the conduct of students." There both sides rested— eyeball to eyeball, heavy-breathing and mutually defiant.

MAY 10 **LIFTING THE SIEGE:** At 2:30 a.m., said one combat-wise cop, "Harlem is asleep." At that propitious hour, 1,000 New York City police, armed with warrants signed by Columbia University trustees, marched on the Morningside Heights campus and dispossessed the student rebels who had occupied five of its buildings for nearly six days. In the inevitable melee, more that 130 people—including twelve policemen—were injured; 698 people, mostly students, were arrested. The action united hopelessly confused Columbia in anger over police brutality. Professors and students were charged by wedges of plain-clothesmen, while other police broke in through underground tunnels.

Initial reaction to the police raid was an emotional tide of sympathy for the protesters. The moderate student government called for resignations of Kirk and Provost David Truman and joined S.D.S. President Mark Rudd in urging a campus strike. Rudd, 20, had recently returned from a three-week visit to Communist Cuba, which he glowingly described as an "extremely humanistic society."

By week's end, tempers had cooled, nearly all police had left campus, and a few professors had even begun to resume classes. Anthropologist Margaret Mead, who has studied and taught at Columbia for 48 years, blamed the demonstration in part on student activists who took advantage of the university's traditional leniency toward campus pranks. But she also accused the administration of failing to recognize the right of students to share in campus authority, and of being unresponsive to community needs. Said she: "We can no longer have privately endowed universities governed by boards of trustees that are not responsive to anyone but themselves."

THE EMERGENCE OF S.D.S.: The Students for a Democratic Society, declared Columbia Provost David B. Truman last week, were deliberately "seeking a confrontation with the university." Thus Truman seemed to support the widespread notion that the wave of recent demonstrations and strikes at Columbia were all part of a conscious conspiracy. That is unlikely. S.D.S. certainly believes in all sorts of radical confrontation, but conspiracy is not really its game. It is a loosely formed amalgam of some 35,000 young people who boast chapters on at least 250 campuses and, if anything, shy away from organization. Opposed to "imperialism" (whatever that means these days), racism and oppression, S.D.S. finds the American university guilty of all three.

What draws young people into S.D.S., says Berkeley Sophomore Peter Stone, 20, is a desire to translate their sense of alienation from society into "a political thing." Products of comfortable, middle-class homes, S.D.S. members typically are disenchanted young liberals who feel that anti-Communism is an irrelevant stance and are animated not by any master plan for revolution but by a sense of moral outrage. For all their talk about "participatory democracy," few members seem prepared to accept, or readily tolerate, anybody else's ideas on how society's ills can best be cured.

30 **A CONVENIENT RETIREMENT:** "It is possible that my retirement at this time might help to ensure the prospect of more normal university operations during the coming academic year." It was not only possible but probable that Grayson Kirk was indulging in understatement when he announced his retirement last week after 15 years as president of Columbia University. For as the start of the new term neared, Kirk's defenders and detractors alike agreed that if he remained on the job, his very presence would provide an excuse for continued controversy on the restless campus. To run the university until a new president takes over, the trustees chose Andrew W. Cordier, dean of Columbia's School of International Affairs and a veteran U.N. official. At 67, Cordier is even older than Kirk.

13 **BACK-TO-SCHOOL BLUES:** Unsoothed by a summer's vacation, the nation's restive schoolteachers last week faced the reopening of classes in a belligerent mood of complaint and protest. Most of the disputes centered on better pay, but that was not the issue in the most serious situation of all: New York City. There, the militant, 55,000-member United Federation of Teachers was threatening to repeat its opening-bell strike of last September. Then, the main issue was more money. This year, the dispute centers on a controversy over efforts to break up the city's huge, bureaucratic system and turn control of the schools over to community-run local boards. Some such decentralization was ordered by New York's state legislature last year in return for providing the city with more state funds.

Most of the anger swirls about a demonstration district in the heavily Negro Ocean Hill-Brownsville section of Brooklyn. Set up last year to test the potential problems of centralization, the project gave a community-controlled committee the right to evaluate teachers, supervise curriculum and spend funds allocated by the central school board. The hope was that community involvement would lead to closer rapport with teachers, more interested students, a better curriculum and, above all, a halt in the steady decline in student skills. But the procedures under which the local committee was to act were never clearly defined. When the committee tried to get rid of 13 teachers and six supervisors last May, New York School Superintendent Bernard E. Donovan called the action illegal. Many outraged parents kept their children out of class, and equally irate teachers walked out in support of their colleagues. The teachers were stoutly backed by U.F.T. President Albert Shanker, who denounced the dismissals as a denial of "due process."

Technically, the community had a weak case. Rhody McCoy, the local Ocean Hill-Brownsville administrator, finally filed charges against ten of the teachers. He cited the "excessive lateness" of one, the failure of four others to maintain class discipline, unspecified opposition to the decentralization experiment by others. A retired Negro judge appointed to hear the cases found that witnesses could not document these incidents and recommended that the ten be retained. McCoy insists that they cannot return. Shanker and the central school board insist that they must. The U.F.T. fears that decentralization would break up its power base and leave teachers vulnerable to the whims of unstable local militants. On the other side, there is the justifiable—but unprovable—contention of Negro parents that too many white teachers consider their children either unteachable or inferior.

TEACHER POWER v. BLACK POWER: For the second year in a SEP row, the school year in New York City opened last week with the teachers on strike. A strike vote had been called by Albert Shanker, the tough, shrewd president of the teachers' union, when the locally elected Ocean Hill-Brownsville committee of Brooklyn refused to reinstate ten ousted teachers.

After two days of round-the-clock negotiations, the school board announced a settlement under which the ousted teachers would "not be prevented" from returning and any teachers dismissed by local boards in the future could appeal to arbitration panels. But the agreement blew up when the affected teachers tried to return to their classrooms and faced a group of angry parents and Negro militants. "They hooted at us, cursed us, called us fagots and honkies," reported one teacher. "They said we'd be going out in pine boxes."

When 15 challenged teachers tried to enter one junior high school, the way was blocked by a jeering crowd. Shanker immediately declared that the agreement had been broken and that the strike was back on. "Mob rule must go," he said.

29 **STRIKE'S END:** The New York City teachers' strike, which denied 1,100,000 children formal schooling for 36 school days in three separate walkouts this fall, finally ended last week. As might be expected in so bitter a battle, the terms of settlement did not really please anyone. And ending the strike still left the schools with a lot of lost time to make up. The Board of Education announced that the school day would be extended 45 minutes daily for 14 weeks. In addition, there would be ten days of extra classes carved out of vacation periods. While the extra sessions cannot compensate for all the instruction time lost, they will provide enough overtime for teachers to recoup most of the pay lost during the strike.

The United Federation of Teachers, which includes 55,000 of the city's 57,000 teachers, wanted to close the schools down completely during its strike. It failed to do so. Perhaps 350,000 students were able to attend classes—either in schools that remained open or in makeshift classrooms staffed by college students and other volunteers. At least 7,500 U.F.T. members violated union orders by teaching outside of union-authorized schools. In many parts of the city, parents improvised schools in churches, storefronts, brownstone basements and apartments. Other parental groups packed the kids off for tours of the city's museums, galleries and exhibit halls. Despite the potential for mischief in so prolonged a period of youthful idleness, police reported that there was no significant rise in juvenile delinquency. A feeling expressed on both sides was that it was the kids who, by their restrained conduct, showed themselves to be the real heroes of the strike.

C. 6 **SEMANTICS IN SAN FRANCISCO:** After two weeks of churning disorder, as black militants campaigned for changes in cur-

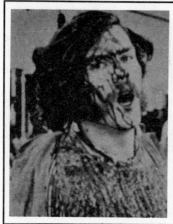 

Demonstrator at San Francisco College. "Shut it down!" they cry.

President Hayakawa: "I stand in the middle. I am neither white nor black."

riculum and admission policy, San Francisco State College President Robert R. Smith reluctantly closed his campus down. Last week he resigned. Named to replace him as acting president was Professor Samuel I. Hayakawa, 62, an internationally recognized expert in general semantics, the study of the interrelationship of language, thought and behavior. Hayakawa, who is the third new president in 27 months, will need a profound understanding of behavior if he is to deal effectively with the convulsed San Francisco campus, where students have been beaten, buildings occupied, fires started, and stink bombs thrown. Last week plainclothes and uniformed police were everywhere.

Hayakawa, who has spoken repeatedly and vigorously on the need for more effective civil rights initiatives, professes some hope that his own color will help him work out a compromise between black militants and whites at S.F. State. "In a very profound sense," said Hayakawa, who was born in Canada of Japanese-American parents, "I stand in the middle. I am neither white nor black." Thus he would like to become "a channel to bring blacks and whites together."

WORD POWER IN ACTION: "Words are remarkably intoxicating," Dr. Samuel I. Hayakawa wrote in *Symbol, Status, and Personality*. "A flood of oratory is capable of producing a DEC mild jag in most people." But as acting president of strife-torn San Francisco State College, which had become quite intoxicated by a month of angry words, Hayakawa last week used deeds rather than rhetoric in an attempt to restore order to the campus. His first decision was to reopen the college despite a student strike organized by black militants demanding a separate black-studies department and unrestricted admission of black students (currently there are 800 in the school's enrollment of 18,000). On the first day that classes resumed, Hayakawa, wearing a jaunty blue-and-red Tam o' Shanter, showed up at a rebel demonstration and climbed upon a truck to welcome returning students. When strikers began blaring their opposition over a loudspeaker on the truck, he ripped out the wires, continued his talk. Although he was jostled and his Tam briefly snatched away, Hayakawa walked calmly through the crowd to his office.

"I am determined to end this reign of terror," said Hayakawa. For most of last week, that was an accurate description of the school's condition. Bands of pickets roamed the campus, trying to prevent nonmilitant students from entering classrooms. Although his predecessors had been reluctant to use police to restore order, Hayakawa had no such compunction. On Tuesday, police arrested 32 protesters, ten of whom were injured in a melee; two days later, 23 more were carted off to jail. The maintenance of order was helped by an organization of proadministration students who confronted strikers in shouting matches—countering "Shut it down!" with "Keep it open!"—and denounced the militants as "Gestapo pigs" for abridging the rights of students who wanted to attend classes. Despite the strike and the sporadic battles between police and militants, Hayakawa claimed that 80% of the college's students were able to attend classes without interruption.

COAST-TO-COAST CASINO: "They're winning at Sunoco!" has JAI
been the come-on TV jingle for Sun Oil Co.'s "Sunny Dollars" game, and each week a high-speed teletype hammers out
the names of winners, followed by amounts ranging from $1
to $1,000. Humble Oil invites drivers to stop by at its filling sta-
tions to play "Tigerama." Mobil's "Winning Line" offers
$1,000 to anybody who completes a card with pictures of three
gas pumps; Sinclair offers up to $1,500 to customers who match
up coupons to spell out a slogan in its "Dino Dollars" contest. With no requirement that the driver buy gas (thus ensuring
that the games will not be classified as lotteries) and with prizes
including watches, luggage, color-TV sets, automobiles and
up to $10,000 in cash, the oil companies' 304 different current
giveaway contests would seem like hard acts to knock.

In fact, the harder the oil companies plug their contests, the
more massive grows the frustration of the players whose glove
compartments are full to overflowing with nonwin coupons.
Nor are players the only ones building up resentments. Gasoline attendants find themselves wasting up to ten minutes
per customer explaining the rules of each new game. America's
service stations stand in danger of becoming "an enormous
coast-to-coast casino," warns E. D. Brockett, chairman of Gulf
Oil Corp., one of the few major oil companies to abstain from
the games. "Costs will rise and service will suffer," says Brockett, who foresees the day when motorists will say, "Fill her
up, check the oil, and where's the roulette wheel?"

MAN!: "We're in a new era of dandyism," proclaims British De- MAI
signer Hardy Amies. Certainly the clothes shown by Amies
and five other leading menswear designers last week at a fashion show in Manhattan's Plaza Hotel were anything but
ordinary. Paris Designer Pierre Cardin's vision of future male
fashion included black leather pants with a matching leather
shirt, laced up the front. For evening, John Weitz, a onetime

race-car driver, showed a Levi-styled dinner jacket worn over a collarless shirt with a red bandanna knotted around the throat.

Mainly responsible for launching men into high fashion is Cardin, who set the styles for subtly belled trousers, zippered "cosmocorps" suits, Nehru coats and velvet dinner jackets. Milan's expatriate American designer, Ken Scott, is showing lounging pajamas and tunic tops for men in clinging jersey. "For my clothes," Scott admits, "a man needs a lot of guts and no gut."

It is lack of guts, thinks Jack Hanson, owner of the celebrated California-based Jax women's sportswear boutiques, that has held men back until now. Says he: "The problem is that so many male homosexuals have always dressed far-out that other men are afraid of being identified as one." Evidently Hanson believes that the old fear is fading, for he has just opened a Jax for Men boutique in Beverly Hills.

JL 5 **THE POLITICS OF YIP:** They poured into the vast main concourse of Manhattan's Grand Central Station 3,000 strong, wearing their customary capes, gowns, feathers and beads. They tossed hot cross buns and firecrackers, and floated balloons upward the celestial blue ceiling. They hummed the cosmic "Ommm," snake-danced to the the tune of *Have a Marijuana,* and proudly unfurled a huge banner emblazoned with a lazy "Y." The Yippies—1968's version of the hippies—were celebrating spring. Hardly had the equinoctial orgy begun, when a dozen youths scaled the information booth, ripped off the clock hands, scribbled graffiti and defiantly passed around lighted marijuana "joints" in full view of the police. The fuzz charged, billy clubs flailing, and arrested 61 demonstrators. Battered but unbowed, the celebrants coursed off to the Central Park Sheep Meadow to "yip up the sun."

After a winter in which the hippie movement seemed so moribund that its own members staged mock burials in honor of its death, the Yippies have suddenly invested it with new life through their special kind of antic political protest. The term Yippie comes from Youth International Party, an amorphous amalgam of the alienated young that coalesced in Manhattan two months ago around a coterie of activist hippies all in their late 20s and early 30s. "The YIP is a party—like the last word says—not a political movement," argues the East Village's Abbie Hoffman, who last fall tried to levitate the Pentagon. Says Yippie Leader Ed Sanders, 28, of the Fugs rock group: "It's the politics of ecstasy."

Ecstasy begins with a platform certain to make any hippie yell yippie: an end to war and pay toilets, legalization of psychedelic drugs, free food, and a heart transplant for L.B.J. Already Yippies have demonstrated their distaste for air pollution by invading the Manhattan offices of Con Ed to hurl soot at executives and detonate smoke bombs. But what the Yippies are really pointing toward is Chicago. There, come the last week of August, they intend to hold a six-day "Festival of Life" in comic contrast to what they call the Democratic Party's "National Death Convention," which will be running concurrently. Among the possibilities being considered: a fleet of fake cabs to pick up convention delegates and dump them off in Wisconsin.

"I TURNED MINE IN": In the toy industry, it has long been an ar- SEP ticle of faith that a youngster who plays with make-believe guns is no more likely to grow up a criminal than a boy who plays with make-believe churches is apt to mature into a saint. Yet as a result of the furor over gun controls that followed the assassinations of Martin Luther King Jr. and Robert Kennedy, toy guns may soon be much harder to obtain. Sears, Roebuck, the world's biggest retailer, has removed toy guns from its Christmas catalogue and ordered its 815 stores to stop advertising guns and "similar toys of violence." In Manhattan, Bloomingdale's and Stern Bros. have even taken their existing stock off the shelves. Payson Sawyer, 35, one of Maine's largest toy distributors and leader of a citizens' group called "Toy Disarmament," has earmarked his entire stock of toy guns for a big bonfire this month. "Everybody talks about disarming the world, but we believe a practical step is to start at home," says Sawyer. His group is sponsoring a campaign in which children who surrender their toy guns receive buttons saying "I turned mine in."

BOOKS

"MYRA BRECKINRIDGE" by Gore Vidal—"It began upstairs when he tore my clothes off in the closet. Then he raped me standing up with the metal clothes hanger twisted around my neck, choking me. I could hardly breathe. It was exquisite! Then one thing led to another. Those small attentions a girl like me cherishes. . . . A lighted cigarette snubbed out on my derriere, a complete beating with his great thick heavy leather belt. . . . All the usual fun things."

Has literary decency fallen so low—or has fashionable camp risen that high? This novel brings up such questions because Gore Vidal is a reasonably serious writer, and nothing in his versatile past will quite prepare the reader for *Myra Breckinridge*. Anyone who has been down to the local fag bar will recognize Myra's true gender long before Vidal coyly pronounces the paradigm. Myra is actually a Myron who has had a Christine Jorgensen-type operation and is passing through Hollywood, trying to rape havoc upon unwary heterosexual males.

What makes the novel a little more than a flighty drag is Vidal's stylish and erudite sense of humor. He offers metaphor after metaphor based upon far-out late-show conceits ("I whispered like Phyllis Thaxter in *Thirty Seconds over Tokyo*"). And he makes it Myra's thesis that the flicks of 1931 to 1945 were certainly the most formative influence upon anyone who came of age during that "post-Gutenberg and pre-Apocalypse" era. This is Vidal's personal notion as well. "Without Bogart," he says, "there could be no Norman Mailer. Without George Arliss," he adds with a Disraeli-ish gleam, "there wouldn't have been me."

"SOUL ON ICE" by Eldridge Cleaver—Prisons are traditional finishing schools of writers and revolutionaries. Eldridge Cleaver is a product of both the black ghettos and the California penal system. Convicted of a marijuana charge at 18 and of assault with intent to kill at 22, Cleaver spent most of the twelve years between 1954 and 1966 in California's state prisons. Now, at 32, he is a *Ramparts* staff writer and a "full-time revolutionary in the struggle for black liberation in America."

Soul on Ice is a collection of impassioned letters and heated essays lamenting the fact that American "negritude" has been forced to cool it for too long. It is Cleaver's thesis—as it is James Baldwin's, among others—that the root cause of racial prejudice in America is sexual. He argues that as a result of the Negro's years of servility, the black male has been systematically robbed of his masculinity. Thus "castrated," the Negro also has been denied his development as a positive intellectual and social force. There is nothing really very new in Cleaver's analysis or black militant ideology. But on the personal level, his chronicles of daily life in prison and his regimen of self-education there are both eloquent and moving.

Gore Vidal: "Without George Arliss, there wouldn't have been me."

John Updike. Beneath the idyl, his couples are caught in a mass of sex.

"COUPLES" by John Updike—In this peaceful town, pretty APRI birds sing and the sumac twines. Church steeples point for all to see toward the virtuous life. This is Tarbox, Mass., the setting of John Updike's new novel *Couples,* where primitive American democracy reveals itself in town meetings, and three streets of the business district are named Hope, Charity and Divinity. Almost any Sunday, one can find a bunch of the fellows tossing around a basketball in somebody's driveway, while the women chat and the children scramble and squabble. Quiet, lovely town, Tarbox. Or so it seems.

The fact is that beneath this suburban idyl, Updike's couples are caught up in a black mass of community sex. With no heat left in the Protestant American crucible, the comfortable couples of Tarbox have reached out for another kind of warmth. Updike is forthright about his purpose. "There's a lot of dry talk around about love and sex being somehow the new ground of our morality," he said. "I thought I should show the ground and ask, is it entirely to be wished for?"

Show the ground he certainly does. Harold Smith is bedding down with Janet Appleby, and Marcia Smith with Frank Appleby; their set calls them the Applesmiths. Eddie Constantine and Irene Saltz make it together, and so do Ben Saltz and Carol Constantine; they are the Saltines. The sexual scenes, and the language that accompanies them, are remarkably explicit, even for this new age of total freedom of expression. Some critics have dismissed *Couples* as an upper-middle-class *Peyton Place*. It isn't, but it is getting a sensational reception all the same. Only three weeks after publication, the novel is on the bestseller lists.

AY 10 **"THE ARMIES OF THE NIGHT"** by Norman Mailer—Early in this book, which is a step-by-step account of the peace march and militant demonstrations in Washington last October, the author reports that Poet Robert Lowell remarked to him: "Norman, I really think you are the best journalist in America." Mailer refused to take it as a compliment. "Well, Cal," he replied, "there are days when I think of myself as being the best writer in America." Lowell was offering up the current intellectuals' line on Mailer, and Norman was mouthing the perennial Mailer line on himself ("Me Mailer, Me champ"). But *The Armies of the Night* suggests that Lowell is wrong, and that Mailer may be closer to the truth. He is a rather lazy and often sloppy journalist, but he can still write like a streak, and this book, which Mailer labels "History as a Novel" and "The Novel as History," is a bravura performance.

UNE 7 **STOP THE PRESSES!**: Nonfiction publishing is rising at a bewildering rate; an average of 351 new nonfiction titles stream off the presses every week, but most of them never get reviewed. Here is a random sampling of titles, issued in the past year or so by reputable publishers, that may have escaped public attention:

Honeybees from Close Up by A. M. Dines.

Water Use Inspector by the Arco Editorial Board.

New Trends in Table Settings by Lucy Staley.

A Trip to the Yellowstone National Park in July, August and September, 1875 by General W. E. Strong.

"TELL ME HOW LONG THE TRAIN'S BEEN GONE"—There are two James Baldwins, equally passionate, at times equally gifted. One is the racial rhetorician, the polished pamphleteer, the literate prophet who warned about *The Fire Next Time* long before the words, "Burn, baby, burn" raged in the land. His preachments remain intensely articulate, painfully—and plainly—relevant. The other James Baldwin is the questing novelist, the private man loaded down with personal problems that he must defeat—or be defeated by. This new book is further evidence that as a fictioneer Baldwin is in great danger of becoming drearily irrelevant. *Tell Me How Long the Train's Been Gone* rambles like a milk train over the same run that Baldwin covered in *Another Country,* sounds the same blast about the Negro's condition, rattles the same rationale for homosexuality: "My terrible need to lie down, to breathe deep, to weep long and loud, to be held in human arms, almost any human arms, to hide my face in any human breast, to tell it all, to let it out, to be brought into the world, and, out of human affection, to be born again."

When he was 14, Baldwin was a boy preacher, a black Cotton Mather, raging against sin, obsessed with guilt. He still is.

"TRUE GRIT" by Charles Portis—Publishers, cowering behind JUNE their accountants' ledgers, aim primarily to pick off winners, not pick up literature. But every once in a while, through the magic of ricochet and carom, they manage to do both with a single resounding shot. Such is the fate of this book. *True Grit* is a lean but plucky novel that has been sold to the movies for $300,000, serialized in the *Saturday Evening Post* and chosen as a Literary Guild selection. It is also gilded with literary quality that can delight book lovers as well as bookkeepers.

Charles Portis, 34, is an Arkansas newspaperman who has

fashioned a pop anti-western in the best tradition of *Cat Ballou*. For openers, his hero is a heroine: Mattie Ross, a sassy, 14-year-old Arkansan whose chief protective girdle is a dry Bible-belt faith, and who is out to avenge the murder of her daddy back in the 1870s. Mattie enlists the aid of Rooster Cogburn, a U.S. marshal who once rode with Quantrill's border gang during the Civil War, but has since become fat and 40, one-eyed and sloppy. Soon they are joined by LaBoeuf, a straight-shooting (but not always accurate) Texas Ranger, who wants to get the same outlaw for an earlier rap and a larger reward.

The burden of the tale is the usual pursuit and chase. What gives the slender story distinction is its unusual style and attitude. It is all rendered from the self-righteously smug "That's the way it was" point of view of the heroine half a century later. Author Portis has succeeded in creating a true mock western: one in which blood flows with the same impact as real tomato soup suddenly gushing out of an Andy Warhol tin.

G. 16 **"DO BUTLERS BURGLE BANKS?"** by P. G. Wodehouse—Which came first, P. G. Wodehouse or the English butler? Wodehouse's publishers confess they are not certain whether he is 87 years old and has written a million books, or a million years old and has written 87 books. Anyhow the figures strain the imagination—but not more so than this potty tale about a bogus butler who sets out to burgle a Worcestershire bank. Connoisseurs of the old master's brand of daffy brouhaha will savor it to the last page.

PT. 20 **"PRESERVE AND PROTECT"**—Taking on an Allen Drury political melodrama is like harpooning a blimp at three feet. It is not only impossible to miss, but every thrust is likely to be fatal. To begin with, there are Drury's characters, a confusion of ideological wind-up toys carelessly slapped down to accommodate the easily distracted. Above all, Drury writes the most impenetrable prose this side of a Japanese motorcycle manual rendered in English: "They all laughed, somewhat ruefully, but dauntless still; not noticing the flurry and excitement and sudden bustling all about that in the jostling, police-held crowd pressed up against the fence behind them, one other, gifted by a sometimes puzzling Almighty with the gift to change the world, laughed too." When will Drury cease and desist?

"THE CANCER WARD" by Aleksandr I. Solzhenitsyn—As a spe- NOV cial kind of literary import, this Soviet novel stands partially obscured by the excess political baggage that has accompanied it. The kinds of labels inevitably suggested by the advance publicity are gross and distracting: savage exposé of Stalinism; revealing political microcosm; old cold-war propaganda. The reader is thus challenged to slip past the luggage and the labels into the heart of the book. It isn't easy. For one thing, cancer makes for strange ward-fellows. The inmates of Solzhenitsyn's ward include men and women from the farthest reaches of the Soviet Union—peasants, ex-prisoners, exiles, bureaucrats, students. When confronted with death, they express jagged—and politically damning—insights into the everyday enormities of life as it had been under Joseph Stalin. Stripped of all illusions by years of war, prison, exile, poverty and sickness, the Solzhenitsyn figure uncompromisingly asserts that modern man can arm himself against the fear of death only with life itself. If Solzhenitsyn is against cruelty, hypocrisy and loss of freedom, he is also against the distracting things that freedom—with its consequent financial inequality—engenders. Snobbery, status seeking, self-importance, the acquisition of consumer goods, materialism—everything, in short, that tends to repress the natural piety of men.

"THE CAT'S PAJAMAS & WITCH'S MILK" by Peter De Vries—At NOV. 58, just 14 years and nine books out of *The Tunnel of Love,* the comic novelist Peter De Vries has grown more dedicated to finding a way through the punishing side of American life. His newest book combines a long short novel with an extended short story. This is an experiment at contrapuntal fiction, for the two tales are linked in a number of ways, including the presence in both of a common character—a slightly rumpled female named Tillie Seltzer.

Hank Tattersall, the anti-hero of *Pajamas,* starts out as a happily married, witty college professor who goes on to explore the U.S. penchant for nerve-racking upward mobility by trying it in reverse. In an excess of whim and *Weltschmerz,* he runs through a job in advertising ("I stink, therefore I am"), a stint as a successful TV singer, and on down through door-to-door salesman, street peddler, gardener, handyman and tramp. He winds up living in a run-down tenement, selling canned "fresh air" door to door to help take care of a mumbling mongoloid boy and a drunken mongrel basset hound. One night he gets his head caught in a dog door that he humanely installed for his basset—and casually freezes to death.

By comparison, Tillie's life has hardly any fizz at all. Serious, well-trained in sociology, she meets a gimp-legged skirt-chaser and hopeless vulgarian named Pete Seltzer. His public wit runs to doubletalk and the invention of nonsense "end" products: after-shaving mints, dietetic shampoo, reversible mayonnaise. "He thinks Cameroons are some kind of cookie," she reflects bitterly. Tillie's matrimonial ordeal in *Witch's Milk* may seem touching, crazily unconvincing, or hopelessly sentimental. But read back to back with *The Cat's Pajamas,* it removes all doubt about De Vries' allegiance to domestic commitment, however grotesque. Tillie appears only at the tag end of *Pajamas,* as a social worker checking on Tattersall. Confronted with the dipsomaniacal dog, a house full of rotting food and stacked dishes, and the mongoloid boy mumbling at the sink, she gets off one of those deadpan lines in which De Vries reveals the madness of the rational world: "Do you think," she asks Tattersall severely, "this is a good environment for an idiot?"

C. 27 **JOHN STEINBECK, 1902-1968:** "This monster of a land," he wrote in 1962, "this mightiest of nations, this spawn of the future, turns out to be the macrocosm of microcosm me."

John Ernst Steinbeck always did have a talent for enlargement. Yet when he died of heart disease in Manhattan last week at 66, Steinbeck left behind a body of novels, short stories, plays and film scripts that were less a spawn of the future than a moral—and often moralizing—record from his special compartment in the nation's past.

Steinbeck was an emotional, sentimental, yet extraordinarily powerful writer who frequently mined his personal experiences for the material of his fiction. He was born in Salinas, Calif., the son of a miller and a Salinas Valley schoolteacher. In New York, he worked briefly for the American and was fired because he seemed incapable of recording facts without rhapsodizing or sermonizing. He then worked for a time as a hod carrier, returned to California and became a caretaker of a lodge in the Sierras. There he completed his first novel, *Cup of*

Gold, which appeared in 1929. Steinbeck published two other novels—*The Pastures of Heaven, To a God Unknown*—before *Tortilla Flat,* in 1935, became a bestseller. *In Dubious Battle,* dealing with an apple pickers' strike in California, further established his reputation, and *Of Mice and Men,* his fable of strength and weakness, solidified it. After 1940, however, Steinbeck produced only two major works—*East of Eden* and *The Winter of Our Discontent*—and neither equaled in power his work during the '30s.

And in 1962, feeling that he had perhaps lost touch with his nation, Steinbeck undertook a cross-country trip in a camper, accompanied by his poodle named Charley. *Travels with Charley* was a bestseller. That same year he became the sixth American author to win the Nobel Prize. (The others: Sinclair Lewis, Pearl S. Buck, William Faulkner, Eugene O'Neill, Ernest Hemingway.)

Edmund Wilson has observed that Steinbeck tended to diminish humans to the condition of animals, to reduce his characters to their simple biological needs and desires. Yet if his stories "animalized" characters, they also animated them with the elemental life of their time and condition. As the preacher in *The Grapes of Wrath* mumbles over Grandpa Joad's grave, "He was alive, an' that's what matters."

MILESTONES

DIED: Ramon Novarro, 69, silent film star, who in the 1920s vied with Rudolph Valentino as the screen's great Latin lover; of injuries suffered when he was bludgeoned in the bedroom of his home; in Hollywood, Calif.

DIED: Shortly before her 88th birthday, Helen Keller; in her home at Easton, Conn. "It is very pleasant to live here in our beautiful world," she once wrote to Poet John Greenleaf Whittier. "I cannot see the lovely things with my eyes, but my mind can see them all, and so I am overjoyed." She was born both blind and deaf. But instead of being condemned to an imbecile's life in an asylum, Helen Keller learned to read and hear with her fingers, and by touching others' throats and lips she was eventually able to verbalize the words she visualized in her mind. Mark Twain named Miss Keller and Napoleon "the two most interesting characters of the 19th century."

Numerals in italics indicate an illustration of subject mentioned.

PICTURE CREDITS

x

PRODUCTION STAFF FOR TIME INCORPORATED
John L. Hallenbeck (Vice President and Director of Production),
Robert E. Foy and Caroline Ferri
Text photocomposed under the direction of Albert J. Dunn

QUOTES OF THE YEAR

President Lyndon Johnson
   (replying to criticism that his Great Society progr
   were being sacrificed to pay for the war in Viet N
   p. 13): "It's just like saying I can't take care of Luci bec
   I have Lynda Bird."

French President Charles de Gaulle
   (delivering his private opinion of Lyndon Johns
   p. 137): "He's a cowboy, and that's saying everything."

Senator Robert F. Kennedy
   (11 weeks before his assassination—p. 33): "If an
   wants to kill me, it won't be difficult."

Republican vice-presidential candidate Spiro T. Agnew
   (during a campaign appearance in Detroit—p. 79)
   you've seen one ghetto area, you've seen them all."

Comedian Bob Hope
   (on Jacqueline Kennedy's marriage to Aristotle On
   —p. 117): "Nixon has a Greek running mate, and now e
   one wants one."

Astronaut James Lovell
   (as the Apollo 8 engine was fired successfully to s
   the spacecraft safely back to earth from the m
   —p. 205): "Please be informed that there is a Santa Cla